Bill Adams'
Yester Days

Bill Adams (signature)

This is a collection of the first 101 columns that began in the Peoria Journal Star on May 9, 1988, including nearly 150 photos. Most of the pictures first appeared with the original columns but many more have been added.

This book is dedicated to Flossie

...for her participation, understanding, support, encouragement and, yes, criticism. But most of all for "being there" these past 48 years, which makes it all...*seem like only yesterday!*

Special thanks

to CILCO and the Peoria Journal Star for their participation in publishing this book. Without their commitment to facilitate its publication, it would have been improbable, if not impossible, to have done so.

ISBN 0-9634793-0-X

Published by the Peoria Journal Star, Inc.
1 News Plaza
Peoria, Illinois 61643

Design and production by Coventry Creative Graphics, Peoria, Illinois
Printed by Logan Printing Company, Peoria, Illinois

Cover photo of the Peoria Skyline by Richard Etter, courtesy of CILCO
Cover design by Coventry Creative Graphics

A portion of the proceeds from the sale of this book will be donated to the Peoria Area Community Foundation for the funding of literacy programs.

Acknowledgements

One of the most dangerous undertakings for this type of book is to thank everyone who participated in providing material and photos, and not forget anyone along the way. Hopefully those who are mentioned in these 101 columns will accept my thanks in that form.

But many others participated with, not only story ideas, but also assisted in collecting (and recollecting) the nearly 150 photos that appear here.

Special thanks to Mrs. Jean Shrier and all her Reference Desk Staff at the Peoria Public Library's downtown branch...especially Mrs. Betty Roberson.

To Chuck Frey and his Special Collections Staff at the Bradley University Library...especially Karen Deller and Sherri Schneider.

To Paul Stringham for all his streetcar, train, traction, and early Peoria photos. And also to H.G. Crawshaw, Bill Janssen and George Krambles for their street car pictures.

To Edna Roten and Dick Deller for their special permission to reuse the photos from Lee Roten's Historic Peoria Photo Files.

To the Journal Star, WMBD, WEEK, WIRL, NBC, CBS and MGM for allowing us to reprint their photos.

To all those individuals who allowed us to borrow their family album photos.

And last, but not least, special thanks to my daughter, Lesa Adams Collier, for her dedicated search for column material over the past four years.

Preface

When I retired from television in 1984, I knew I had to do something to keep busy. In reflecting back over my career, I decided it might be fun to put down on paper some of my experiences, especially those halcyon days at the Madison Theater. I knew I'd personally enjoy the nostalgic trip back, but I also thought, if nothing else, my family might enjoy it, too. So I began what was to be a short story about the Madison and its people during my 17 years there.

But while doing this little story, I decided I might as well go back and document the history of the Madison, from its opening day. Having done that, I thought it would be interesting to include the Madison's competition at the time of its grand opening on October 16, 1920. By now I was so involved (and had collected so much material) I felt compelled to detail the history of all of the Peoria Area's known theaters, from the very beginning. I wound up documenting over 130 of them, dating back to 1836.

And so, what began as a small booklet of my theater experiences, evolved into (as of this printing) a 15-chapter book on the history of theaters and showbusiness in "our town." That book, by the way, is still growing but hasn't made it into print as yet, primarily because a column called *Yester Days* got in the way.

While collecting and documenting this wealth of information for the book, the Journal Star began publishing a tabloid section each Monday called *Vintage Point*. It immediately struck me that all the material I was finding at the Peoria Public Library, the Bradley University Library, and other places, might be of interest to the older folks who would be reading the newspaper's new senior citizen section.

I contacted my friend, Jack Brimeyer, who was then assistant managing editor (and has since become managing editor), who apparently liked what he saw. Enough so, at least, to take my humble effort to the editorial staff, and a few days later, I received a call from the Journal Star's managing editor, Marge Fanning.

The Journal Star began with that first column on May 9, 1988 (which is the first column in this book), and *Yester Days* has been running ever since.

So, here's the first 101 of those columns in book form, with most of the original photos, and many more. I hope they will, once again, take you back to some of those bygone days and beyond, many of which...*seem like only yesterday!*

Bill Adams

Table of Contents

First Column, May 9, 1988

Shows began playing in Peoria 150 years ago

Bill Adams

Native Peorian William R. Adams, better known as Bill, is the retired president of Mid-America Television and LDX Broadcast Inc. and is the former general manager of WEEK-TV, Channel 25. He is on the Public Building Commission and has served on local and National Better Business Bureau boards and councils.

Before joining WEEK-TV in 1960, Bill managed the Madison Theater for 15 years and was production manager for TV TimeTab. He also served in the U.S. Navy from 1944-46.

A Woodruff High School graduate, Bill is married to the former Florence Castle, also a native Peorian. They have three daughters, two sons and four grandsons and reside in Peoria. (At book publishing time, six grandsons and one grand-daughter...and twins on the way.)

This column is dedicated to the history of our Greater-Peoria Area. Although it will touch upon all facets of that history, it will deal mainly with the entertainment business, since that was my background and interest all my adult life. It's written for young and old alike...but it's nostalgia only if you're old enough!

If anyone waxes nostalgic over this one, get to the "Guiness Book of Records" people *fast*. You'd have to be more than a century and a half in age, because it was just 150 years ago last February when showbusiness began in Peoria, at least as far as our documentation goes.

The first known theatrical performance in Peoria dates back to 1838...in a new courthouse, built between 1834 and 1836. (As far as I know, the "Grassy Knoll" problem hadn't come up yet but then we're talking three courthouses ago.)

"Feb. 17, 1838 - A benefit performance was given at the courthouse tonight for Mr. Childs, tickets cost 50 and 75 cents." (A lot of money at the time. I'm sure much more than normal but, then, this *was* a benefit) "and the performance opened at 7 p.m."

At least one other known presentation was made in this same courthouse in 1853. I'm sure there were many others, too, because there were no known public halls in Peoria until about 1850. When traveling shows came to town, they would perform at the courthouse or in the dining and ballrooms of the leading downtown hotels. Two of which were the Clinton House, at South Adams and Liberty, now occupied by the Jefferson Bank Building, and the Planter's House at Northeast Adams and Hamilton, now the location of Security Savings. (This was even before the time of Bob Jamieson.)

My interest in the history of the entertainment business is so intense, I guess, because I was fortunate enough to have had a "plum" job when I was 16 — usher at the Madison Theater. (You remember ushers? They were the ones who showed you to your seat. They even assisted you with a flashlight so you didn't break your neck in a darkened theater.)

But where else could you work while seeing the best Hollywood had to offer week after week, plus all the double-features and stage shows you could handle at the other three "Great States" theaters, the Palace, Rialto and Apollo...and Oh Yeah!, get paid 25¢ an hour to boot!

My interest in "big bands" began then, too. I never missed a show change at the Madison or the Palace. All the bands played the Palace...Benny Goodman,

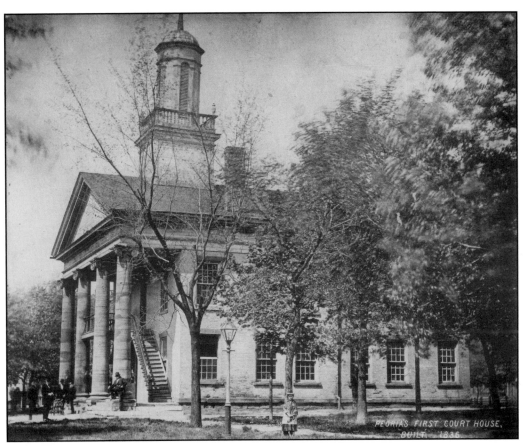

The Peoria County Court House, completed in 1836. It was the location of the first known theatrical performance in Peoria, on February 17, 1838. *(Picture courtesy of Peoria Public Library)*

Glenn Miller, Duke Ellington, Gene Krupa, Louie Armstrong, Horace Heidt, and Tiny Hill. I can still remember sitting down front, watching and listening to the pit orchestra below stage level, during intermissions and before and after shows.

You know what? It was worth the 30 or 40¢ admission, even if you didn't get in free.

...and it seems like only yesterday!

Rouse's Hall opened in 1857

TODAY AND YESTERDAY - Monday, May 16...1873!

A band of 25 Indians, fresh from the wild and wooly West, stopped in Peoria for an exhibition at Rouse's Hall before traveling on to the International Fair in Vienna to become part of P.T. Barnum's show; real, live Comanche Indians, chiefs and braves mostly.

About Rouse's Hall...it was by no means a new showplace when Barnum's Comanches descended upon it.

It was opened on May 18, 1857, at Main and Jefferson, with the entrance at 404 Main...built by Dr. Rudolphus Rouse, a prominent Peoria physician at the time. The opening production was a play titled "Charles II or The Merry Monarch," starring Broadway favorites Mr. and Mrs. Henry Howard.

Around the turn of the century, it became the Main Street Theater, giving way to silent motion pictures and vaudeville.

The theater was razed in 1920 to make way for the Peoria Life Building, later known as the Alliance Life Building. You know it today as The First National Bank Building.

Rouse's Hall wasn't the only Peoria theater to present wild Indians - or at least try..."Sept. 4, 1917 - Wild Indians were hunted on the streets of Peoria last night by motorcycle police. The fugitive redskins were sons of Chief Bull Bear (no stockmarket pun intended) of the Arapahoes. They went wild after sampling Peoria's firewater and failed to show up for their act at the 'Hippodrome.' "

You know how you can remember exactly where you were and what you were doing at the time of some major historic event? Like President Kennedy's assassination for example!

That's why I can remember so vividly Sunday, Dec. 7, 1941. I was just 16 at the time of that day that would "live in infamy," working Aisle Two at the Madison Theater as the "rookie" usher.

Bob Hagen, assistant manager, came running excitedly out of the manager's office, telling everyone in hearing distance that the Japanese had bombed Pearl Harbor! This 16-year-old man of the world commented..."Who's she?"

...and it seems like only yesterday!

Tearing down Rouse's Hall, at the corner of Main and Jefferson. Built by Dr. Rudolphus Rouse, it was one of Peoria's first theaters. *(Picture courtesy of Peoria Public Library)*

Marian & Jim became Molly & Fibber McGee

Our first Yester Days column has already struck a responsive chord with Aaron Drake of Pekin. The mention of big bands caused Mr. Drake to call to give the "Inglaterra Ballroom" equal time. (We'll cover this grand old ballroom along Peoria's Main Street in future articles.)

He says the "Ing" had more big-name bands than the Palace in those days...and he's right, of course. Not only that, you could also dance to your favorites as well as listen. This, however, was a little before my dancing days. I was married 10 years before my wife convinced me that dancing to the big-band sound was fun, too...and we still do. I'm a theater man at heart, though. I still prefer to sit and listen. (But don't tell her!)

Good Friday and April Fool's Day came together this year and to add a bit of irony to it...it was the day Fibber McGee passed away. Jim Jordan and his wife, Marian Driscoll Jordan (who died of cancer 27 years ago), were great former Peorians and good friends of our town until the end. During their many years at the top of the heap in the Golden Days of Radio, they continually mentioned Peoria on their "Fibber McGee and Molly" show. Jim was born and raised on a farm about six miles out Farmington Road from Peoria. He met the young Marian Driscoll while she was singing in the choir at St. John's Church in the "South End," where he and a friend were performing.

He and Marian later married and had two children, Jim Jr. and Kathryn. The Jordan family later lived at 601 Bradley Ave. across from the Bradley campus. Jim had lived in the neighborhood as a child and admitted playing in tunnels under the field that would later be the location of Robertson Memorial Field House. The Jordan's put together a song-and-dance act and traveled the circuit, performing at theaters throughout the country. They would return to Peoria from time to time and played the Madison and Palace on several occasions.

When radio came into vogue in the 1920's, Jim and Marian were given the opportunity to work long hours (for no pay in the beginning) on WENR in Chicago. They were making big money in theater appearances but were getting more exposure on radio. With their future producer, Don Quinn, they put together a show called "Smackout," a format not unlike Fibber McGee. The young Jim Jordan had developed an old man's voice for radio and used it later on this show as the proprietor of a grocery store that, when someone wanted to buy something, he was always "smack out" of that particular item.

They moved from WENR to WMAQ, where they first met another struggling entertainer from Peoria by the name of Charles Correll. He became the "Andy" of "Amos 'n' Andy" but that's another story.

They eventually developed "Fibber McGee and Molly" with Don Quinn and sold it to the Johnson's Wax Co. It soon went on the NBC network and the rest is history. It was the No. 1 radio show for several years and was in the "top 10" for many more. I had the honor and extreme pleasure of interviewing Jim Jordan in his Beverly Hills home for a television show in 1984. Jim was 87 then and was the recipient that year of the Illinois Broadcaster's Association "Outstanding Achievement" award. He was old in years but still had the quick wit of youth.

Jim Jordan died April 1, 1988...at the age of 91. I like to think that Jim smiled a little that it was Good Friday, but I would bet my first usher's paycheck that he laughed out loud when told it was April Fool's Day.

...and this time it was only yesterday!

Marian and Jim Jordan in an October, 1941 publicity photo to promote their radio program.
(An NBC photo)

Bob Hope's career took off on old radio

In the year following World War II, Memorial Day was a pretty busy time for those honoring our military heroes. On this date, observance began with memorial services on Legion Hill in Springdale Cemetery, followed in the afternoon by a mammoth parade of the downtown area.

Then another service in the Court House Square at 2:30 p.m. Prior to the parade, combined units of the military conducted services at noon on the East Peoria side of the Franklin Street Bridge, in honor of the men who lost their lives at sea. Speaker was the Rev. Joseph Gerber, a former naval chaplain.

What better day to remember the man who did more to raise the morale of the fighting men and women through World War II, Korea, Vietnam and right on to our Persian Gulf protectors of today.

I "hope" you didn't miss "Happy Birthday, Bob: 50 Stars Salute Your 50 Years with NBC." (Now that's a title!) It aired a couple Monday nights ago on NBC and WEEK-TV. It not only celebrated Mr. Leslie Townes Hope's association with the network, first on radio and then television, but also his 85th birthday.

Now, everyone today is probably familiar with Bob's TV career, but do you recall his meteoric rise in radio? His radio premiere was on NBC's Blue Network (they had two, the Blue and the Red), on January 4, 1935. It was on a show called "The Intimate Review" which already starred James Melton and Jane Froman and the Al Goodman Bromo Seltzer Orchestra. Also in 1935, he briefly appeared on "Atlantic Family" for Atlantic Oil (How about that, Texaco?), along with Red Nichols and his Orchestra. In 1936 he joined the "Rippling Rhythm Revue" featuring Shep Fields and his Orchestra, of course. All these associations were brief, but two years later Robert was a hit in "The Big Broadcast of 1938" movie, singing his soon-to-become theme song, "Thanks for the Memory" (not Memories), with Shirley Ross. It starred W.C. Fields and also featured Martha Raye and Dorothy Lamour.

This became Bob's big break and he signed with Pepsodent Toothpaste (remember poor Miriam, who neglected using Irium?), to do his own show which began on NBC Sept. 27, 1938. By 1940, the show moved into fourth place behind Edgar Bergan, Jack Benny and Fibber McGee and Molly. By 1943, Hope's show was No. 1 in the country, with a fabulous 40-plus Hooper rating.

Bob used many big-name stars on his show from Al Jolson, to Judy Garland, to Bing Crosby, but his regular cast was Barbara Jo Allen as "Vera Vague," Blanche Stewart and Elvia Allman as "Brenda and Cobina," vocalist Frances Langford, side-kick Jerry Colonna and Skinnay (not Skinny) Ennis and his Orchestra.

Which brings me to my first "look" at Mr. America. My dad was a big fan of Bob Hope's radio show from the beginning ...and in the summer of 1939, after its first season on the air, my parents and I were on our way to a two-week fishing vacation at Nisswa, Minn. There were no super-expressways in those days. If your route went through town, you went through town, which we did in Minneapolis. As we were stopping and starting with the traffic downtown, I spied the Orpheum Theater marquee featuring Bob Hope and his entire radio cast "On Stage-In Person!" Dad could go no farther. He went around the block, parked the car and we went down to see the stage show...the fishing could wait.

They put on a great show, and as I recall, Bob and Vera Vague got a little risqué, or so it seemed to a 14-year-old kid. I was not only hooked on Bob Hope from then on...but Skinnay Ennis became one of my favorite bands. Ennis was also a vocalist with a breathless singing style, who sang with Hal Kemp before leading his own band. He also did comedy on the radio program. His most famous song became his theme song. Remember "Got a Date With An Angel"?

So no matter what NBC says, Bob Hope hasn't been associated with the network for 50 years. It's really 53 years...but his NBC success began 50 years ago.

...and it seems like only yesterday!

Bob Hope and Jerry Colonna on Bob's NBC radio show. *(An NBC photo)*

Sander Vanocur ushered at the Madison

...and a tribute to Bob Jamieson, Sr.

Robert A. (Bob) Jamieson

(A Journal Star photo)

Tuesday, May 17th was just another of many Red Letter Days for Mr. Robert A. Jamieson. Our good friend Bob received another major award (I think this makes three) from the Salvation Army ...their most prestigious "OTHERS" award. To help celebrate the occasion was Robert A.'s son, young Bob Jamieson, NBC correspondent who heads up the network's "Sunrise" news program weekday mornings and backstops John Palmer on the "Today" show among his other duties. If anyone in our town deserves the accolades he receives, it's the senior Bob Jamieson, including a school named for him. The Army is well aware of this because Bob has served for over 40 years on their advisory board and I've never known him when he wasn't concerned for the "other" less fortunate people in our society.

I've never heard a finer tribute paid to a father from a son than young Bob's to end his keynote address at the packed house in the Civic Center. After turning many nice phrases about his dad, this 45-year-old man of the world said, "...and when I grow up, I want to be just like him!" — and that's just about the best "award" of all.

All this reminds me of an association I had with another NBC-TV news correspondent with a Peoria connection many years ago. In 1961, the year after I joined WEEK-TV as promotion manager, I had the good fortune to attend an NBC Promotion Manager's Conference in New York City. Fred Mueller, WEEK's first general manager (who, incidentally put the first Peoria TV station on the air in 1953), joined me on the trip. Fred tended to his N.Y. business while I attended the meetings but we would meet each night, and he bought us tickets to Broadway shows three nights in a row...and I've been a stage play addict ever since.

The last night in N.Y., the network's news department hosted a cocktail party for all the affiliate promotion managers and I asked Fred to join me (as if he couldn't wrangle an invitation without my help). As we entered the room, we were greeted by all the NBC-TV and Radio news anchors and reporters except David Brinkley. David was the Washington, D.C. half of the "Huntley-Brinkley Report" so he was, obviously, not in town, but we had the chance to meet and visit with Chet Huntley, Frank McGee, Sander Vanocur and many others. I don't know about Fred...but this kid was impressed!

My biggest surprise of the evening came from Sander Vanocur. Sander was a new, rising news reporter and news anchor at the time. He later became a personal friend of President Kennedy and the family. As I walked up to him to shake hands, he read my name tag and said, "Peoria, my old home town!"

Reading the surprise on my face, he explained that it wasn't really his hometown but he had spent a couple happy years in Peoria. He and his mother had moved to Peoria and she operated a diner restaurant in the 100 block of Northeast Monroe Street, next to the old Peoria Public Library Building. In our conversation, he mentioned that to help out with the living expenses he had a part-time job as usher at a local theater. My antenna went up immediately. Without indicating my interest at this news, I began quizzing him as to where and when he ushered. Sander couldn't, off-hand, remember the name of the theater but said it was across the street from the Père Marquette Hotel. I mentioned the Madison and he said, "Yeah, that's the one...the Madison!"

When I asked him when this was, he thought a moment and indicated he must have started about the beginning of 1944. I was nearly afraid to ask the next question but said, "Do you, by any chance, remember the manager of the theater?" Vanocur

Sander Vanocur in 1963
(An NBC photo)

said, "I don't remember his name but he was a tall, skinny black-haired young guy, as I recall." I stuck out my hand and said, "Shake hands with Skinny!" This time it was Vanocur who registered complete surprise.

...and it seems like only yesterday!

Remembering when dad's presents were 'cheap'

From one father to another (well, some of you anyway), it just occurred to me that, because I'm an only child, my dad was robbed! He received only one Father's Day gift each year. That's why I had five kids.

And that one gift my father received was a pretty cheap one, too. Now, it wasn't that I was cheap, it was just that, when I was young, prices were a little more reasonable than they are today. A *little* more?

For instance...in 1935, Peoria Dry Goods was selling men's polo shirts or sweaters - two for $1. Also, men's hosiery - four pairs for $1; Clark's Department Store had Essley shirts for $1.65; Block and Kuhl's Father's Day Necktie Sale 55¢; Cohen's Furniture - electric fans (8 inch) $1.19, deck chairs 98¢; Szold's - men's straw hats 78¢, washable ties 9¢ each (now, that's more in my price range); Klein's Basement - fine dress shirts 79¢; Sears - genuine overalls $1.10; plain socks 10¢; The Bee Hive - fine pipes 37¢.

Or, if you were a little flush and wanted to treat Dad to some entertainment in June of 1935, buy him a couple tickets to take Mom to see, hear and dance to Isham Jones and his 17 Columbia Artists at the Inglaterra or Chick Stephan's Orchestra in the Seneca Hotel or McKinney's Original Cotton Pickers at the National Roof.

Or, how about a stage show at the Palace, featuring the rage of the 1933-34 Chicago World's Fair - fan dancer Sally Rand and her Revue. Oh well, forget that; Mom wouldn't let him go anyway!

Five years later, in 1940, Dad was forced to accept a more expensive gift. Fredman Brothers - lawn mowers $2.98; The B & M offered a Swank cigarette case for $1, and Palm Beach ties for $1; Block and Kuhl's advertised Wilson Brothers pajamas for $2 (the Wilson Brothers weren't in them, of course), Beau Brummel ties $1, Manhattan shirts $2 (Now, who wants a shirt you can only wear in New York?) and Walgreen's (remember where they were located in 1940?) had Golden Crown golf balls for 49¢ each, seven jewel Tyson watches $6, a pound of Prince Albert tobacco 67¢. And Walgreen's took the prize for the best gift of all. They loaned you a free camera...if you bought and developed your film with them!

By 1953, I could afford to pay a little more for Dad but prices were getting completely out of hand. O'Brien-Jobst had 100 percent Dacron suits for $89.50 or slacks for $28.75; year-round suits for $22.50; Block and Kuhl's offered Lytton's summer suits for $25 and summer slacks two for $11; Peoria Furniture Mart was selling modern chairs at $29.95 and Schradzki's featured Prince Gardner wallets and billfolds (I always thought they were the same thing) and key chain sets for $5 (regular $6.75). Also, blue denim slacks $4.95.

But if my two (by then) kids wanted to make me happy, all they had to do was buy me a special 2-door, 6-passenger Salon Buick for just $2,263.88. The dollars weren't bad, it was the additional 88¢ that killed you! So, sit back, relax and try to keep cool, Dad. Look how much more expensive your gift will be next Sunday. YOU NEVER HAD IT SO GOOD!

...and it seems like only yesterday!

A Ray Barclay photo of Block & Kuhl's "Big White Store," one of several local stores offering "cheap" Father's Day gifts back in 1935.
(Photo courtesy of R. W. Deller from Lee Roten's Historic Peoria Photo File)

The June 20 & June 27, 1988 columns were rewritten and reprinted on July 10 & July 17, 1989. Please see pages 132 & 134.

Remembering some glorious old Fourths

Years ago, a show business name that became synonymous with the Fourth of July was George M. Cohan. Mr. C. was an all-time great of the Broadway stage. Not only an outstanding song-and-dance man, he was also a composer-lyricist-librettist-director-producer.

Some of his big hit songs were "Give My Regards to Broadway," "Forty-five Minutes From Broadway," "Harrigan," and "Mary's A Grand Old Name." But what tied him closely to the holiday were "I'm A Yankee Doodle Dandy," "You're A Grand Old Flag," and "Over There." George received the Congressional Medal for "Over There," which became the rallying cry of our troops in World War I. Younger readers will relate to Mr. Cohan through the Academy Award-winning portrayal of him by James Cagney in 1942. (The "Yankee Doodle Dandy" movie is still being shown on TV.) Joel Grey also portrayed Cohan in the 1968 Broadway stage musical, "George M!"

Remember his words, "I'm a Yankee Doodle Dandy...born on the Fourth of July...."? George was so patriotic, he stretched his birthdate a little, because he was actually born on July 3, 1878, in Providence, R.I. He died in New York City on Nov. 5, 1942.

Thinking back on our personal "Independence Day" celebrations though, the fireworks were what made for a "Glorious Fourth." It was difficult to get to sleep the night before just thinking about it. Unfortunately, however, July 5 wasn't so glorious for many youngsters and adults, alike, as horrors of the previous day were reported.

It's because of the many accidents that always occurred, that local governments stepped in and banned fireworks as a personal privilege. Peoria and East Peoria were the first to ban the personal use of fireworks in this area in 1940. To compensate for this, the American Legion staged its first big fireworks demonstration that year at Peoria Stadium, with the cooperation of the Peoria Journal-Transcript.

The Peoria Star of July 4, 1940, showed pictures of kids outside the city limits, shooting off fireworks "as usual," while another classic and, I'm sure, posed, photo showed kids on the West Peoria side of Western Avenue enjoying the thrills of firecrackers, while kids on the Peoria side sat, wistfully, on the curb watching them. The reason for the ban, though, must have had something to do with the way we youngsters created new ways of abusing the privilege. Torpedoes, for instance, were designed to explode when thrown on a hard surface. But another, more exciting way to explode them (and scare more people in the process), was to place them on streetcar tracks, to explode as the next streetcar came by.

One-incher firecrackers were held at the end while they exploded, by some of the braver (and dumber) kids. One-, two-, and three-inchers were placed under inverted tin cans, to see how high they would go. No wonder they were banned!

From about 8 to 12 years of age, I lived with my parents "up the river," north of Mossville. My dad (with the help of an uncle) built a house in Holmes Center, on the Illinois River. What a great place to live at that age. Country life, but without the work of a farm. Our place was an ideal spot to have a picnic and my family and their friends were picnic addicts. Every Fourth of July they would assemble for one (or, maybe two) days.

One night, shortly after dark, my dad and uncles were shooting the big night-time stuff. (We kids were not allowed to handle these.) Dad had a bunch of "farmer" matches in his shirt pocket. He was holding a Roman candle while it shot various-colored balls of fire into the sky. It backfired, and a fireball went into his pocket of wooden matches. He dropped the candle, tore off his shirt, buttons and all and, fortunately, avoided a serious chest burn, or worse. Exciting times? You bet, but dangerous, too.

...and it seems like only yesterday!

George M. Cohan - the legendary Broadway performer who wrote so many old favorite songs, including "Give My Regards to Broadway" and "You're A Grand Old Flag."

(Photo courtesy of Peoria Public Library)

The July 11, 1988 column was rewritten and reprinted on July 24, 1989. Please see page 136.

'36 a scorcher, too

Last week's column, covering the World Premiere of "Earthworm Tractors" at the Madison on July 14, 1936 (the day before the hottest day on record), reminded us that there was more to the story regarding hot weather in the '30's. Although it won't make us feel any cooler in this drought year of 1988, there may be a little comfort in knowing that it was considerably hotter then than it has been so far this year.

But 1936 wasn't the only scorcher. For instance, 1931 broke a record with seven straight days of 100° plus. Then in 1934 a June 26th headline in the Peoria Star gave an indication of what was in store for the summer: PEORIA STEAMS IN "WET HEAT" AS MERCURY HITS 101°.

The heat wave had started in May and the temperature steadily climbed to 104° by June 27 and 28.

The year 1934 had another similarity to 1936. It also boasted of a historical day in association with a hot spell. July 4 marked the opening of a "gigantic distillery." The world's largest...the 22-acre Hiram Walker & Sons opened with a bang (pardon the pun) on that date. By July 21, the weather was back on the front page and dominated the local news until July 26, when it finally dropped below 100°. Local heat-related deaths reached 21 with 500 nationally. During May, June and July, 16 days of 100-to-105° temps were recorded. The year 1934 was just a curtain-raiser, though, for 1936. As we mentioned last week, the all-time record high temperature for Peoria was achieved on July 15, peaking just after the Madison's World Premiere. The string of 100° days began on July 4 and continued through July 17, 14 straight days, doubling the previous record of seven set in 1931. A total of 167 people died of heat-related causes.

Among the dead was retired vice president of the First National Bank, George M. Bush, at his 310 N. Perry residence. Another was Fire Chief Dennis E. O'Connell, found dead the next day at his home at 617 Frye Ave. by an ice delivery man.

It was so hot that Caterpillar temporarily laid off 9,000 workers in the factory area and the iron workers were forced to quit work on a new rack-house under construction at the two-year-old Hiram Walker Distillery.

People trying to endure the heat, in those days before air-conditioning, were sleeping outside in places like Eckwood Park on the riverfront and on Northmoor Golf Course.

To give one example of how hot it was: Peoria attorney E. Bentley Hamilton was playing golf at Peoria Country Club. He reached into his bag for a ball and came out with a "sticky mass" instead. The extreme heat had broken the covering of the ball, allowing the liquid center to leak out. Now that's what I call hot! But the big question is...why in the world was he playing golf in that heat, anyway? That's a silly question, and can only be answered by another golfer.

The one big difference between the heat of the '30's and the heat of 1988 is...air-conditioning! It was long before homes were air-conditioned and little else, for that matter. Even electric fans were scarce, which was why so many people fell victim to heat prostration. Even years later, in the '40's and '50's, one of the few air-conditioned places was the theater, and during the day, we'd sell more tickets because of air-conditioning than because of the movie.

Opening night of the brand new Hiram Walker's Distillery on July 4, 1934, another one of Peoria's hottest days.
(Photo courtesy of Peoria Public Library)

Every morning during hot weather, we'd start up the big air-conditioner in the basement of the Madison around 9 a.m. It had a huge fly-wheel about 25 feet in diameter. We'd close all the windows and doors and let'er run full-blast until the box office opened at 11:45 a.m. By then it would be cold enough to "hang meat" in the auditorium. When the cashier was ready, we'd open the doors across the front of the theater. People walking up and down Main Street would get hit with that cold air, turn immediately into the box office and buy a ticket. They wouldn't even look to see what was playing or the price of a ticket. They just wanted to get inside.

...and it seems like only yesterday!

Madison Theater beat Palace in race to open

A later photo of The Magnificent Madison Theater which opened October 16, 1920.
(Photo courtesy of Peoria Public Library)

Russ Sweeney of East Peoria answered our inquiry about who remembered the opening of the Madison Theater in 1920. He wasn't at the opening, but as a 7-year-old, he remembers the crowd in front of the theater that day. Russ also says his father was a projectionist at the Lyceum Theater in the early days. He sent us a copy of "Moving Picture World" dated Jan. 29, 1921, which features the grand opening of the Palace Theater on Thursday night, Jan. 6, 1921. It opened as Ascher's Palace, about three months after the Madison, across the street. Some old-timers may recall these two grand old theaters being built simultaneously, but did you know there was a race to see which one would open first?

Dee Robinson was president of Robinson Amusement Co., the firm that developed and built the Madison. Dee was a modest man and, when he was young, traveled with many theatrical companies. But he tired of life on the road and decided to settle down. He settled in Peoria, which he later called "the greatest city in the world." He must have truly believed that, too, because he gave up a traveling job, making $200 to $300 per week, and became a Peoria factory bookkeeper for $9 per week. He soon opened his own theater, built a theater chain, until the building of his "dream theater," the magnificent Madison. But another prominent Peorian was also dreaming at the same time. William E. Hull was building

Ascher's Palace Theater lost the race. It opened on January 6, 1921.
(Photo courtesy of Peoria Public Library)

his beautiful theater and apartment complex just across the street. In addition to being a U.S. representative, Mr. Hull was a local man who believed in Peoria and proved it by developing his "palace" structure. He, too, was high in praise of Peoria, calling it "the greatest city of its size in America."

Robinson leaned heavily on local Peoria businesses to develop his project. He hired Frederic J. Klein as Madison architect, whose offices were just a little over a block down Main Street. Mr. Klein earlier designed the Hippodrome Theater (later, the Rialto). Fred Harbers and Sons were hired as general contractors. Dee also hired a local man, Herbert D. McNally, as general manager. Mac had previously managed the old Empress Theater, below the site of the new Palace, in the 400 block of Main, among others.

Rep. Hull, on the other hand, not being a theatrical man, leased his theater to Ascher Bros., a Chicago chain headed by Nathan Ascher and his brothers, Harry and Max. The Chicago influence carried over in the designing by hiring J. E. O. Pridmore, a Chicago theater architect. The general contractor, however, was a Peoria firm, Val Jobst & Sons. But Ascher Bros. also hired Chicagoan Charles F. Manzing as manager, plus Chicago's Harry Rogers as musical director, and Rogers recruited most of his musicians from Ascher's Chicago theaters.

For a time it appeared a toss-up as to which theater would open first. It's impossible to read someone's mind 68 years later, but Mr. R. obviously, gave a lot of thought to the future of the business and where it was headed. In 1920, movies were getting better and better. They were already cutting heavily into vaudeville. It was now becoming possible to show a quality film for three or four days and capture a large audience, without the addition of vaudeville, for about the same competitive price. So, why pay the added cost of a backstage capable of "flying" scenery, not to mention the additional time to build it? So the Madison plans were altered. The stage area was capped off and the race to open first was won by nearly three months!

Mr. Robinson's philosophy proved correct over the years because, from the beginning, until it closed in 1983, the Madison was always considered the quality motion-picture theater in Peoria. It was the flagship theater in Central Illinois for years. Even in the late '30's and early '40's (the heyday of the double-feature) the Madison was the only Peoria theater able to maintain its quality status by showing a single top movie every week, for a full seven days, sometimes more, and demanding the highest box-office prices at the same time. Dee Robinson was, truly, a genius of his time.

The big race was a little before my time, but I fondly remember those early '40's years.

...and it seems like only yesterday!

Over 125 "showplaces" grace Peoria's history

We've talked about Peoria's show business legend and pinpointed a few examples of its very early development. Searching for material for this column (and a book that may, or may not, ever get published), has presented us with information on over 125 "showplaces" in the Greater Peoria area that had something to do with this town's great interest in entertainment. To select a few of the major ones that, no doubt, contributed to the "live" side of the business, I've chosen these: Parmely's Hall (later Howard's Theater); Rouse's Hall (later Main Street Theater); Grand Opera House; Pete Weast's Theater (later Lyceum Theater); Majestic Theater; Orpheum Theater; Shrine Temple (later Shrine Mosque); Hippodrome Theater (later Rialto); Princess Theater; Apollo Theater; Madison Theater and Palace Theater.

Now, wait! Before you start questioning three of the last five (which were known mostly as movie theaters) they did, at one time or other, present live entertainment. We'll cover some of them later, but it was the performers that contributed most, and here's some early newspaper quotes documenting them.

Feb. 1, 1882 - "General Tom Thumb, the midget, made his first appearance in Peoria, playing in the two-a-day vaudeville at Rouse's Hall. He sang a few comic songs and cracked a few jokes and was well received. Before the performance, he put on a smart publicity build-up by driving through the streets in a midget-sized coach, drawn by four small ponies, and attended by an undersized coachman in livery...."

Jan. 23, 1878 - "The Wild West was represented by Buffalo Bill (William J.) Cody and Company played at Rouse's Hall the other night in the melodrama, 'Life on the Border'...."

April 5, 1892 - "John L. Sullivan, king of the heavyweight prizefighters, played at the Grand Opera House today in the melodrama 'Honest Hearts and Willing Hands.' He brought down the house at the climax when he stepped forward in the role of the hero, shook his fist under the nose of the snarling villain, placed a brawny arm around the waist and shoulders of a sobbing old woman and orated - 'Fear not, Mudder, I'm wid yez.'"

April 13, 1902 - "Eva Tanguay, the 'I Don't Care' girl of burlesque, appeared in Peoria for the first time. She played at the Grand Opera House in 'Chaperones'...."

Jan. 18, 1911 - "Lillian Russell, famous beauty of the day, was playing at the Majestic Theater in 'In Search of a Sinner.'"

March 4, 1915 - "Norman Hackett played at the Orpheum Theater in 'The Mystery of the Hot Biscuit.'"

March 24, 1915 - "Sophie Tucker was wowing 'em in vaudeville at the Hippodrome."

Oct. 20, 1917 - "Thrice did Madame Sarah Bernhardt die on the stage of the Majestic Theater this day, each time investing that sordid and commonplace function of shuffling off with fresh modesty. Aged and crippled, the great actress proved again she still had what it took to make her the toast of the stage in all lands."

April 8, 1935 - "Irene Vermillion, whose home town is Peoria, although she has headlined vaudeville bills all over the United States and only recently returned from a successful London appearance, will bring her Revue Continental to the Palace stage today for a one-day showing.

With her act is Kemit Dart's orchestra. Mr. Dart, also a former Peorian, whose dance music was widely popular over Central Illinois before he went into

The Grand Opera House, where John L. Sullivan appeared on April 5, 1892.
(Photo courtesy of R. W. Deller from Lee Roten's Historic Peoria Photo File)

vaudeville, and Miss Vermillion's revue. Mr. Dart and Miss Vermillion are husband and wife, and he manages Miss Vermillion's revue. Dart's orchestra was a striking success in London and furnishes accompaniment for Miss Vermillion's dancing, which has been so widely praised by critics."

April 30, 1931 - "Rear Admiral Richard E. Byrd, USN, explorer of the wastelands around the North and South Poles, spoke at the Rialto Theater before an audience of some 3,000. He appeared under the auspices of the Inter-Civic Council."

...and it seems like only yesterday!

Radio star Charles Correll never forgot Peoria

Back in 1949, former Peorian Charles J. Correll was quoted as saying, "You can take the boy out of Peoria, but you can't take Peoria out of the boy." He and Jim Jordan were perfect examples of that and both were (along with Marian Dricoll Jordan) very proud of their Peoria roots. Jim and Marian, of course, went on to fame as "Fibber McGee and Molly," but Charles Correll was already a big-time personality as Andy of "Amos and Andy" by that time. He often reminisced about his hometown, saying that he never had the town out of his mind. Charley was born at 711 Hancock St. (now a vacant lot), on Feb. 3, 1890, the son of Joseph B. and Stella Fiss Correll. He was the oldest of three boys and a girl. His brother, Joseph B. "Red" Correll, was the long-time superintendent of building and grounds for Peoria public schools while his kid brother, Thomas, made a career coaching in Peoria-area schools, first at Averyville and Kingman and then as coach and athletic director of Woodruff High School. (Tommy was my coach at Woodruff.) His sister, Alice, married Charles Roszell.

When Charles Correll was an infant, the family moved to 507 Bigelow. By the time he was four or five, they moved to 1318 N. Adams, where they lived the entire time he went to school. He started grade school at the old Jefferson School at the corner of Mary and Jefferson. Later, he attended Longfellow School. After Longfellow, he attended Greeley and graduated there. While in eighth grade, young Charles started carrying papers for the Peoria Journal and carried for either the Journal or Star all the time he went to Peoria High, where he graduated in 1907. He recalled that their home on N. Adams was next to the firehouse and he loved to watch them train the horses that pulled the fire wagons.

Following graduation, Charley went to Springfield and worked as a stenographer for the state superintendent of construction until 1908. Then he returned to Peoria to learn the bricklaying trade with V. Jobst and Son, where his dad was a bricklayer.

His folks gave him piano lessons for ten months when he was thirteen. He readily admitted he liked music (and everything) better than bricklaying, so by 1911 he was playing the piano for the silent movies at the Columbia Theater in the evening while laying brick during the day. Some of those days in 1911 he was associated with another Peoria theater, too, but as a bricklayer, not as a piano player. Len Worley told the story for years, that Charley Correll laid brick on the Orpheum Theater that opened April 24, 1911. Correll moved to Rock Island in 1914 and played piano in the Majestic Theater there in the winter and laid brick in the summer. It was about this time he got into all the local talent shows in town. Through those, he went to work for a Chicago road company, putting on home talent shows around the country. He finally quit the bricklaying trade in 1918. It was that year he met Freeman Gosden (Amos of "Amos and Andy") in Durham, N.C., who was also a member of the same home talent company. They worked together from 1918 to 1924, when they started in radio.

The two future radio pioneers moved to Chicago. They lived together and began fooling around with a ukulele and piano. They learned a few songs and started in radio (for no pay) on a New Orleans station. They created a couple Negro characters and cut some talking records for Victor. They began the black dialect in 1925 and went on the air on WGN Chicago on Jan. 12, 1926, as "Sam and Henry." The show shortly became a solid hit. It was so well received in Chicago that, when the boys left WGN two years later, the station decided to keep the name.

On March 19, 1928, they moved over to WMAQ, which was to become the CBS outlet for Chicago. Since they lost the rights to "Sam and Henry," they began putting together a new show and called it "Amos and Andy." It went on the NBC Red Network on Aug. 19, 1929, sponsored by Pepsodent toothpaste.

Our good friend Bill Brown, former general manager of WMBD and now a broker for Merrill-Lynch, is the proud possessor of an original letter written by Charles Correll to his "Uncle Joe and Aunt Maggie," dated June 17, 1929. It was written the day that final arrangements were made for "Amos and Andy" to go on the network. It tells the inside story of this historic event. Bill has given us a copy of that letter and we'll cover it next week.

...and it seems (at least to some of us) like only yesterday!

Charley Correll and his wife on a return visit to Peoria on January 14, 1936, to celebrate his father's 70th birthday.
(Photo courtesy of Peoria Public Library)

On the road with Charles Correll...

Last week's column covered Charles Correll's Peoria connection up to his beginning in radio as Andy of "Amos and Andy." As we mentioned, Bill Brown, former general manager of WMBD, has an original letter from Charles Correll to his uncle and aunt back in Peoria. (We don't know their last name, but I believe "Aunt Maggie" was his father's sister.) It's so interesting from a personal, as well as historic point of view, we asked Bill to let us share it with you.

The letter was found in the Majestic Theater Building where the WMBD studios were for many years. It was written on Hotel Muehlebach stationery in Kansas City, where Amos and Andy were doing a personal appearance at a local theater:

"June 17th, 1929

"Dear Uncle Joe and Aunt Maggie:

"Just wrote my Dad a letter and while I have a little time between shows here I will drop you a few lines because I have some news and you are generally very much interested in what is happening to us.

"You know we all wondered what would happen when we quit the Tribune and went to the News. Well, it has happened. That syndicating of records that we started got us exactly what we wanted and today the final arrangements were made for us to go with the National Broadcasting Co., starting on the chain on Aug. 19th, and Pepsodent Co. will sponsor us. We've been dickering with them for the last two months hot and heavy and the delay was because we wanted certain things in our contract that they didn't want to put in so we finally told them to either put them in or tear up their contract and today we got the contract we wanted.

"I suppose Dad has told you all about this before but he didn't know much more than we did and that wasn't much up till now. There have been several stories in various papers saying we were going with them and the news has been out all over for quite a while but it was just a lot of hot air until now. They are paying the News $16,500 for our contract and they pay us $100,000 for the year and in addition to that we'll work for another program for an additional $50,000 so it looks like a pretty nice year. That doesn't include personal appearances and personal appearances right now are paying us $5,000 a week as you probably know. Don't think I'm blowing my horn but I am very happy over it all and I know you always show very keen interest in what is going to happen and how we are going to come out, so I'm telling you the facts even though it may sound egotistical but don't get that idea. God knows that's the last thing I want anyone to think or ever expect to be. I'm just damn lucky, that's all. The Lord has his arms around me plenty and nobody knows it more than I do. We just happened to light on something that happens once in a lifetime.

"We have been getting receptions all along the way that were marvelous. The one here in Kansas City outdid the one in San Francisco and they say that Lindbergh had nothing on us in San Francisco. I have a lot of moving pictures of the whole trip and you'll see them before long because I'm going to bring them with me when I come down and that won't be long because we are going to Chicago at the end of this week for one week, then to Minneapolis for one week and then back to Chicago to stay with the exception of probably spending a couple weeks in New York before we go on the chain.

Charles Correll.
(Photos courtesy Peoria Public Library)

Charles Correll as "Andy".

"I've got lots to tell about our trip West. It was great and we both like the West very much, especially the climate. The cities of the East are better, but the climate out there is just too bad. We've had great success in our appearances and have been advertised like a circus every-place, and while we have spent a lot of money stopping at expensive places, still we have come out way ahead so that's that.

"Well, the first act of the last show of the day is on right now so I'll have to quit and get into my clothes for our share of the show. I'll be seeing you soon and if you have a chance, drop me a letter. I'll be home by Saturday and maybe Friday of this week. Love to both of you from both of us."

(Signed) "Chas."

Next week we'll conclude Charles Correll's great success by recalling the fame of "Amos and Andy".

...and it seems like only yesterday!

"I'd like to have you and Aunt Maggie come up and visit us for a few days if you can. But don't come up and visit some-body else and only run and see us once in a while. I mean come to our house and *stay there*. We can show you a good time and we have lots of good drinks so whatever you want and if we haven't got it, we'll get it. What do you you think of that?

"Both of us are well. Gosden and I have been working very hard on this trip but we're standing it all right. The girls are all right, too. We hope both of you are well, also. It's terribly hot here in Kansas City and I hope you are not quite so hot in Peoria. I'm quite sure that Chicago isn't this bad and I *know* absolutely that our apartment is cooler than any of these hotels we've been in.

Nobody, but nobody, missed "Amos and Andy"

When "Amos and Andy" first went on the NBC network on Aug. 19, 1929, Amos Jones and Andrew H. Brown were using blackface gags developed earlier. Freeman Gosden of Richmond, Va., played Amos, while our "Peoria boy," Charles Correll, played Andy. The characters were two Harlem blacks who bought an old car with no windshield and went into the cab business, calling it the Fresh Air Taxi Co., "Incorpolated." Andy carried the comedy and Amos was the straightman. Amos' appeal declined and was, later, used only occasionally. In his place Gosden created a new character, George "Kingfish" Stevens, head of the "Mystic Knights of the Sea" lodge. The show's plots revolved around the conniving Kingfish's double-dealing and, usually, Andy was the victim.

In the program's early years, Correll and Gosden did all the voices, more than 100 of them. Later on, other actors and actresses were brought in, but Gosden still played Lightnin' and Correll played Henry Van Porter.

Radio was still an infant when "Amos and Andy" came on the scene, just before the market crash of 1929. The Depression continued through most of the '30's, but for 15 minutes each weeknight, some of the bitterness was eased by these two common men. They epitomized the masses with no jobs, no money and no foreseeable future. At first the show was on late-night, 10 to 10:15. Later it was scheduled from 6 to 6:15 and ran as a serial, Monday through Friday until 1943.

And did you know it was once broadcast from WMBD? In 1943, the pair had been out west. Their train was delayed for six hours by snow storms in Kansas and they were unable to reach Chicago in time for their broadcast. They detrained, rushed to the WMBD studios and aired the program from here.

"Amos and Andy" was an absolute phenomenon! The listening audience exceeded 40 million a night, six nights a week. Around 1931, theaters advertised that the movie would stop at 6 p.m. so the audience could hear the show over the P.A. system. Otherwise the public would stay home rather than miss one episode.

Newspapers published daily accounts of the program. Taxis, streetcars and busses had no passengers. People didn't run water or flush toilets during the 15 minutes. Auto theft increased. Robbers knew that almost everyone was at the radio set from 6 to 6:15. People could walk down the street on warm spring and summer evenings and listen to the show through open windows because every radio was turned to "Amos and Andy."

Pepsodent ended its sponsorship on Dec. 31, 1937, but Campbell Soups immediately picked it up on Jan. 3, 1938. The program combined the best of situation comedy and soap opera. Many episodes had cliff-hanger endings. This happened in 1939 when Andy went through an entire wedding ceremony, up to the words, "I do." Before the minister could make the final pronouncement, a shot rang out, Andy fell wounded, and Amos wailed, "Ow-wah! Ow-wah!" The next day newspapers were in controversy. Was Andy married or not? Lawyers bickered over the fine points of the law. But Correll and Gosden let it drop and Andy continued his single, woman-chasing ways. By now the boys' salary was over $7,000 per week.

Freeman Gosden (left) and Charles Correll (right) in front of the Peoria Star's downtown office on Madison Avenue.

(A Peoria Star photo courtesy of the Peoria Public Library)

By the 1940's, radio competition was increasing. The show fell victim to a new era. It slipped to 60th place in the ratings. So, on Oct. 8, 1943, Amos and Andy began a weekly 30-minute variety show for Rinso on Friday nights, then moving to Tuesday night from 1945 through

1948. Their early-day announcer, Bill Hay, was replaced by Harlow Wilcox of Fibber McGee and Molly fame. The show also featured Jeff Alexander's Orchestra and Chorus. It worked and Amos and Andy, again, found themselves in the top ten throughout the 1940's. When CBS raided NBC's shows in 1948, Correll and Gosden made the jump with many others, pocketing $2.5 million.

Hard times fell again in the '50's. Ratings slipped. Rexall Drugs (now sponsoring) canceled in '54 and radio stars were trying to get on TV. Correll and Gosden tried, but soon found they couldn't play the TV roles, so blacks were hired and the boys supervised. Conflicts began between the cast and creators. No one was happy with the show. Blacks charged it was a disgrace to their race and protests from the NAACP helped force it off the air.

Correll and Gosden were personally hurt by the conflict. As early as 1948, Gosden told Newsweek magazine, "What we've tried to do over the years is mirror the trials and tribulations of Negroes of whom we're very fond." Their characters could never be malicious or evil. If there was a villain on the show, he had to be white. But by 1954 they were just glorified disc jockeys on CBS Radio and survived until Nov. 25, 1960.

Both men retired then, living near one another in Beverly Hills. They remained close friends until Charley's death on Sept. 26, 1972, at the age of 82. Ironically, he suffered a heart attack and died on a visit back to Chicago, the town where it all began in 1926. He was survived by his second wife, Alyce McLaughlin Correll; two sons, Charles and Richard; and two daughters, Dorothy and Barbara.

Freeman Fisher Gosden died of heart failure 10 years later, on Dec. 10, 1982, at the UCLA Medical Center in L.A. He suffered from heart trouble for 12 years and had undergone several major operations. He was survived by his wife, Jane Elizabeth Stoneham Gosden; two sons, Craig and Freeman, Jr.; and two daughters, Virginia and Linda.

George Bernard Shaw gave them their finest tribute. He said, "There are three things I'll never forget about America: The Rocky Mountains, Niagara Falls, and Amos and Andy!"

...and it seems like only yesterday!

A. J. Robertson stands tall in hilltop history

One of Peoria's biggest legendary figures of those great "yester days" was in the entertainment business but not show business. His is probably the most cherished name in Bradley sports history, A. J. Robertson.

"Robbie," as he was fondly known, was more than a coach and athletic director of Bradley Polytechnic Institute. According to our friend Bob Leu, whose own personal history with Bradley dates back to the '30's, "Robbie was the most outstanding leader of young men I ever met."

Bob should know because he was, for years, Bradley's public address "voice" of major sporting events and may be best known for his coverage of Bradley basketball. Bob reminded us that it was just 50 years ago this week that A. J. "Robbie" Robertson was elected to the coaching staff of the College All-Star Football Team as the first (and only) small college coach to be so honored.

It was the fifth annual All-Star Football Game and was held in Soldier's Field the night of Wednesday, Aug. 31, 1938. Arch Ward, sports editor of the Chicago Tribune, was the creator of the charity game in conjunction with the 1933-34 Chicago World's Fair. (Ward was also the father of the All-Star baseball game and the Golden Gloves.)

Back then, coaches and athletes were elected to the team by the fans in a coast-to-coast poll conducted by the Chicago Tribune and 150 associated newspapers and radio (before TV) stations. Robertson was selected as one of five (out of 64 coaches receiving votes) to be on the staff. He was in pretty "heady" company, too.

The head coach was first-place winner Bo McMillan of Indiana. His assistants were second-place winner Harry Kipke, who had been coach of Michigan but was "unattached" at voting time; Raymond Pond of Yale; the great Elmer Layden of Notre Dame, finishing just ahead of Robbie; and A. J. Robertson of Bradley Polytechnic Institute. The balloting wasn't just to select coaches, though. All player positions were voted on, too, and along with A. J., the captain of the team, Bill McClarence, was also

elected, placing eighth out of 34 college halfbacks in the country. Was Bradley "Tech" qualified to be in the running for such a prestigious national event? After all, it had just 940 students in '38. Well, A. J. had just guided it to the state championship in 1937 and, later, in September of 1939, his team tied the legendary Bob Zuppke's U of I team 0 to 0. Was Illinois any good that year? A month later, Illinois beat Michigan, coached by Forrest Evashevski and halfbacked by Tom Harmon by a score of 16 to 7. (Young readers won't remember Tommy, but he's the daddy of movie and TV star, Mark Harmon.)

Yes, B.P.I. was qualified, but that in itself doesn't get you on the All-Star team. It took a monumental effort on the part of Bradley boosters at home and all over the country to pull it off, over 5,000 workers all told. They were headed by David B. Owen, Bradley president and general chairman; Robert D. Morgan, president-alumni association; Frank Finney, alumni chairman; and Bob Leu, student chairman. (Bob had just graduated in the junior class.) Kenny Jones, Journal-Transcript sports editor, handled the publicity and the votes to the Tribune, while the Journal-Transcript covered the costs.

Every Bradley graduate was sent a ballot. Sorority coeds ran the downtown booths in front of the old Journal-Transcript building and Madison Theater.

The U of I joined in. Fred Vance, sports editor of the Daily Illini, led the Champaign drive. The Bloomington Pantagraph, Decatur Review, Springfield Register and St. Louis Globe-Democrat printed ballots. The Minneapolis Star promoted Robbie and Robbie's home town paper, The St. Cloud, Minn. Times-Journal, came through with 2,000 votes.

Peoria Mayor Dave McClugage declared a "Robertson Day," while U.S. Rep. Everett Dirksen promoted the cause in Washington.

The alumni voted from all over the world. Peoria groups traveled to various locations, one of which was Pittsburg, where they solicited ballots, including one from the famous baseball star, Honus Wagner, according to Bob Leu. Votes were received from 39 states and from Hawaii, England, France and Mexico. The final count showed Robertson with 769,208 first-place votes and 2,867,410 points. Capt. McClarence garnered 721,476 votes.

Chuck Ginoli remembers it well. Although he attended that "other" school, the U of I, he was working that summer as a "gopher" for V. Jobst and Son, doing work on the men's gym on Bradley campus. He remembers Robbie and assistant coach "Dutch" Meinen talking about the event.

Bradley Athletic Director and Coach, A. J. Robertson.
(Photo from Bob Leu's book, "Good Evening Bradley Basketball Fans.")

We can't say it was because A.J. Robertson was involved, but 1938 was the first time the college team man-handled the pros, by the tune of 28 to 16. And the team they beat? The professional champion Washington Redskins, quarter-backed by the great Sammy Baugh.

...and it seems like only yesterday!

Our 45th high school class reunions

...and Uncle Joe and Aunt Maggie identified

Thanks to Helen Gallagher and Mrs. Robert Birkel for solving the mystery of "Uncle Joe and Aunt Maggie." The Aug. 15th column was a letter from Charles Correll to his uncle and aunt but mentioned no last name. Both ladies identified them as Joe and Maggie Fiss. Joe Fiss was the brother of Charley's mother, Stella Fiss Correll, and also a brother to Mr. Birkel's mother, Emily Fiss Birkel.

Helen says she remembers Joe Fiss well from her Block and Kuhl days. He manned the lower Fulton Street side door of B & K for many years. (I had made a calculated guess that Aunt Maggie might have been Charley's father's sister but, instead, Uncle Joe was his mother's brother. — Who's on first?)

As I write this, I'm looking forward to attending my 45th high school class reunion, but when you read it, it will have already happened. The big event is Sunday, Sept. 4th (yesterday) and it's the celebration of Woodruff High's Class of 1943. I was, actually, a member of Woodruff's last mid-year class of January, 1944, but have celebrated in the past with either the '43 or '44 class. That way I visit with twice as many old friends.

1944, by the way, was a big year in my life, for three major reasons. I graduated from high school in January...joined the Navy (drafted) in March...and got married in July. That's what a world war can do for an average teenager!

I don't remember much about the first two events but I do vividly recall getting married. That experience can be a little traumatic at 19, especially when you do it on a 44-hour liberty.

But, as I said, this is not my first high school reunion. I attended the 35th and 40th, which were fun. I also attended past reunions with my wife, Flossie (Castle), who graduated from Manual in the Class of '43. Her 45th was celebrated last June 11th at Mount Hawley Country Club, which was a grand affair. Our Woodruff event begins with a river cruise on the new "Spirit of Peoria" riverboat, leaving the Boatworks at 3 p.m. It takes us for a ride up the river, docking later at the Ivy Club for cocktails and dinner with our old (let's make that mature) classmates.

When I first attended one of these parties, I'll admit I felt a little uncomfortable and ill-at-ease. I'm not sure why. Maybe it's because that with all the time that's elapsed, it's difficult to identify some of the "kids." After all, people do change. The ladies probably come closer to looking as they did back then...but the men!

Well, what with gray hair, and no hair, and chests that have slipped down to their belt-buckles, it's sometimes hard, if not downright impossible, to identify one another.

One big saver, though, is having nametags with yearbook pictures on them and names in big bold letters, so you can easily read them, even without your glasses. There's nothing worse than squinting at someone's lapel (or bust) as though you were checking for lint. And did you ever notice, that, although we've all aged a bit, we never "think" that old? Oh sure, we know it every time we look in a mirror, but the person trapped inside that body never seems to mentally age beyond a certain point. I'd guess somewhere between 30 and 40.

The class officers of the Woodruff High School Class of 1943. (left to right) Bill Buster, treasurer; Betty Hoskins, president; John Lang, vice president; and Glen Perdue, secretary.

(Photo from the 1943 Talisman yearbook)

Now, some people avoid reunions like the plague, and that's too bad. It's really enjoyable to get back together with friends of an earlier time and reminisce...and, yes, maybe even lie a little. Why not? No one's going to remember exactly how it was, anyway. Well, no one except Flossie. (It's not easy being married to someone for 44 years who has total recall!)

Anyway, it's fun to remember how it was with old classmate friends, and when you do

...it seems like only yesterday!

Come to think of it, it *was* yesterday.

Broadcast career born from a neighbor's odd sense of humor

We bought our first home back in 1952; a small two bedroom Best Home at 5108 Harvard Ave. (now Glen Elm Drive). Our real estate agent was a man between broadcast duties. His name was Hank Fisher.

Unfortunately, Hank died of a heart attack a number of years ago while sports director of WEEK-TV. But in his day, he was one of the best play-by-play announcers in the business. In the early '50's, he was WIRL Radio's voice of Bradley basketball and he gave WEEK's Chick Hearn all the competition he wanted. Hank was a native of Effingham and came to WIRL by way of WLW in Cincinnati. This was his second stint in Peoria, having been at WMBD before the war. He had worked at WLW with some other struggling broadcasters. A couple of them went on to national fame. They were Durward Kirby, later right-hand man for Gary Moore on CBS Radio and TV, and Rosemary Clooney. Rosie and her younger sister, Betty, sang on WLW as The Clooney Sisters and Hank loved to tell how he and his wife, Mary, used to baby-sit the Clooney girls.

In 1952, Hank decided to leave broadcasting and make his fortune in real estate. Our house was his first (and maybe his last) sale. A short time later he was lured back to his first love, sports announcing. But selling us that house is probably why I wound up in the broadcasting business for 25 years.

As it turned out, that house was next door to another radio personality, WEEK's Bob Burton. Remember "Burton the Bounder"? Now, at the time, Bob Burton was *the* early morning radio show host in Peoria and his was a household name. He had, previously, been named one of the top disc-jockeys in the country. He made the national news and was featured in the theater newsreels. Bob was the local Arthur Godfrey with great appeal, especially with housewives. Living next door to this man and his wife, Jean, was some kind of wild experience.

It was also where the idea to get into broadcasting began with me. I met many of the people I later worked with at the Burton's. I first met Bill Houlihan in Bob's kitchen.

Burton was a fun-loving guy with more energy than anyone I ever knew. He was either at a party or having a party, almost every night. This became very difficult for me. With the long hours I put in at the Madison Theater, what I didn't need when I came home late at night was a party. But Bob would wait for me to drive in. Then he'd insist we join the festivities. It was fun at first but soon grew old.

Finally, an idea came to mind. I'd call home when I was leaving work, so my wife could have the garage door up. (We couldn't afford an automatic door in those days.) I'd drive up near our house with enough speed to make it into the garage. Then I'd turn off the headlights, put the car in neutral, turn off the engine and coast, quietly, into the garage. I'd slowly drop the the garage door and sneak into the house. *My own house!* It worked for a while but Bob soon caught on.

Bob was a notorious practical joker and he got back at me, in spades! One hot, stifling August night, I came home about midnight and we went to bed. We didn't have air conditioning in those days and with all the windows and doors open, there wasn't a breath of air stirring.

I finally began falling asleep about 2 a.m. when a vehicle came speeding up our street with its siren wide open. It sounded as though it came right through our window. I sat bolt upright in bed, jumped up and stumbled out the front door, trying to run and put on my pants at the same time. I was at the curb in seconds. But I looked up and down the street and there was nothing. Absolutely nothing! Burton's house was dark with no activity, so he was probably still out partying. Other neighbors were out now and we were all scratching our heads.

The next day I was out cutting the grass in all the heat, when Burton came over. We made small talk about the heat and he casually mentioned how hot it was sleeping last night. I took the bait. I said, "How would you know, you weren't home last night." He started to howl with laughter and I knew I'd "been had."

When he was able to talk, he said, "That siren was me. Jimmy Costello and I rigged a siren on my red convertible. When I hit our street, I turned it on, killed the engine, and drove into the garage. Boy, Bill, you sure looked funny zipping up your pants at the curb." After I fumed for awhile, he continued, "I don't know why you're so upset. After all, you're the one who taught me how to coast into a garage!"

...and it seems like only yesterday!

A Friday the 13th promotion photo of WEEK's sports director, Hank Fisher, surrounded by newsmen Tom Connor (left) and Bob Arthur (right). *(Photo courtesy of WEEK-TV)*

1930's and '40's were boom times for local radio

In addition to movies, stage shows, vaudeville and dance bands, the 1930's and '40's were a time of another great form of live entertainment - local radio.

Last week we talked about a couple of people who were closely identified with WEEK in the '50's, Hank Fisher (also with WIRL) and Bob Burton. But since the earliest days, until 1947 when WEEK-Radio went on the air, WMBD-Radio was the only station in town. This was also before television came on the scene in 1953 and just about everything WMBD did was, by necessity, done live. It required a large staff of announcers, entertainers, engineers and administrators, and a lot of local people were associated in one way or another.

Some of the names that readily come to mind are Milton Budd, Emil "Farmer" Bill, Jack Brickhouse, Brooks Watson, Harry and Florence Luedeke, Gomer Bath, Marv Hult, Irene Kircher, Phil Gibson, Wayne West, and Jack Lyon, just to name a few.

To me, one of the outstanding and genuinely entertaining shows of the '30's and early '40's was Juvenile Theater. What a scintillating collection of young, local entertainers that show brought to the air over many years. Twins, Billy and Bobby Mauch and Jackie Otten, who went on to make Hollywood motion pictures, all performed on WMBD. The Mauch twins were a little ahead of Juvenile Theater but Otten appeared on the show.

Milton Budd was credited with developing Juvenile Theater. Milton was first heard on WMBD in June, 1932. The Peoria Journal of that year listed J-T for the first time on Saturday, July 9, at 1:30 p.m. Later, it became a Saturday morning program.

The stars of Juvenile Theater were local youngsters from, just old enough to sing, dance or play an instrument, to 16 — the age limit for the show.

There were probably hundreds of kids on it over the years. As early as 1935 it boasted Betsy Ross, Doris and Margaret Ehrhart, David Kaplan, Neil Catton, Dorothy June Ristic, Gale and Dean Howard, Buddy Butler, Ann Dooley, and Jimmie Gent. Jack Lyon was musical director and Harvey Muncie accompanied the kids on piano. Later years found Wayne West and Ozzie Osborne providing background music. Milton Budd was M.C. over all its years.

By 1938 there also were Jimmie Bickel, Marjorie Burling (who went on to sing with the Eddy Howard orchestra), Jack Tiemeyer, Donna Lou Coffman, Myerlene Wabel, Dale and Donald DeWitt, Joanne Snyder, Nelma June Dugan, Judith Ann McDuff, and Marilyn Linden; then in 1939, Hazel Forde, Thelma Jean Paugh, Harold Wright, Charles "Tiny" Timm, and Jane Power, and later, Patsy Campbell.

Betsy Ross Schumaker Bachtel was in the Manual Training High School graduating class of 1943 and was a friend and classmate of my wife, so I had the opportunity of visiting with her about the program. She has many memories of that show and others over the years.

She has special feelings about Milton Budd, whom she described as being like a second father to her and all the kids on the show. Another special man in her memory book is musical director, Jack Lyon.

Betsy began on J-T in May, 1934, at nine years of age, and continued until she was 16 in 1940. She had a beautiful singing voice, sounding older than her tender years. She remembers that when she began on the show, the WMBD studios were located on the second floor of the Orpheum Theater building on Madison Street. WMBD moved to the Alliance Life Building, now First National Bank, in 1935, and Betsy's mother's diary lists the dedication date of the new studios as May 11.

After Betsy Ross graduated out of J-T, she sang for various local orchestras and decided to try her hand at producing a local variety show. It was during World War II. She collected the talent, scenery and props and produced the show. She went to Len Worley, city manager of Great States Theaters, who gave her the use of the closed Majestic Theater. She talked Cilco into donating the electricity. The local unions cooperated with the music and stagehands, and the show was on. The price of admission? Two packs of cigarettes for our fighting men overseas. (We didn't know about smoking problems then.) The show was a sell-out. As a matter of fact, it had to be repeated to handle the overflow demand.

An enterprising young lady, this Betsy Ross, and she still is. I'm happy to report that she is fine, well, and active today, and still looking much like that pretty, young child star of Juvenile Theater with the mature singing voice who entertained thousands of Central Illinoians back in those "thrilling thirties."

...and it seems like only yesterday!

Betsy Ross
(Photo courtesy of Betsy Ross Bachtel)

Milton Budd
(Photo courtesy of WMBD)

The unforgettable Len Worley

Most everyone is familiar with "The Most Unforgettable Character I've Met," a feature carried in Reader's Digest for many years. Every time I hear the phrase, I'm reminded of one person...Leonard C. Worley.

I worked for Len over a 17-year-span. When I began as an usher in 1941, he was already a living legend in local theatrical circles. Len demanded a lot. He gave his all to the business and expected no less from you. If your performance was not what he thought it should be, you, and everyone in earshot, heard about it loud and clear. There was no doubt in your mind when Mr. Worley was unhappy.

Len was a local area boy, born in Henry in 1882. He, his brother, Francis, and their parents moved to Peoria in 1897 when Len was 15. On Sept. 11, 1903, Len, described as "a stagestruck boy," achieved an early ambition to become an usher at the Grand Opera House. Once bitten by the show business bug, he never left the business he loved so much.

Worley went up through the ranks at the Grand Opera House, from usher to doorman to treasurer, which he was when the theater burned down on Dec. 14, 1909. He married Charlotte Davis, a native Peorian, in 1904 and the Worley's were living at the Niagara Hotel at the time of the fire. The theater building was in the 300 block of Hamilton, next to the old Peoria County Jail. Also housed in the building and destroyed in the fire, were the Peoria Journal and the German Demokrat newspapers.

Mr. W. left Peoria after the fire to manage the Opera House in Keokuk, Iowa, then moved to Aurora to manage the Grand Theater there. He was fast becoming known as an outstanding theater authority and was gaining respect from actors and show people throughout the business.

From Aurora, he returned to Peoria at the request of Charles Nathan and Felix Greenberg, as treasurer of the Orpheum Theater. In 1925, he became manager and director of stage shows at

Len Worley, city manager for Publix Great States Theaters.

(Photo from Bill Adams' private collection)

the Palace. Later, when Publix Great States bought out Theaters Operating Co., they began using him as a troubleshooter, sending him to "sick" theaters around the circuit and whipping them back into shape. In 1927, Great

States named him city manager of their Peoria theaters, a position he held for the remainder of his career.

During his many years as city manager, he brought nearly every big name in show business to town. Such stars as Van and Schenk, Jack Benny, Sophie Tucker, Ben Bernie, Helen Kane, Duke Ellington, Pat Rooney, Eva Tanguay, Sally Rand, Ben Blue, Eddie Cantor, Will Rogers, Amos and Andy, Jim and Marian Jordan (before Fibber McGee and Molly), Faith Bacon, Ina Rae Hutton, Olson and Johnson, Bill "Bojangles" Robinson, and so many more.

Len became so synonymous with show business over the years that by 1938 the company honored him for his 35 years in show business with a "Len Worley Appreciation Week." It was celebrated Sunday, Sept. 11, through Saturday, Sept. 17, at the Madison, Palace, Rialto, and Apollo. The Madison and Palace began with special midnight shows, with added musical entertainment. Madison organist, Russell Fielder, held a songfest and played the "Mighty Hinners Organ," while the Palace Theater Orchestra furnished music in the foyer. Earlier in the evening, high school bands presented concerts in front of the two theaters.

The climax of the week's celebration took place the following Friday night, when 300 of Len's friends, associates and employees, including B & K President John Balaban, gathered at the Hotel Père Marquette for a testimonial supper with entertainment and dancing.

This all occurred up to three years before I knew Len Worley...but this legendary gentleman would see more tributes over the years, and I participated in one in 1947.

World War II was over. Everyone who was going to return had returned. Len had now been city manager for 20 years and it was his 65th birthday, so the employees decided to throw a surprise party for him, again, at the Père Marquette.

We knew that "Mr. Worley" was fond of dogs. Years before, he had befriended a mangy old cur he named Rags. He took him in out of the cold one winter night and after that, Rags became the "King of the Madison."

Merle Eagle, manager of the Palace, came up with the idea to give him a dog as a gift, but not a mutt...a pedigreed Sealyham Terrier. It was a great idea, but a $500 one. It wasn't easy getting that much money together in 1947, but we finally did and Len's dog arrived from California

in time to surprise "the boss." And it really was a surprise. Len was overwhelmed. Mr. Frost was the dog's name and the Worleys spoiled him as much as any parent ever spoiled a child.

By now we had our two oldest daughters, so when we decorated the Madison lobby for Christmas, we would hang two stockings over the fireplace mantel. They were specially made by Flossie with "Kimmy" and "Kerry" spelled out in sparkle dust. When the Worley's dog came along, a third stocking went up for "Frosty."

By 1955, Len was 73 and the Journal Star paid another tribute to him for his 50 years in show business. He stayed on the job until retiring at 78. Three years later, his wife died. His health declined, his eyesight failed.

He passed away, totally blind, on April 14, 1972, at the age of 90.

The living legend was now, simply, a legend, but a most colorful one. Leonard Cecil Worley was truly an "unforgettable character."

...and it seems like only yesterday!

The Orpheum Theater had its ups and downs

The Orpheum Theater was located at 108 NE Madison and opened on April 24, 1911. It was built by Albert E. and Edward C. Leisy (of the Leisy Brewery family), at a cost of $100,000 and opened under the management of Charles Bray. It was the Peoria connection of the Orpheum Vaudeville Circuit. But Mr. Bray failed to make a success of it and it closed the next year.

At that time, Charles Nathan and Felix Greenberg were operating the Lyceum (formerly Pete Weast's Theater), and others. They were interested in building their own chain, so they took possession of the Orpheum, reopened it and began booking good, quality vaudeville. Under their supervision, it proved very successful.

Len Worley, later the longtime Peoria city manager for Publix Great States Theaters, came back to Peoria as treasurer of the Orpheum, after working out of town for several years. He came at the request of Nathan and Greenberg, as we mentioned last week.

Years later, Len would reminisce about those early years at the Orpheum. He said there were two shows a day when the theater first opened, but Nathan and Greenberg instituted three-a-day vaudeville, one show in the afternoon and two shows at night. In the mid-'20's, Theaters Operating Co., a local group of showmen, assumed operation of nearly all the downtown theaters, including the Orpheum. They continued the three-a-day policy with all seats reserved. By now the vaudeville was augmented with a newsreel and other screen features, such as Pearl White serials, all silent, of course.

Worley indicated that every big-name act in the country played the Orpheum at one time or another. Names such as Will Rogers, Al Jolson, Sophie Tucker, Fannie Brice, Jack Benny, Eddie Cantor, Moran and Mack, and Gallagher and Shean. He also recalled that the Orpheum was not just a vaudeville house. During the days when it was considered one of the best-known entertainment houses in the country, it also played summer stock, musical productions, and legitimate plays.

By the mid-'20's, motion pictures were affecting the entertainment business, causing a decline in vaudeville and legit shows. In an attempt to offset this, the Orpheum began offering dishes and silverware as give-away incentives to attend. By 1927, sound was installed at the Madison, just across the street. Regular Orpheum stage show and vaudeville performances probably discontinued on Feb. 12, 1927. An ad appeared in the local papers on that date, stating "the last performance of the season." It, like the Majestic, would only be used after that for special bookings.

By 1929, the stock market crash took its toll on all show business in town, but it tolled the death knell for theaters such as the Orpheum and Majestic.

By the end of the Orpheum's reign, vaudeville had moved to the Palace, forcing the end of a short but illustrious life of the grand old theater. It remained intact for many more years, but the dust and cobwebs slowly took over and the onetime pride of Peoria vaudeville became a warehouse for storing old furnishings, sets, draperies and the like from other Great States Theaters.

In the 1930's and '40's, the basement of the Orpheum was utilized by Publix Great States Theaters Art Department. It was headed up by a talented genius of an artist named C.J. "Dusty" Rhodes. Johnny Duncan, who was also a top-flight stagehand and stage manager, worked for Dusty for several years. It was out of this department that Dusty, among many other things, designed and built the last marquee for the Palace, which was installed on the newly remodeled theater in November, 1936.

I was too young to remember the Orpheum as a regular performing theater, but I vividly recall my dad talking about the great days of vaudeville there, which he loved so much as a young man. He said he couldn't afford the regular price for a seat at the Orpheum, so he and his friends shelled out five cents to sit in the gallery on wooden benches to see all the great performers of the day. He became quite taken by one of the acts that came there. It was a ventriloquist by the name of Edgar Bergan and his dummy, Charlie McCarthy. This was long before the two (plus Mortimer Snerd and Effie Klinker) became so popular on radio.

By the time I began at the Madison, the Leisy Estate still owned the Orpheum Building and Publix Great States had acquired the lease on it and the Majestic, but they were "closed houses." The company held the leases and paid them each week so that competition didn't come in and open theaters against them.

A startling fact about the Orpheum. From its opening in 1911 until its demolition in January, 1952, it had a total history of only 41 years. But an even more startling fact is that, although it played a very prominent part in our town's rich show business history, especially as a top-flight vaudeville house, it was a "continuous" theater for a mere 16 years. A very short life span, but a gloriously legendary one.

...and it seems like only yesterday!

Opening day of the Orpheum Theater, April 24, 1911.
(A Bert Powers photo, courtesy Peoria Public Library)

Madison Theater had plenty of competition

Earlier this summer we discussed the grand opening of the Madison Theater on Saturday, Oct. 16, 1920, with the silent movie "Humoresque." The Madison was a plush theater featuring a 20-piece orchestra, which gives us an idea of what a top-flight theater could be in those days.

But when silent movies came on the scene in such grand style, they had to compete with legitimate stage shows, vaudeville, burlesque and even movies in smaller, less impressive theaters but with cheaper prices. It really proved to be a mixed bag of entertainment.

Which brings up the question...what was the competition offering as entertainment that week the Madison opened? Here's a look at some of them. The **Majestic** at 212 SW Jefferson was having a busy week. On Wednesday and Thursday, Oct. 13 & 14, it was featuring a big musical revue, "Hello Jazzbo," with a cast of 35 people, billed as a riot of fun with a Creole Beauty Chorus and their own "Jazzonian" orchestra. Prices: 50¢, 75¢, and $1.

Friday, Oct. 15, the night before the Madison opening, the Majestic presented a one-time-only performance of one of the greatest musicians of all time, John Philip Sousa and his march band. He was billed as conductor and Lieutenant-Commander, USNRF. Tickets: 50¢, $1, $1.50, and $2. He *must* have been good, at those prices.

Day-and-date with the Madison opening, the Majestic presented a silent motion picture, "Ireland A Nation," billed as the sweetest Irish story ever told, with All-Star Irish vaudeville. It was accompanied by Bae Pierre Brook Hart, a French-Indian Mentallist, assisted by Princess Parilla. Matinee: 25¢ and 50¢. Evening: 25¢, 50¢, 75¢, and $1.

Across the street at 207-09 SW Jefferson, the **Hippodrome** was offering a silent movie on Sunday, Oct. 10, through the Wednesday preceding the Madison's opening. It starred the great baseball hero himself in "Babe Ruth in Action." On Thursday the 14th and ending on the Madison's big day was a stage presentation of Manual Alexander & Co. in "The New Stenographer," a breezy comedy sketch. Supporting acts were: "Four Old Veterans," a quartet of Civil War Vets, singing and dancing songs popular in the 1850's and '60's; "Wiki Bird," singing guitarist; "Ritter and Weis," comedy song and dance; and "Leonard Trio," an aerial and ground novelty act. All this plus on the screen, Neal Hart in the western, "Get Your Man," and Earl Williams in "The Fortune Hunter." Also, "kinograms" of a big Indianapolis parade...and the price? 10¢, 20¢, and 30¢.

The **Orpheum** at 108 NE Madison, the closest competitor to the Madison (until Ascher's Palace opened a few weeks later), was being advertised as "Peoria's Vaudeville Palace." On the previous Thursday, and continuing through the Madison's opening day, were "Bert Earl and 8-Girls-8," a spectacular, offering Mirth and Melody; Ray Conlin with his Sob-Vocal Comedy; Rice and Newton, with Songs and Patter; Earle and Sunshine, in a character sketch, "Today and Yesterday"; Jordan and Tyler, the composer and the violinist; and a special offering of George Roland & Co. in a farce, "Fixing the Furnace." News Views, a silent newsreel, was also being shown. Matinees, weekdays at 2:30 p.m.; evenings, 7:30 p.m. and 9:15 p.m.

The following Sunday, for four days, offered "Davigneau's Celestials" with Borromeo, Oriental Jazz Pianist, assisted by Miss Men Toy, Geisha Dance; and Shun Tok Seth, tenor; "The International Nine," the World's Fastest Tumblers; Ray and Emma Dean, in an original skit, "Alpheas"; "Cervo," on the Piano Accordion; "Crawley and West," Artists Supreme; and "Salle and Robles," Comedy Team.

The Madison Theater Concert Orchestra, with its second director Jacques Beaucaire (real name Jack Baker), on December 1, 1920.
(A Bert Powers photo, courtesy of Peoria Public Library)

The front of the Majestic Theater before the Jefferson Building was extended.
(A Bert Powers photo, courtesy of Peoria Public Library)

The **Shrine Temple** was dark on the day of the Madison's opening, but earlier in the month, it featured the personal appearance of Henry Burr and Billy Murray. Burr, of course, was a very famous singer of the day, who was well known, not only for his stage work, but as an early phonograph recording star. He was one of the first singers to record. His career began around 1910 and lasted until the early '40's.

Billy Murray was also an early, prolific recording entertainer. His career began shortly after the turn of the century with a recording career from about 1909 until the early '30's. Billy specialized in humorous novelty and topical songs. About a week and a half after the Madison's opening, the Shrine Temple would feature presentations from four operas from the Metropolitan Opera of New York. The Scotti Grand Opera Co. would perform "La Boheme," "Madame Butterfly," "L'Oracolo," and I'Pagliacci," over two days.

The **Apollo** at 313 Main, began on Thursday, the 14th, and ending the night the Madison opened, with Olive Thomas in the silent feature, "Darling Mine," plus a Mack Sennett comedy, "Fresh From the City." The following day, Sunday, they began playing the famous D.W. Griffith's "The Live Flower," plus an added comedy, "She's a Vamp."

The **Duchess Theater** at 309 SW Adams (where the Commercial National Bank now stands) began a three-day run starting William Farnum in an action-packed adventure, "Drag Harlan," on Friday, Oct. 15. Monday and Tuesday, Tom Moore starred in "Stop Thief." It was accompanied by Episode Three of a serial, "Bride 13."

The **Princess Theater**, 227 SW Adams (now the location of CILCO), was also offering a silent movie. Beginning Friday, Oct. 15, and running through Sunday, the "New" Princess, according to its logo, was featuring Charles Ray in "The Deserter."

So, there you have it. The Madison's competition on Oct. 16, 1920.

...and it seems like only yesterday!

Local TV burst on scene at WEEK 35 years ago

What were you doing between 6:30 and 7 p.m. on Sunday, Feb. 1, 1953? It was a historic moment in Peoria, but even if you were here, chances are you missed it. It was the first image and sound ever telecast on local TV.

Bob Fransen, program director, of WEEK-TV sat in an easy chair before the cameras and said: "We know you've been waiting a long time. So have we. We're going to try to get through this without too many fluffs." And with this relaxed approach, WEEK-TV, Channel 43 (remember?), went on the air in living black and white.

Fransen proceeded to introduce some of the station's personnel, beginning with its first news director. Remember his name? Bob Arthur, of course. Along with Arthur, he introduced "Red" Engle, news photographer, and Bob Bath, news reporter. (Bath was the son of another well-known newsman, Gomer Bath.)

After the news team, Fransen introduced Fred Mueller, general manager, and Bill Flynn, sales manager. Fred was also G.M. of WEEK-Radio, and had been for the past five years. Following these two, Bob turned to Joan Ehrens, whom he referred to as "our gal Friday" and Kitty Kolby, women's director.

Next on camera was Bill Oakley, "The Stroller" of the Peoria Star. Oakley made the wry comment that he felt "historic." Fransen countered that "hysteric" might better describe his feelings.

At this point, Bob introduced four more gentlemen whose voices were well known over WEEK-Radio, by asking the audience to guess "who's who." The four were George Baseleon (later "Salty Sam" on the "Captain Jinks Show"), Bob Burton (my next door neighbor), Bill Houlihan (no introduction necessary), and Stu Armstrong (a "jack-of-all-trades" announcer at the radio station). Finally the floor director, Bill Dorn, was introduced.

At 7 p. m. the first night's regular programming began consisting of "Stagecoach," "Ellery Queen," and "The Pretender."

Some of the first week's shows were:

Monday — "What's My Name?" Paul Winchell and Jerry Mahoney; "I Love Lucy"; "Robert Montgomery Presents" and "Douglas Fairbanks Presents."

Tuesday — "Texaco Star Theater," Milton Berle; "Life is Worth Living," Bishop Sheen, (another Peoria boy); "Two for the Money," Herb Shriner; "Club Embassy," Mindy Carson.

Wednesday — "Kraft Music Hall"; "Dangerous Assignment."

Thursday — "You Bet Your Life," Groucho Marx; "Cisco Kid"; "Dragnet," Jack Webb; "My Little Margie," Gale Storm.

Friday — "Dennis Day"; "March of Time"; "Big Story"; "Old American Barn Dance."

Saturday — "Big Top," Jack Sterling, (formerly of WMBD); "My Hero," Robert Cummings; "Your Show of Shows," Sid Caesar & Imogene Coca, (just appeared at the Civic Center); "Wrestling"; "Your Hit Parade."

But one reason you may have missed the historic moment in 1953 is because WEEK wasn't at full power that first day at 2907 Springfield Road, East Peoria. It only had a range of about 12 miles. Another reason was because you'd have had to have a UHF converter on your VHF set, if you had a set. And there was no microwave connection with the networks.

Also, since it was the only local station, it didn't limit itself to NBC programming. It carried programs from three networks, NBC, CBS, and Dumont, via the kinescope process (filmed off a TV screen).

Who was the first news, weather and sports team on Peoria TV? You're probably ahead of me. We've already mentioned two of them. They were Bob Arthur, Bill Houlihan and Chick Hearn. By the way, Chick wasn't mentioned as part of the opening night festivities. It may have been that he was on the road covering Bradley basketball, but he was on hand to do the sports the following night.

About six months later, on Aug. 14, 1953, WEEK-TV telecast the first "live" network program. It was the College All-Star football game from Soldier's Field in Chicago.

In 1960, Fred Mueller, in one of his weaker moments, hired me as promotion manager. I joined the staff on Sept. 1 of that year, one month after a young fella by the name of Chuck Harrison had moved over from WMBD to replace Bob Arthur. Fred was a wonderful man. As fine a human being as I've ever met, let alone work for. He was G.M. until he retired in 1973.

Four years later, in October, 1964, a major change occurred at WEEK-TV. I was moving over to sales but had handled much of the promotion and publicity for the event. Channel 43 became Channel 25. A new antenna was installed. It not only changed the channel number, it also boosted the power, and allowed us to telecast in "living color" for the first time.

Veteran weatherman Bill Houlihan on the job in 1953. *(Photo courtesy of WEEK-TV)*

General manager Fred C. Mueller (left), seated on the set with Chief Engineer Wayne Lovely. WEEK-TV originally went on the air as Channel 43. *(Photo courtesy of WEEK-TV)*

In 1960, when Chuck Harrison came, he joined Tom Connor as our powerful news team. Tom did the 6 o'clock and Chuck did the 10 o'clock. Houli was still on weather, but Chick had left in 1956 to become the "voice" of the L.A. Lakers basketball team, and my "old real estate agent," Hank Fisher, was now the sports director. What a great news team...and fun to be around.

Chuck Harrison and Tom Connor were very serious-minded, no nonsense, news people on the air, but both had great

fun off-camera. You wouldn't believe it, but Tom Connor (real name Emil Sepich, Jr. from Canton) was one of the funniest men on two feet. Houli held his own with them too, but Hank Fisher? Well, Hank was one of the World's top all-time practical jokers. But don't take my word for it. Ask Ducky Anthony. He can tell you one I can't write about here.

It was a fun business to be in for all my 25 years, and you know what?

...it seems like only yesterday!

Remember Kramer's?

If you've been around "our town" anywhere near the time my wife and I have, you remember, as a teenager, a few places to go and things to do other than the theater. But a couple of those places that were high on our list required a car. So you couldn't wait until you were 16, got your driver's license and borrowed Dad's car. Why? So you could take your "best girl" to one of the two best drive-ins in town. No, not a theater drive-in...a restaurant. Yes, I'm talking about Kramer's along Western at Moss and Hunt's along Farmington Road, and it could be anywhere from 1937 to 1960. (Hunt's is still there and still serving those great big ice cream sodas and tenderloins the size of pizzas!)

The thing that jogged my memory was a phone call from Florida earlier this month from Erwin Kramer, who owned and operated that drive-in along Western. He and Al Hunt were big competitors, but there was room for both of them, and both ran quality operations. Kramer and his wife, Erma Davis Kramer, retired to the warmer climes after 1960 and now reside at Lighthouse Point (Island), just south of Boca Raton, Fla.

Erwin called me after reading the column on Len Worley to tell me that Len was indirectly responsible for his success in the restaurant business. It's so interesting, I asked his permission to share it with you.

The year 1932 was probably the deepest time of the Depression, but he decided to open Kramer's Grill at 415 Main St., next to Webb's Loan Bank and just down from the Palace Theater. Things were so bad he was offering breakfast of two eggs, choice of ham, bacon or sausage, orange juice, toast and coffee...for 15¢. His luncheon menu was varied with everything except the price...25¢. The topper, though, was his highest priced evening meal. A T-bone steak dinner...35¢!

Now, he was doing a reasonably good business, but at these prices, his daily receipts only ran around $23 or $28. The restaurant seated 33 people. In addition to his rent, he had to pay his cook $11 per week and the waitresses $6. He wasn't making it, and foreclosure was staring him in the face.

In desperation, Erwin went over to talk to Len Worley with an idea. Was there some way they could strike a deal to have the entertainers who appeared at the Palace each week, eat their meals at Kramer's Grill? It was handy enough. All they had to do was come out the alley stage door and walk up one door to the restaurant.

As was so often the case, Len wanted to help out a friend, so he contacted the manager of the midgets that were to appear at the Palace the following week, and he agreed to have them eat there and pick up the tab at the end of the week. The midgets would come in and nearly fill the little cafe. People walking up and down Main Street would stop and gawk at these little people while they ate.

The next week the theater featured a freak show called the "Freaks of Nature." All these people ate at the grill and the same thing happened, only more so. Crowds would build on the sidewalk, five and six deep, watching these unusual people eating in Kramer's.

The extra business, plus all the publicity, immediately showed up in the daily receipts. Suddenly they were doing $35 a day, then $50. Pretty soon it grew to $150 to $160. The future of Mr. Kramer as a restaurateur was assured and he credits Len Worley for helping him over a rough time of the Depression.

But that's not all. Here's "the rest of the story," as Paul Harvey would say. While Kramer was struggling downtown, Al Hunt (who had previously run a tire company at Hamilton and Madison, remember "Hunt for Tires"?), was running a drive-in along Western and Moss. According to Erwin, Hunt was apparently having a problem with the owner of the land, so, one midnight in the mid-1930's,

This is Kramer's Drive-In in its first year of operation at the Western Avenue site. The year was 1937. *(Photo courtesy of Erwin Kramer)*

This shot, taken in 1940, shows expansion of the successful restaurant along Western into its familiar log-cabin design, hallmark of Kramer's for a couple generations of Peoria-area people.
(Photo courtesy of Erwin Kramer)

he had a crew come in after closing, jack up the building onto a flat-bed truck and haul it out to the current location on Farmington Road, and the business has flourished there ever since.

Another drive-in was built on Western and was operated for a time by Bill Call, who had been a violinist at the Palace. But he apparently lacked the experience to make it go and it closed.

Kramer ran his downtown grill from 1932 until 1936, when he sold out to Emil Pitsch. Then he negotiated for the Western Avenue property and opened Kramer's Drive-In in 1937. He operated a very successful business until he sold out to Jim Jumer in 1960. Jumer operated

under the Kramer name until 1970, when he built his hotel next door and changed the name to Jumer's Castle Lodge.

But that's still not all. Over the years, Kramer hired many young teen-agers and young ladies as curbies, waitresses and the like...and four of them are still there, working for Jim Jumer.

They are:

• Betty Swan Czerwinski, who started in 1940 at age 15 as a curbie and is now a waitress.

• Lulubelle Hafsted Hill started at age 16 in 1951 as a salad carrier and for years has been a waitress for both Kramer's and Jumer's.

• Joyce Keogeol Wallace began as a waitress in 1957. Later she was in catering and for 25 years has been head hostess.

• Grace Brady Simmons also started at Kramer's in 1957, first filling curb-side orders, then moving over to steamtable operator. She also helped open kitchens and train kitchen staffs in other Jumer hotels.

Top that, Paul Harvey!

Needless to say, when Mr. and Mrs. Kramer come back to visit Peoria, which they often do, they stay at Jumer's Castle Lodge. Erwin admits to 86 years of age but, somehow, I didn't ask Erma's age.

...and it seems like only yesterday!

"War of the Worlds"

Fictitious program caused real panic

It was just 50 years ago last night that the world came to an end! Well, not really...or we wouldn't be here talking about it. You probably know by now, I'm talking about the most famous single radio program ever aired..."The Mercury Theater on the Air," and its adaptation of H. G. Wells' "War of the Worlds." It was produced, directed, partially rewritten and acted in by a 23-year-old genius, Orson Welles. (Note the name similarity? Wells and Welles.)

Orson was born not far away, in Kenosha, Wis., on May 6, 1915, the son of a pianist-inventor, and his love of acting came early. At 10 he played Peter Rabbit at a Chicago department store, was paid $25 a day, and thus became a professional. At 12, he staged a school production of "Julius Caesar," and (naturally) played three of the major roles himself.

In 1931, Orson went to Ireland and wound up broke. He returned home and, after several more disappointments, met Thornton Wilder. Through him he met Alexander Woollcott, who got him a tour with Katherine Cornell.

The tour ended in New York in 1934 with "Romeo and Juliet." Backstage, Wells met a young, former businessman-turned-theater-enthusiast, by the name of John Houseman. (Yes, he did it the old-fashioned way, he *earned* it.) Houseman was producing Archibald MacLeish's play, "Panic," and was so impressed with Welles he offered him the lead.

They worked together on WPA project shows in 1936, and in 1937 did an ambitious radio production of "Les Miserables" for Mutual. They leased New York's old Comedy Theater, renamed it Mercury Theater, and opened with their modern version of "Julius Caesar."

The early actors who developed around Welles' acting ability were Joseph Cotton, Agnes Moorehead, Martin Gable and George Coulouris, with others later. Welles produced and directed, and Houseman handled the business details. At 22, Orson was already dubbed "genius" and "wonder boy" by the critics.

In the summer of 1938, CBS-Radio offered the group a series of Monday-night, 60-minute programs, dramatizing literature classics. Orson was already a radio veteran. He'd been on the "March of Time" by 1935 and since March 1937, had been Lamont Cranston, "The Shadow." He was now averaging $1,000 per week, but "Mercury Theater" would be his baby. He would star, write, narrate, produce and direct...and continue his stage career. (And you think *you're* busy!) On Sept. 11th, the show became a CBS regular of the new fall season. It moved into a Sunday night slot against Edgar Bergan's "Chase and Sanborn Hour," on NBC. This was a top-rated show with an estimated 34.7 percent of the total audience. After the first seven Sunday broadcasts, Mercury Theater was rated a paltry 3.6. So how did the show create so much havoc nationally?

H. G. Wells' version of "War of the Worlds" was updated to fit with 1938's times. The English setting was changed to Grover's Mill, N.J.

The narrative was changed to radio news bulletins. The Hotel Biltmore changed to Park Plaza. Although Kenny Delmar did the voice of the anonymous "Secretary of the Interior," he did it with a great imitation of President Roosevelt's voice. Frank Readick, who played the newsman in the field, copied Herb Morrison's style of an earlier actual radio report of the Hindenberg crash.

The show went on the air with practically no one listening. So they missed the opening which established the program's name and fictitious presentation announcement.

Meanwhile, 12 minutes into the popular Bergan broadcast, an evidently not-too-popular singer was introduced.

Orson Welles in 1938 on the Mercury Theater.
(A CBS photo)

more bulletins. Monsters in control of middle New Jersey. Lines down in Pennsylvania.

Soon real panic began happening throughout the country. In Newark, people actually wrapped their faces in wet towels and fled into the streets. In Boston, families on rooftops imagined they could see the red glow as New York burned. In Pittsburgh, a woman was saved in an attempt to swallow poison.

Inside CBS, Welles and his group went blissfully on, ignorant of the havoc they were creating. Later, Welles suspected all wasn't right with the world when he noticed police with billy clubs swarming through the halls.

After the show, hearing what happened, Welles thought his career was finished. He faced police interrogations and press interviews. Reporters grilled them about reports of deaths and suicides. Later they learned that no one had died. Orson's career wasn't finished...it was made!

I'm sure someone out there remembers hearing the original program. Unfortunately (or maybe fortunately), I missed it. Why? Simply because our family were big Edgar Bergan fans. But "War of the Worlds" certainly stimulated a nation's imagination.

...and it seems like only yesterday!

HAPPY HALLOWEEN!

An estimated three to six million listeners started dial-twisting.

When CBS-Radio was tuned in, the restless listeners froze to what they thought were news bulletins about something happening on Mars. As reports continued to interrupt what these millions thought was a remote broadcast of an orchestra playing from a New York hotel, most of them stayed to hear the startling news. Some of the dialog: "Ladies and gentlemen, this is the most terrifying thing I have ever witnessed — wait a minute! Someone's crawling out of the hollow top — someone or...something...

"...something's wriggling out of the shadow like a gray snake. Now another one...they look like tentacles...." The announcer began describing the chaos occurring. Heat rays turned soldiers into screaming flames. Suddenly he was cut off the air. A piano interlude was heard, then

Edgar and Charlie made mark in unlikely media

Last week, while reminiscing about "The War of the Worlds," I mentioned that my family and I missed the original radio program because we were such big Edgar Bergan and Charlie McCarthy fans. Theirs was the NBC show with a huge audience opposite CBS's "Mercury Theater on the Air."

That fact, and remembering my father's infatuation with Edgar Bergan ever since he saw him perform at the old Orpheum Theater, brings to mind what a great popularity this ventriloquist garnered on, of all things, radio. Ventriloquists depend on visual contact with their audience, since they do what they do without moving their lips. But Bergan proved to the entertainment world that being visible wasn't necessary. All you had to do was create a character voice so real that even unseeing radio listeners could believe it was another person.

Born in Chicago (a Peoria suburb) on Feb. 16, 1903, Edgar developed an early interest in magic and ventriloquism, while still in grammar school. He paid 25¢ for a booklet on how to "throw your voice," and it turned out to be the best I investment in his life. He soon began using it to play jokes on his family, sending his parents to the door, only to find no one there.

By the time he was in high school, he sketched the face of a "dummy." It was the likeness of a neighborhood newspaper boy named Charlie. Later, he paid a carpenter named Theodore Mack $35 to carve the face out of pine. So the enterprising young Bergan named him Charlie after the newsboy, and McCarthy (a derivative of Mack), after the carpenter.

But Edgar still had plans to be a doctor and entered Northwestern as a pre-med student. He and his "friend" Charlie began entertaining at parties and other gatherings to help pay his way through school. In the summers he went on the Chautauque Circuit and, by the mid-'20's, dropped his medical plans to go on the road full time, traveling North and South America and Europe.

Edgar Bergan and Charlie McCarthy were first heard on radio Dec. 17, 1936, on Rudy Vallee's "Royal Gelatin Hour." Rudy had seen the act at a party and invited him to appear on his Thursday night NBC variety show. He accepted, but then had second thoughts about a ventriloquist doing a radio show. Vallee finally insisted that they try it. Charlie and his friend were a sensation and were brought back several times.

Chase and Sanborn decided to sponsor Bergan on his own show beginning May 9, 1937. A big cast was built around the two including the, then, top comedian in America, W. C. Fields and the sarong girl, Dorothy Lamour. Don Ameche, who had been a leading man on "The First Nighter" program, was a member of the cast and announcer. In a few short weeks the "Chase and Sanborn Hour" was leading such other established programs as Jack Benny, Eddie Cantor, Fred Allen's "Town Hall Tonight" and "The Kraft Music Hall." Bergan stayed No. 1 for nearly three years.

W. C. Fields started an immediate feud with Charlie and developed a hatred of the dummy, who continually topped him on the show. Fields left the show after the first five months, but in December of 1937 Edgar hired Mae West, who made headlines with an infamous skit on "Adam and Eve." Her script had been approved by the NBC censor, so it wasn't so much the words, but the sensuous way she read the lines that created a furor among the listening audience. Before the show was off the air, the NBC switchboard was jammed with calls of protest. NBC also heard from the FCC and the aftermath of it all caused the network to ban Mae West for 15 years, not even allowing the mention of her name.

In 1939, Bergan created another dummy, a slow-talking "nerd" of a character he named Mortimer Snerd. By 1940, Ameche and Lamour were dropped. The show was shortened to 30 minutes and the new format included Ray Noble's Orchestra, a weekly guest, and Bergan, Charlie and Mortimer. Abbott and Costello became regulars until they got their own show in 1942. Later, Don Ameche returned, teaming up with Frances Langford, to create their argumentative husband and wife team, "The Bickersons."

Edgar created another dummy in 1944. He named her Effie Klinker, an old-maid type. He later created a fourth one, Podine Puffington, but neither became as popular as Charlie and Mortimer.

By 1945, Bergan was making $10,000 a week on radio, plus another $100,000 a year on Charlie McCarthy dolls and mementos. Bergan did his last NBC show for Chase and Sanborn on Dec. 26, 1948. A year later he returned on CBS and immediately began recapturing his old Sunday night audience. Finally, he reverted back to a 60-minute format in 1954 and lasted until 1956. Candice Bergan, Edgar's daughter, frequently appeared on his 1956 shows as a child.

Edgar remained semi-active after his radio career, doing personal appearances and managing his enterprises until he passed away in his sleep on Sept. 30, 1978.

In 1964, NBC broadcast the highlights of the Chase and Sanborn Hour hosted in the '30's and '40's by Edgar Bergan, with help from Charlie McCarthy.
Other guest regulars included (clockwise from top:) Rudy Vallee, Eddie Cantor, Don Ameche, W.C. Fields and Dorothy Lamour.
(An NBC photo)

And just think, if Edgar Bergan hadn't introduced an unpopular singer, (I wonder who it was?) on Oct. 30, 1938, America might not have spun the radio dial and may have been spared the panic that night on CBS's "War of the Worlds." Worse yet, we might never have heard from Orson Welles again. Well, maybe, but somehow I doubt that. Anyway

...it seems like only yesterday!

Dick and Marian Coffeen struck a special chord

Sometimes the "small world department" works to great advantage. Such is the case this week. My daughter, Lesa, who does research for the column, has a friend, Ginny. As it turns out, Ginny is the daughter of Dick Coffeen who formerly worked at WMBD and I have been looking for background on Dick. He was musical director at the time of his death in 1968.

Our recent column on "Juvenile Theater" rang a bell with Dick's widow, Marian Harvey Coffeen, and she has a family association with WMBD-Radio that dates back to before she ever knew her future husband.

Marian was born in Peoria in 1916. Her grandfather, Paul DeNufrio, was a violinist for the original group of musicians in Peoria. Other members of that group were Salvatore LaRocca, father of Roxy, Joe, Paul and Frank LaRocca. A man by the name of Henry Fosco, another member, was the grandfather of Ed Fosco, who originally established Fosco's Restaurant on Western. This early band used to ride a buggy to perform at Al Fresco Park (circa late 1880's).

Paul DeNufrio's sons, Frank and Danny, both played piano, as did his daughter, Anna. Anna was Marian's mother, and she played piano for the silent movies at the Lyceum Theater in 1912, when she was 18.

Marian's Uncle Danny played in the Palace Theater pit orchestra and later was the first piano player for Juvenile Theater, according to Marian. He died of a heart condition in 1947, at the age of 49. Brother Frank, nicknamed "Dud," died in 1978 at age 72. He played locally for Joe Kilton's Orchestra and owned a photo service on Main Street.

Danny DeNufrio also had a cousin-in-law who played with him in the Palace pit, by the name of Tony Marinello. Tony's daughter, Mildred Marinello, was, later, famous around Peoria as a dancer and singer, and was in vaudeville with harp player-entertainer Roxie LaRocca.

So it wasn't surprising, with her musical background, that Marian would become involved in the business. In the spring of 1932, while attending Roosevelt Junior High, she entered a radio opportunity contest sponsored by Publix Great States Theaters and WLS-Radio.

Wayne Matheney, Arnold Wahlfeld and Milton Budd, imitating Tom, Dick and Harry, a famous trio of the day, won first prize of $40. Marian Harvey, impersonating Ruth Etting, won second prize of $20. Both winners, representing Peoria in the district contest finals, appeared at the Madison Theater on Thursday night, Aug. 25.

The two Peoria acts joined four other district winners to go on a tour of the Publix Illinois circuit. Other Peorians accompanying the troupe were Lewin Neff, announcer, and (Uncle) Danny DeNufrio, pianist.

The following year, in August 1933, Marian Harvey joined the WMBD cast of "Grab Bag," a one-hour Saturday night program from 11 p.m. to midnight. She joined local favorites, Wayne West and Irene Kircher, who had been on the program for several weeks. Also in the summer of '33, Marian sang with Wayne West on the WMBD show, "Old Man Sunshine and Little Girl Bluebird," a 15-minute popular music show on Tuesday mornings at 8:30.

When WMBD moved to the Alliance Life Building in 1934, Marian had her own program, "Sunbonnet Sue," accompanied by Jack Lyons on the organ. It was on this program that band leader Jack

Dick and Marian Coffeen (left) at the Biltmore Bowl with Phil Harris, Tiny Hill and Mrs. Hill.
(Photo courtesy of Marian Coffeen)

Wedell heard her sing. He hired her to tour for the summer with his orchestra as female vocalist. Another musician touring with the band that summer was Dick Coffeen. That's how Marian and Dick first met.

K. Richard (Dick) Coffeen was born at Blue Mound, just outside Decatur, in 1911, the son of William and Estelle Thornell Coffeen. After he had taken piano lessons, he bought a shiny new trumpet from Sears Roebuck, and taught himself how to play. He was 11 years old. After high school, he joined Charley Wortham's orchestra and toured the Chautauqua Circuit, playing little towns in Illinois.

After that, Dick joined a five-piece group that played around Decatur called the Brian Dunbar Band. Another couple young lads around the Decatur countryside also played in the band. One later became a household word in the Peoria musical world. His name is Ozzie Osborne. And guess who the drummer was in that group? None other than the big man himself, Tiny Hill.

Dick joined the Jack Wedell band in 1934, where he met Marian, and toured that season. In 1935, Tiny Hill took over the five-piece Decatur band and asked Coffeen to play for him, but Wedell asked Dick to stay because he was going into the

Père Marquette the following winter. Dick opted to go back with Tiny, however, and the Tiny Hill band went into the Inglaterra for the fall of 1935 and winter of 1936. Dick and Marian were married in 1936 and Dick toured with, first, the five-piece Tiny Hill band and, later, with the expanded big band the next eight years.

Ozzie Osborne left the Tiny Hill organization after a few years and came to WMBD-Radio, where he remained for quite some time as musical director. In 1944, Dick Coffeen joined WMBD as Ozzie's assistant. Then, when Ozzie left the station to go into business for himself, selling organs and pianos, Dick took over as musical director. He held that title until his death in 1968, at the age of 56.

Dick was a very handsome and talented man. He was well-liked and left many memories along his musical path as he played with numerous groups around Peoria. His music, and Marian's, brought much joy to so many of us throughout Central Illinois.

Dick and Marian had two daughters, Virginia Anne and Mary Elizabeth, and one son, William Richard Coffeen. Marian and Ginny still reside on North Sheridan Road.

Great memories from two special people.

....and it seems like only yesterday!

Remembering Tom Connor: A "newsman's newsman"

We've talked before about unforgettable characters. One that has to be high on my list is one you'd never suspect from seeing him on TV. His name was Emil Sepich, Jr., but you knew him as Tom Connor. Emil passed away at the early age of 52.

It's appropriate that we remember Tom today, because last Friday was the Peoria Area Chamber of Commerce's 13th Annual Community Thanksgiving Luncheon at the Peoria Civic Center. Tom Connor gave the narrative on what we had to be thankful for at the first annual luncheon in 1976. Tragically, Tom died in August of the following year.

At that time, a group of Chamber members was so impressed with Tom's personal concern for others and his silent approach to helping those less fortunate than himself, that they created a special "Tom Connor Service Award" to be presented to the volunteer each year who best epitomized Connor's attitude for service to the community. The first award was presented just three months after his death, at the second annual luncheon.

Now, how can you describe a man with this depth as a "character"? Well, you really had to know him to understand. This serious-minded, hardworking radio and TV newsman was one of the driest, most genuinely funny people I've ever known.

Emil Jr. was the son of Emil and Margaret Sepich, who still reside in Canton. After his Canton schooling, he attended Southwestern College at Memphis and the Columbia School of Journalism. He received camera experience in both production and acting at WGN-TV in Chicago, and he served a hitch in the Air Force.

Emil began his news career at WBYS-Radio in Canton in 1947. Two years later, he became news director at WKBV in Richmond, Ind. In 1950, he was named news director at WIRL-Radio. As the story goes, it was here at WIRL that he acquired the "on-air" name of Tom Connor. He told me he went by Todd Fallon in Richmond. Apparently, WIRL owned the rights to "Tom Connor." Since people couldn't be seen on radio, it was the station's policy that when they hired a new newsman, they'd hire someone with a voice similar to the previous one and continue with the same name. But Emil changed all that. He stayed with WIRL until 1954, when he became news director of the Peoria Journal Star's new, and Peoria's second, TV station, WTVH-TV, Channel 19. He began on TV as Tom Connor, but WIRL "blew the whistle" on using the name. So he assumed the name Tom Conrad. This name was so similar that WIRL saw the futility of it and gave him the name. He, of course, kept the name for the rest of his career.

When I first met the man, I had been working at WEEK for just a couple weeks in 1960. Tom had been there since 1956. We became nodding acquaintances in the hall. One day he stopped me (since we hadn't been introduced) and said, "Say, do you work here? I keep seeing you around but we've never met. My name's Tom Connor...but my friends call me Emil." From that moment on, we were friends.

But the "character" part of Emil is what's hard to explain. He was so serious and businesslike during his newscasts it's hard to convey how absolutely funny he could be when the red light went off. I think he used his humor to keep the staff loose, especially during a hectic day in the newsroom. He also enjoyed it if you gave it back to him, which I did after I knew him well enough.

Example: Tom loved to call you on the phone, using a "masked" voice to put you on, or maybe sing a song he claimed was his favorite, "Ramona." He would sing it off-key in the worst voice imaginable, then act as though he'd sung it beautifully. If you laughed (which you had to do) he'd act hurt, stomp off and pout until you apologized.

My way to get back at him was this. I'd run into him somewhere in the building, hopefully in front of others, and say, "Oh, Emil...I mean Tom...no, I mean Todd...oh, whatever the h--- your name is..." And he loved it. He'd go through all the antics of a "star personality" that no one could remember.

But Tom Connor was one of the ablest, dedicated, hard-working journalists I've ever known. He could smell a story with his eyes closed. He could have gone anywhere in the country in TV, including the networks. But this Canton boy loved Central Illinois. I don't think, although he had offers, that he ever wanted to leave. Unfortunately, he did though, the hard way. He suffered a massive heart attack, sometime after his Friday night broadcast in August 1977.

When I retired in 1984, I felt Tom Connor's ghost still walked the halls at WEEK. I'll bet, if you ask Tom McIntyre, Chris Zak, Bill Houlihan, or some of the other folks still around who worked with him, they'll tell you it still does.

Journal Star editor, Chuck Dancey, paid him a fine tribute as far back as 1955, when he said, "...Tom Connor is a newsman's newsman. He's neither pompous nor does he hammer out his words. He tells the news with quiet, confident, fluent authority — and invariably closes with a smile and an item that has a trace of humor in it. His passion is for accuracy."

I felt compelled to write about Emil today, in association with the 12th Annual Tom Connor Service Award. What a professional...What a character...What a great human being.

Emil, if you can hear me

...it seems like only yesterday!

Emil Sepich Jr. was better known as Tom Connor. *(Photo courtesy of WIRL-Radio)*

Friend's death brings back memories of showman

Flossie and I lost a dear friend recently ...Dan McGrath. Danny was not only a close friend, he was my godfather. But his passing reminded me that he and his wife, Pauline, were very close friends of Ralph and Marie Lawler, who now live in Tucson, Arizona.

Ralph Lawler was a boss of mine when I managed the Madison Theater, and he reminded me, after reading the column on Len Worley, that Len played an important role in his life, too. Lawler came from our neighboring city, Galesburg, and as a young lad of 14 he began his show business career as an (underaged) usher at the old Auditorium Theater there. Later, the Auditorium was renovated, remodeled and renamed the Plaza.

But Ralph, with his pal "Dutch" Peterson and two of their buddies, "Buck" and "Wes," all got jobs ushering the Auditorium for a number of big road show attractions. A man by the name of Jericho hired them, the only requirement being ownership of a long pair of pants. Ralph's older brother provided a pair of ill-fitting ones and another showman was born. It only lasted long enough for state inspectors to catch them working nights under age 16, and Ralph's career ended abruptly, but not for long.

He was so smitten with show business he got a job working days (which was legal) at a local movie house peddling handbills for 50¢. Throughout high school he helped the janitor in the mornings, before classes, and ushered at night. Following graduation, he became assistant treasurer at the remodeled Plaza for many of the better road shows.

It was here he met Eskel Gifford of the Gifford Players, whose group came and played 26 consecutive weeks, offering weekly changes of popular Broadway plays. Ralph became close friends with Gifford and Robert Emmet Jones, his producer, director, and actor.

When Gifford Players left Galesburg for Peoria, Ralph went with them. They played one season at the Hippodrome, followed by another at the Orpheum. It was here in Peoria that Ralph met Marie Segg and fell in love.

Gifford's left the Orpheum and went to Springfield and Lawler with them, again, but life was tough without Marie. So he phoned Len Worley and, once again, Len helped change someone's life and career.

Worley told him they were looking for a manager of the Apollo Theater and he might have a chance for it. Late that night Lawler returned to Peoria and met Leonard at the Sugar Bowl. He was hired for his first managerial assignment as Apollo manager. Now he and Marie could get married, and to this day Ralph credits Len Worley for making it all possible. The next 14 years Lawler was shuffled from Peoria to Bloomington to Springfield to Kansas City to Toledo and back to Peoria, where he established a district office for Publix Great States Theaters during World War II.

The district office and Lawler moved to Peoria while I was serving in the Navy. His offices were on the third floor of the Madison Theater, above the mezzanine. When I returned to get my $40-a-week job back in 1946, I met Ralph Lawler for the first time. He was very personable. We had an enjoyable meeting, but after some small talk, he indicated a problem. He'd put me back managing the Madison if I wanted (it was the law) but Paul Morgan, an older man, was now there. He asked if I'd consider Pekin. He'd be able to pay me more, possibly moving me into the Pekin city manager title.

Ralph Lawler with his two managers, Jack Geltmaker, top, and Bob Hagen, bottom, as they appeared managing Shakey's.

Ralph and Marie Lawler.
(Photos courtesy of Ralph Lawler)

I thought it over but told him I'd been gone from Peoria long enough and wanted to come back to the Madison. He readily agreed, and moved Morgan to Pekin. Then he said, "Let's see, I have to pay you your previous salary...that was $45 a week, wasn't it?" I was "flabbergasted." I was now married and really needed the extra five bucks. I mumbled something unintelligible, without revealing the truth, and walked out with a raise. No one will ever tell me Mr. Lawler didn't deliberately make an error in favor of a returning vet.

Ralph was also the first theater boss to soften a strict rule of managers and their assistants both working all day and night on holidays.

He came into my office one day, just before Christmas, and closed my door for me. I thought I was being fired, but instead, he told me to decide which day I wanted off, Christmas Day or Christmas Eve. Take my choice, then give the other one to my assistant. I can't explain what this meant to me, but it was worth much more than money. After that I was a big Ralph Lawler fan. By the way, I still am.

But Lawler left shortly after that. He had a yen to own his own theater. So, when the outdoor theater craze took over after the war, he and Mehlenbeck Brothers built the Peoria Drive-In on Glen Avenue. It opened in October, 1947. A couple of my best theater friends, Jack Geltmaker and Bob Hagen, went with him as managers.

Later, he also built and operated another drive-in theater in Delavan, Wisconsin. Geltmaker stayed and managed the Peoria operation and Hagen moved to Wisconsin to manage that theater.

After operating first-class drive-in theaters for a number of years, Ralph sold them at their peak. The fast-food franchise business was now coming on strong and after much close observation, he opened the first Shakey's Pizza Parlor in Peoria on University. This was followed by others in Springfield and Rockford. Hagen and Geltmaker again joined him in the pizza business.

For the past several years now, after several successful careers, Ralph and Marie are retired in the sunny warmth of Tucson. They still keep in touch, though, and return each year for visits, which gives us a chance to reminisce and lie about those good old theater days.

And I'll bet if you asked him, Ralph Lawler would tell you

...it seems like only yesterday!

"Day of Infamy" found author ushering at Madison

It doesn't seem possible but Wednesday is the 47th anniversary of the bombing of Pearl Harbor. Would someone remind President-Elect George Bush?

I couldn't forget that Sunday in 1941. I was ushering Aisle Two at the Madison that day, the newest member of that ushering fraternity, about six months after turning 16. I saw all the great Class "A" movies because they all played the Madison. The big premium, though, was free employee passes to see any of the other movies and stage shows at the Palace, Rialto, and Apollo, and the Palace stage shows were the absolute best. Oh yeah, they also paid me 25¢ an hour to usher, too.

I met my future wife at the Madison. She was 15 and dating another usher. She didn't know it at the time, but I had my eye on her. She'd come in on Saturday or Sunday afternoons, and would sit in the balcony. (Maybe that's why I wanted balcony duty so badly.) We probably would have never met if it were not for the Madison, because she went to Manual and I attended Woodruff.

When I began, we wore white gloves and stood at "parade-rest" at the head of the aisle, and God help you if Chief-of-Service Bob Ringle caught you letting anyone go down your aisle without you and your flashlight. Talking was strictly forbidden, unless you did your talking with hand signals, and you could because we had a signal for just about everything.

The "rookie" on the staff had to work Aisle Two because it was the busiest aisle in the theater. When I started I remember that George Marshall was on Aisle One, Vern Wasson was on Aisle Four. Other ushers I can remember then and a little later included Hank Willoughby, Jim Hankins, Dean Kendall, Bill Blair, Bob Smith, Dick Scherer, and Gil Crotty. Gil was a neighbor of mine and my closest friend.

In addition to Chief-of-Service Ringle, there were Ed Rogers, balcony captain, and doormen, Bob Hagen and Don Grieser. The theater manager was Bill Harding, and, of course, Len Worley was city manager.

Our payday was Saturday mornings at 10 a.m. We were paid in cash in a pay envelope but before we received it, we attended an usher's meeting, and it was mandatory...if we missed the meeting without excuse, no pay.

Bob Ringle was a strict disciplinarian, not unlike an army top sergeant. One day after I'd been there awhile (I was promoted to Aisle Three) Dick Scherer came on duty about 2 p.m. on a Sunday afternoon, assigned to Aisle Four. He proceeded to whisper to me out of the side of his mouth. Ringle was at the chief's post all the way across the inner lobby, but he must have heard him. He walked slowly across to Dick and said, in a low, quiet voice, "Mr. Scherer, we do not talk on duty. If you want anything, use your hand signals. If you talk again, you will no longer work here."

He turned around and headed back across the lobby, when Scherer whispered something else to me. Ringle turned around, came back and said, "Mr. Scherer, you're fired. Give me your flashlight." Dick gave him the light, but couldn't believe he was totally serious, so he remained standing without saying a word for about 15 minutes. Ringle finally walked back over and Dick was sure he was returning his flashlight. Instead he quietly said, "Mr. Scherer, you don't work here anymore. If you want to continue to stand there for free, it's ok with me, but your pay stopped 15 minutes ago." And he was right. Dick didn't work there anymore, and there were teen-agers virtually standing in line for usher's jobs.

Usher Bill Adams promoting the motion picture, "Ship Ahoy" in 1942.

Madison Theater ushers (Bill Adams third from left) promoting the short-running "Ship Ahoy" outside the theater's side doors.

(Photos from Bill Adams' private collection)

Another duty assigned to the ushers was sign change. The night before a new show was to start, all three sides of the canopy had to be changed plus all the signs and stills on the theater front, in the outer lobby, along with two six-sheet boards outside the Madison exit doors. Also, when the Rialto was closed, as it was occasionally, we had to change part of that canopy, which advertised "Now playing at the Madison."

This job was done regardless of the weather, and the weather didn't always cooperate, especially in the winter. They did pay us extra for it, though, and after awhile I looked forward to it. I used to take pride in how fast I could change a canopy.

The usher staff would, occasionally, get into the act in other ways of advertising coming attractions, as the accompanying photos will attest. Lapel badges were often worn along with other things, such as the navy cap promoting "Ship Ahoy." I hated to wear a hat and do to this day, but you either wore it or you turned in your flashlight, and lots of luck on your new job.

All the promotion that was done to sell the public on "Ship Ahoy," must not have been enough, though. It opened with a midnight show on Saturday, May 30, 1942, and ran just four days, through Wednesday, June 3rd. Most of our movies ran at least a week.

It's hard to figure, too. It was a big MGM musical, starring Eleanor Powell, Red Skelton, Bert Lahr and Virginia O'Brien, with Tommy Dorsey and his

orchestra. It was also supported by three short subjects and the Paramount newsreel. Well, you win some and you lose some.

It's interesting to note it was preceded the week before by "Rio Rita," starring Abbott and Costello and Kathryn Grayson. It was followed by a nine-day run of "Reap the Wild Wind," with (are you ready for this cast?) Ray Milland, John Wayne, Paulette Goddard, Raymond Massey, Lynne Overman, Robert Preston, Susan Hayward, and Charles Bickford.

Maybe I'm wrong, but could it be we were spoiled with the great movies of the '40's?

Well, anyway...it seems like only yesterday!

Ozzie Osborne retains passion for entertaining

When you think of big bands, small bands, radio music or just music in general 40 or 50 years ago around Central Illinois, you have to think of Ozzie Osborne. What a fine musician and what a great guy he is.

Ozzie was born in Macon, Ill., on Jan. 31, 1913, the son of Claude and Anna Faye Lancaster Osborne. Ten years later, his sister Virginia was born. Macon is a small community just outside Decatur. When Ozzie was three, the Osbornes moved to Storm Lake Iowa and, later, moved back to Decatur. His father became fire chief of Decatur.

It was there he attended Oakland Grade School, Roosevelt Junior High and Decatur High. He played a little basketball in high school, but like so many of us teen-agers, he, too, got a job ushering — at the Avon Theater there.

But Ozzie's real passion was music, and over the years he played guitar, banjo, bass fiddle, vibraharp, piano and organ. He even sang a little. "Not very good," by his own admission, but on occasion, he'd come out of the band section and sing.

He recalls playing in the early days with Byron Dunbar's 11 or 12-piece band. They played in and around Decatur. One place he vividly recalls was a bootleg joint on Lake Decatur, operated by Butch Blenz.

It was out of the Dunbar band that a five-piece group evolved called "The Five Jacks." Ozzie played guitar and banjo, Warren Doss was on bass fiddle, and the drummer? None other than the big one himself, Tiny Hill.

Osborne has many interesting stories about Tiny. He'll never forget the first time he met Harry L. Hill. Oz was at his Decatur home one day, when a heavyset man walked up on the front porch and knocked on the door. He was in bib overalls and had a piece of straw sticking out of his mouth. It was, of course, Tiny Hill.

Tiny eventually began fronting the five-piece band and it became the Harry Hill Band. Dick Coffeen, described by Ozzie as his very best friend, was also a member of the group. In 1935, Hill approached Ozzie and suggested that they move to Peoria. There wasn't enough work in Decatur. In Peoria, he felt they could at least get bookings for three or four nights a week. So, the group came to Peoria.

Ozzie was still single when he first moved here and for awhile he dated Marion Harvey's sister, Virginia. Marion, as mentioned in an earlier column, later married Dick Coffeen. At first Ozzie lived in a tenement-type apartment house on Fayette Street, not far from Spalding. After that, he moved to the Kickapoo Hotel at Main and Knoxville.

One night in 1937 the Tiny Hill Band was playing at the Inglaterra. A group of people was milling around in front of the bandstand. Ozzie began talking from the bandstand to a pretty girl in the crowd. During the break he found her and introduced himself. She was Ellen Marjanovitch, by then a Peoria girl, but formerly from Danville. They began dating, and a year later they were married. He was 25, she was just 18.

Oz stayed with Tiny Hill for several years after he expanded to the big band. He played guitar and vibraharp and sang occasionally, but Tiny did most of the vocalizing. One of Osborne's special memories is the recording sessions with the group and, yes, Ozzie was with him when they recorded the one and only, "Angry." It became their theme song. By 1940, Ozzie grew weary of the life on the road, so he settled back in Peoria and went to work for WMBD-Radio. He replaced Bob Black in a four-piece group at the station. The piano player was Marion Coffeen's uncle, Dan DeNufrio.

He stayed with WMBD for the next ten years, becoming musical director.

But later, he decided he not only wanted to play music, he wanted to sell musical instruments. He began selling for Byerly Music in the 200 block Main Street. Then he moved up to the 500 block and went to work for Charley Adams' store. Later, he moved back down Main to Mathews Music.

By the early '60's, Ozzie yearned for his own business. He decided he'd be better off away from the downtown competition, so he opened "Ozzie's Music" on Main Street, but up on the bluff near Sheridan. Another young musician by the name of Rox Bucklin worked for him there. Oz says they "sold the heck out of organs." One month they sold 80 of them.

After a few years he moved the business out on Sterling Avenue near the mall. Then, the last six years of his business life, he had his own carpet company and finally retired a couple years ago.

A few years ago, Oz and his wife, Ellen, bought a new home on Rochelle. Sadly, Ellen passed away in January 1985, but he still resides at the same address. The other day, when I called Ozzie about doing this column he invited me over. His daughter, Judy, was visiting from Pittsburgh, and the three of us relived some of those great WMBD and Tiny Hill days.

But Ozzie Osborne doesn't live in the past. He, like most of us, enjoys remem-

Ozzie Osborne (left) with the WMBD-Radio band and the Raye (Rashid) Sisters.
(A George W. Sommer photo, courtesy of WMBD)

bering the good times, and he still writes beautiful music. In 1958, he wrote a song titled, "Lady With the Dreamy Eyes." It, like most of his 138 songs, was about Ellen. Then, just the past year, he wrote a new song titled "All I Can Think Of Is Love." It was my pleasure to have him play it on the organ. It was so beautiful, I strongly suggested that he have it published. But he was one ahead of me, he already had.

All the years I've known Ozzie Osborne, he's been a quiet, soft-spoken man who genuinely enjoyed entertaining people with his beautiful music. It's nice to know he hasn't changed. When he sits down at the organ in his living room, you can see how much he still enjoys the experience. May he experience it for many more years to come.

...and it seems like only yesterday!

"The Big White Store" just a joyful memory now

It's sometime in the middle '30's, on an evening during the Christmas shopping season. A light, fluffy snow is falling. You hop off the streetcar in the 100 block of South Adams Street, and you head for the one place that the entire season revolves around..."The Big White Store"...Block & Kuhl's.

In my mind's eye and ear I can envision that scene, with all the hustle and bustle of busy shoppers and the cheery ringing of the bell in the hand of a Salvation Army Volunteer who stood shivering at the traditional kettle, accepting money for the needy, on every street corner.

As a child of nine or ten, I remember approaching Block & Kuhl's corner window at Adams and Fulton, with chills of anticipation, to see all the animation within a beautiful Christmas scene. And in its midst, the jolly old man himself, sitting in his throne chair, surrounded by all the dazzling toys available that year.

Upon entering the revolving doors, you saw the brightly decorated main floor, and you knew at a glance why this store was referred to as "downstate's Marshall Fields." It not only looked it, it carried the merchandise you'd expect to find there, in all departments.

As likely as not, the first person you'd see as you entered was a tall, stately man with a florid face and a tall, majestic carriage, the floorwalker, Mr. Frank Bush, and always with the traditional carnation in his lapel. When you reached the elevators, you were greeted by Hazel Scott, head elevator starter. All elevators were personally run by lady operators, in uniform, as well as Hazel. But no elevator moved up or down until Hazel Scott pressed her hand-held clicker, to indicate it could proceed. Once in motion, the operator would call off each floor and the departments on it.

Another Block & Kuhl employee in those days was one we all knew later, Helen Gallagher. Helen began working at the big white store in 1929. She worked in (what else?) the gift department. It was a "leased" department, operated by Edward Gumplo of New York. She became buyer and manager of the department and remained until 1950, when she left to open her "Helen Gallagher Gift Shop."

Her pink shop was located at 417 Fulton and, later, she was a major partner in the Foster-Gallagher Co.

But for a child in the '30's, there was really only one floor where you wanted the elevator to stop. The fifth floor... *Toytown!* When the doors opened to that happy sight and sound, it was similar to the experience of Alice in Wonderland, only not as scary. You virtually stepped into another world...Santa's Wonderland. As you slowly took in the scene, it seemed all the toys in the world were there, and they were all working, or moving, or doing whatever they were supposed to do.

Now, I know kids today have their malls and exclusive toy stores and, I'm sure, a much bigger variety of toys with a lot more sophistication. But when I walk into one of them, I wish my grandkids could experience Block & Kuhl's fifth floor, just once. The first thing you might see and hear was the organ-grinder man and his monkey. If you put a penny in the monkey's tin cup, he'd pour it into his pocket, tip his little "bell hop" hat to you in thanks, and move on to the next child who had money tightly clutched in a small fist.

Then there was a merry-go-round to ride and a Christmas Carnival of clowns, monkeys and elephants, all moving. For the girls there was "Aunt Patsy," who was there to demonstrate all the dolls for them (and their mothers, too). There were also demonstrators in individual booths to show kids and parents how to operate all the mechanical toys.

A Ray Barclay photo of a huge crowd gathered around "The Big White Store" in the late '30's after the Santa parade. From the Peoria Historical Society Collection in the Bradley University library. *(Photo courtesy of R. W. Deller from Lee Roten's Historic Peoria Photo File)*

Toytown traditionally opened the Saturday before Thanksgiving and in 1935, as an inducement to get there for the 8:45 a.m. opening, they offered free tickets for a special kids' show at the Madison Theater. All you had to do was come to Toytown and get your free ticket.

But as is still the case today, the Christmas shopping season didn't officially begin until Friday, the day after Thanksgiving, when Santa (and he was Block & Kuhl's Santa) came to town. The parade that continues today, which this year celebrated 101 years as a continuing parade, is the oldest in the United States. It began in 1887 (without Santa) to celebrate the start of construction of a bridge across the Illinois River here. The next year a bigger parade, with merchants along the parade route entering in with special decorations, celebrated the completion of that "Upper Free Bridge."

Then two years later, in 1889, Schipper & Block, the predecessor to Block & Kuhl's, began its sponsorship, and this is probably when Santa entered the festivities. These two companies sponsored the parade for the next 72 years. In the early days store employees participated. One such, in the '30's and '40's was house detective Molly Werner, who was "Mother Goose" on that special float.

No doubt about it, Block & Kuhl's big white store was a great institution, and fondly remembered as part of my Peoria childhood.

...and it seems like only yesterday!

Although I had no interest in prices at that age, here's some that Block & Kuhl's was advertising in 1935, at a time when wages were pretty small: Lionel streamline electric train, $5.98; Shirley Temple dolls, $2.98; life-like Dy-Dee baby, drinks water from bottle, wets, $2.98; a real moving picture projector, sturdy steel with cord, 59 cents; Mickey Mouse Lionel Train outfit, $1.98; boys cowboy suit, including gun and holster, neckerchief, cowboy hat, vest, lariat, $2.98. Fred DeBord, by the way, was toy buyer in those days.

And the adults of that day, especially mothers, had an added treat in the store. They could drop the kids off on five and then ride up two more floors to have a leisurely lunch or dinner in the beautifully decorated seventh-floor dining room. It was an exquisitely furnished room, using silver-trimmed china, silverware, and linen table cloths. The waitresses (as were all female employees) were dressed in black or navy blue with white blouses. The menus were exceptional and desserts a specialty. The seventh floor offered more than a meal, it was an event!

Pipe organ poured out a musical adventure

Picture yourself sitting in a packed Madison Theater sometime in the late 1920's or during the 1930's...or even the early '40's. The feature picture has just ended. The big velvet curtain has closed with "The End" still projected on its rippling surface. A small light can be seen flickering down to the right of the orchestra pit.

Suddenly a reverberating musical sound begins pulsing and throbbing from the very walls of the theater. A spotlight suddenly hits a golden object rising out of the depths. A moving figure takes form...it's the organist playing at the triple keyboard of the "Mighty Hinners Organ" as it rises to a level above the orchestra pit. The musical portion of the evening's entertainment has begun. The curtain reopens and the lyrics of the song being played is flashed on the screen. The audience begins to sing along by following the bouncing ball as it passes over the words. If you haven't experienced this musical adventure (or something similar to it) then, my friend...*you haven't lived!* The Hinners pipe organ was installed in the Madison in the summer of 1927, during the first major remodeling of the theater.

Since its 1920 opening, the Madison's main musical thrust was a 20-piece, and a little later, a 25-piece orchestra, which accompanied the silent films.

But in 1927 sound was about to break upon the scene. All-talking...all-singing...all-dancing motion pictures, and the Madison wasn't built for the medium. The orchestra platform had to be removed and a pit built in its place. The new organ was installed on a lift platform, so it could be raised and lowered into the pit.

The back wall of the auditorium had to be changed from a partial, to a complete wall, so sound could be contained for better acoustics. Since a big orchestra would no longer be needed to accompany the "talkies," a pipe organ would be used for special musical entertainment, and during intermissions. The Madison pipe organ was one of the last two theater pipe organs built by the Hinners Organ Company in Pekin in 1926. The other, a smaller one, was installed in the Pekin Theater, which was practically around the corner from the Hinners factory.

The first person to play the new $25,000 Madison organ was Ralph Brigham, a well-known organist of the period. He was hired as a guest organist to reopen the newly remodeled theater, which had been closed from June 4 to Sept. 18, 1927. Since the movies were still silent, however, the theater reopened with Clara Bow in "Hula" and with the Madison Theater Symphony Orchestra, with Forest Woodman conducting.

Mr. Brigham was a "guest" organist, however, so the honor of being the first Madison staff organist for the "Mighty Hinners" went to Mr. F. Dawson Fenton, who took over ten days later. Fenton had formerly been the organist at the Palace.

Many organists followed Mr. Fenton, who played it from Sept. 28 to Nov. 27, 1927. On Nov. 28, Leonard Leigh was introduced as a "guest" but he became so popular, he stayed as a regular until Oct. 26, 1929, which was about a year after "talking" pictures came to the Madison. Leonard Leigh was a very gifted and entertaining organist who went on to bigger things. Radio was now beginning to make a big impact, and Leonard became musical director of the NBC Radio Network. It was fitting since early radio programs were mainly accompanied by organ music. Gomer Bath was the fourth Madison organist. Gomer was another Canton boy, whose first job was organist at a theater in Paducah, Ky. He was first mentioned as organist at the Madison on June 24, 1928.

A 1927 photo of Leonard Leigh, Madison Theater organist, with the "Mighty Hinners Organ."
(Photo from Bill Adams' personal collection.)

Then on Aug. 12 of that year, he began playing daily concerts at 12:45 p.m., while Leigh played the regular shows. Later, he worked at WMBD-Radio where he originated the "Man on the Street" program. After that, Bath was a Peoria Journal editor and columnist. He wrote the "Straws in the Wind" column for several years.

Another musician of considerable note (pardon the pun) who played the Madison's mighty console, was Milt Herth. He began on Nov. 24, 1929, and played until August, 1930. Milt went on to considerable fame with his "Milt Herth Trio" and an impressive recording career.

After closing for the summer of 1931 the Madison reopened on Aug. 16 with another new organist, Jimmy Huffman. Huffman, who had been on radio, was a guest organist until Oct. 14 of that year.

The organ continued to be featured as part of the Madison program in 1932 and 1933. On April 16, 1933, Leo Terry, "Famous Master of the Organ," was guest for two weeks.

On March 11, 1934, Russell Fielder, "The Smiling Star of the Console," began an indefinite engagement. In addition to Russell, different local singers were featured singing specialty songs. Some of these singers were Norman Davis, Lyle Pilcher, Milton Budd and Wayne West. Fielder's "Fairwell Week" began July 8, 1934. But Russell was brought back each New Year's Eve beginning in 1936, until the early '40's.

The year I began working at the Madison, 1941, Russell Fielder and Milton Budd teamed up to lead "Community Sing" every Friday night at 9 p.m. This special feature began on Nov. 14 and continued until April 1942. Community singing occurred occasionally until 1946, but it was the end of an era.

The main reason, other than the changing times, was the deteriorating condition of the organ. The leather bellows were in constant need of repair and other parts were worn beyond use. By the early '40's, we had to have a man come in each year to patch it up enough to use on New Year's Eve. He, by the way, was the only person capable of repairing it, because he was a dwarf. With his knowledge and small size, he was the only one who could do the work in the small areas in the walls containing the pipes, bellows and moving parts.

What a grand old organ, and great musicians.

...and it seems like only yesterday!

"The Ing" was a favorite of New Year's revelers

Happy New Year! We're only a day late with that salutation, although we actually celebrated New Year's Eve in this column last week by talking about the Mighty Hinners Organ at the Madison. It was appropriate since the organ had been part of the more sober celebrations over the years.

But there was another place known for New Year's reveling back then, too, and ironically, it began the same year as the Madison, only about eight months earlier. I'm referring to the one and only...Inglaterra Ballroom.

"The Ing," as everyone lovingly referred to it, was built by Ross Amusement Co. for around $60,000. It opened with a big ball on Feb. 17, 1920, and, althought the ballroom was the victim of three major fires over the next 31 years, it was the center of a major part of the big band activity in Central Illinois from 1920 until 1951.

That era was also the time of other great ballrooms and theaters, and they drew the big bands like magnets. The theaters, mainly, were the Orpheum, Majestic and Hippodrome, then the Madison, Palace, Shrine Auditorium and, later, the Shrine Mosque. The big bands came, and the audiences enjoyed.

But that was also a time to dance, and with the quality as well as quantity, of the dance music available, there was a veritable dance craze across the country. There were many ballrooms, dance halls and nightclubs around the area. Places like Fernwood Gardens out Farmington Road, The Hub Ballroom (still packing them in) at Edelstein, and Mackinaw Dells, for those who had the transportation.

Then there was the Winter Gardens, The Triangle Gardens and right downtown, in the 200 block of North Adams, was the National Roof Garden. All the major hotels had their rooms for dancing, too. The Jefferson Hotel's Gold Room and also the Tropics nightspot, downstairs, drew big crowds. *The* place to dance in the Père Marquette was the Peoria Room, and it had its Rendezvous Room, too. But the "grand" of the ballrooms was "The Ing."

It was a big band music haven, in the 900 block of Main Street at the foot of the hill. All the best orchestras played there, from the top-name national bands to the regional and local groups.

We've already talked about Tiny Hill's band playing the Ing, beginning in 1935, but here's some more you might remember playing there in the '30's and '40's: Jan Garber, Vincent Lopez's Debutantes, Red Nichols, "Peoria's own" Charley Cartwright, Henry Busse, Jack Wedell, Art Kassel, Freddy Martin, Ted Weems, Carl Engles and his Royal Aces, and Johnny "Scat" Davis.

Although it wasn't a band as such, a lot of country and western music was presented in February 1935, when Gene Autry and his Round-Up appeared twice, on Feb. 15th with the WLS Radio Stars, and again on Feb. 20th with the WMBD Barn Dance.

My parents were avid dancers, especially during the '20's and '30's, during their dating days and early married years. I can remember, as a child, hearing them recall going to the Inglaterra and other places. They remembered another Peoria couple who used to go to some of the same dances, Jim and Marian Jordan. The Jordans, of course, went on to radio fame as Fibber McGee and Molly.

And those early 1920's were also a time when my dad began listening to a band on the radio, back when they had to use headsets to listen. He and his brothers would tune in WDAF in Kansas City late at night, then pass the earphones around the table to hear the Coon-Sanders

"The Ing," at the foot of Main Street hill during its 31-year history as a ballroom.

(Photo from the Grassel Collection/Peoria Public Library)

Ozzie Osborne at the vibraharp with Tiny Hill during the Inglaterra Ball-room days.

(Photo from Ozzie Osborne's personal collection)

orchestra, known as "The Kansas City Nighthawks." The band boasted not one, but two leaders. They were Carleton Coon and Joe Sanders.

Carleton Coon died suddenly while the band appeared at the Hotel Sherman's College Inn in Chicago in 1932, at the age of 38. A few years later, Joe Sanders formed his own band and "The Old Lefthander" would play the Inglaterra or Palace Theater whenever he was in the area.

It was in the late '30's when my parents took me along with them to see and meet this great entertainer at the Ing. It was my first visit to the ballroom, but I'll never forget it. I still have his autograph.

Many local and regional big bands headquartered at the Ing. One of those in the '40's was Peoria's Joe Kilton. Joe has been playing with bands in Peoria and around Central Illinois since his high school days. As early as 1927, he was playing trumpet with Paul Mehlenbeck's band. In 1936 and '37 he played with Bob Black's band in the Père Marquette's Peoria Room.

Kilton formed his own band in 1943 and, shortly, was playing regularly at the Inglaterra. He appeared weekly on Thursday nights and some weekends.

But, as mentioned before, The Ing had a history of fire problems over the years. About 3 1/2 years after its opening, on June 19, 1923, it suffered its first fire. The second fire occurred ten years later, on March 10, 1933. This time it required $20,000 (one third of its original cost) to remodel it. Finally, on Jan. 23, 1951, it suffered a devastating fire, estimated at $100,000 in damage, which virtually destroyed the interior. The Grand (not so old) Lady never reopened again as a ball-room. The interior was, later, remodeled and it became "Downtown Chevrolet." Years later, it housed the Peoria Board of Education-Adult Continuing Education Center, but it was vacant for its several final years. Then, in July of 1987, the wrecking ball turned it to rubble, to make way for a new building as part of the Methodist Medical Center Complex.

Wrecking balls can turn buildings to rubble, but they can never destroy the memories of those who came to dance and to listen to the swinging big bands. Did they play in Peoria? You bet! And most of them played at the Inglaterra Ballroom.

...it truly seems like only yesterday!

Ho Toy Lo a favorite

The column on Kramer's Cafe and Drive-In a few weeks ago registered with many people around town, as well as those scattered from California to Florida. Many didn't know, or had forgotten, that Mr. Kramer got his start downtown on Main Street. But this reminded us that Kramer's Cafe wasn't the only eatery in that area by far.

Right across the street was Lekas' Sugar Bowl, and the Bee Hive was down at the corner of Main and Jefferson. At Madison and Hamilton was The Diner, with The White Hut half a block down Hamilton. The area had many others over the years, and I suspect the location of the Madison, Palace and Apollo Theaters has much to do with it. Why, the Palace Cafeteria was right in the same building of the Palace Theater. It was downstairs, with the entrance on South Madison, next to the theater side doors.

One that became a haunt of mine in the '40's was just three doors up Main Street from the Madison. It was not only a very nice family-operated restaurant, for my money, it had the best Chinese food in town. You've probably already guessed, I'm talking about Ho Toy Lo.

Flossie and I became close friends with the folks who ran it, Paul and Susie Chan. We're still good friends and just the other day we had the chance to visit and reminisce about the good old yester-days.

Richie Frasco was the night bartender at Ho Toy Lo back then, and he and his wife, Mildred, joined us. Among the six of us, there were a lot of memories that came flowing back from the past.

Paul Chan was born in Montoon, Canton, China, in 1903. He and his family came here in 1919. Susie Quon was born in Gunnison, Miss. As a girl, she moved to southern Canton, China, where she attended school for six years. Then she moved back to Gunnison. After a sister was married in Portland, Oregon, she moved there to live. Paul's aunt in Portland knew Susie's sister. While visiting his aunt, Paul met Susie and, soon, they were married, on Aug. 4, 1936.

Paul, though, was involved with the restaurant before it became Ho Toy Lo. It was, originally, En Joy Lo, and it's an interesting story of how it evolved. Paul, along with his father, Tom Chan and another Chan, by the name of John, went into partnership and opened En Joy Lo at 508 Main, on April 14, 1928. Paul operated it, with John as chef, along with Raymond Choy, (who's real name was Chan, but that's another story). The restaurant operated successfully for ten years, even though a few of them were pretty lean, especially right after the market crash.

In 1938, Paul bought out his father, Tom, and John Chan and he and Susie became proprietors. They wanted to change the name, but with no extra money, they weren't in a position to buy new signs, especially the neon sign in front. Paul decided that, if they didn't change the name too drastically, maybe they could get by without too big an outlay. So, by simply changing the first three letters in the name, En Joy Lo, rough translation, "enjoy yourself while you dine," to Ho Toy Lo, meaning "good luck restaurant," a new business was launched and the old sign was saved.

After Paul's dad, Tom, sold him his interest in En Joy Lo, he remained in the carry-out business for many years. He operated Tom Chan's Chinese Food on Franklin, near Logan Printing Co. Then he moved to the 400 block of South Adams, and later, he located on State Street.

Rich Frasco began tending the Ho Toy Lo bar at nights in 1941. During the day, he and his family operated Frasco's Grocery Store at 3001 NE Adams. Then in March, 1945, he and Millie bought "Louie's Tap" from Louie Cornish, in the

An H. G. Crawshaw photo of the Ho Toy Lo Restaurant (right) at 508 Main St. before the devastating fire in May, 1951. *(Photo courtesy of R. W. Deller from Lee Roten's Historic Peoria Photo File)*

But back to Main Street. Paul and Susie prospered there for many years. My wife and I started going there during our dating days and continued after we were married. We watched the Chan family prosper and grow. They had three children. Howard, the oldest, was followed by another son, Phillip, and later, baby daughter Mavis was born.

Then in April 1951, the restaurant suffered an early morning fire. Paul left for home about 2 a.m. About 7 a.m., Richie received a call from Karl Wild, who operated a jewelry store in the next block. By the time he and Paul got there, smoke was rolling out of the building. Paul had difficulty negotiating a lease with a term long enough to remodel and reopen, so he bought a building at 515 N. Jefferson. He took his original sign with him and opened a new Ho Toy Lo at that location in May, 1953. He and Susie continued their great food and service at that location until they sold in 1974.

Over the years, Peoria has had many fine Chinese restaurants, and there are quite a few excellent ones today. But then, or now, there are none finer than Ho Toy Lo.

...and it seems like only yesterday!

2700 block of North University. They operated under that name until they retired on March 20, 1985.

Another side story about the Frascos. We ran into them at a party several years after Ho Toy Lo. They mentioned that they lived up on the river near Mossville. I told them I lived in "Holmes Center" as a child, and that's where their home was. After describing the exact location, I yelled, "Hey, that's where I lived. My dad and uncle built that house in the early '30's." The Frascos have invited us to visit them several times since, and I'm always thrilled to see my old home, although they have done much remodeling and improving since then.

"Burton the Bounder" remembered for his antics

A few weeks back we talked about living next door to the man who first got me interested in the broadcasting business. Our next door neighbor, Bob Burton. "Burton the Bounder" as he was known to his thousands of fans, signed WEEK-Radio (1350) on the air each weekday morning, with his "Breakfast with Burton" program. Bob's show was so popular, especially with the housewives, in the late '40's and early '50's, he was sometimes referred to as Peoria's Arthur Godfrey, and he was, at least, as unpredictable as Arthur, if not more so.

He was a real character on the air as well as off. During the cold winter months, for example, he'd frequently remind his lady listeners that freezing weather was on its way, so "...you'd better bring your brass monkeys in off the lawn." He was nearly always coming from a party, so the station had a stand-by tape of Bob prerecorded, in case he didn't make it in time to sign on at 6 a.m.

But Bob was equally unpredictable off the air. He was an excellent pilot and had a commercial license. After partying for several hours one day, he decided to take a little spin, but not in the normal way. He actually flew, not over, but *under* the Cedar Street Bridge! Not only that, he did it the hard way. He rolled the plane over and flew under the bridge *upside down*! I'm not sure if the authorities found out who it was or not.

I do remember another time, when we were neighbors, that Bob was grounded. He decided to fly over his house to say "hello" to his wife, Jean. He came down at tree-top level and "buzzed," not only his house, but the neighborhood as well. Mothers were running outside, grabbing their children and "hitting the dirt."

All the time we were neighbors, Bob tried his level best to get Flossie and/or me to take a ride with him in his plane. I had never been up and Flossie's only experience was a sightseeing trip around Peoria on a teen-age date. Knowing what we knew, though, there was no way he was going to sell either of us on that idea.

For many years I've heard a story about Burton, having to do with his radio show. To be sure of my facts, I called Arvid "Swede" Nelson, an engineer at WEEK-TV, who worked with Bob in those early radio days, to verify the story. As close as we can remember, it went something like this:

Bob was constantly thinking of ways to promote his show on the air. One day he mentioned that he was planning something special, a "first" for Peoria radio. Then, on the Monday before, he announced that the big event was going to happen on his program the coming Friday. Every morning that week he kept talking about it, "teasing" the audience without actually telling them what it was. He kept building it bigger and bigger. Thursday, of course, he signed off by saying to be sure to listen the next day for the "first on Peoria radio."

By now the town was buzzing about his Friday show. What was it going to be? Bob would tell no one, including the staff. But the day before, he did tell Swede to have a couple hundred feet of cable on a portable "mike" for the next day. Friday's show came but, naturally, Bob kept up the suspense all morning long, up to the very end of the show. Then he began.

He told his audience that he was now using a portable microphone with a very long cable. (This was way before wireless "mikes.") He described leaving the sound-proof studio, walking through the station halls, out into the lobby, saying "hello" to the receptionist, then through the glass doors into the hallway on the 10th floor of the Commercial Bank Building. He said he was turning left into the hall, past the elevators, to the end of the hall. Then left, again, down another hall. A few doors down, he turned into a doorway and through swinging doors, into another room.

He described going into a cubicle in the room and shutting the door, and then he said; "...and now ladies and gentlemen, the moment you've all been waiting for. A 'first' on Peoria radio..." He leaned over, stuck the microphone down into the receptacle, and flushed the toilet!

That was the sign-off of Friday's show, so Bob was off until Monday morning, and I'm told there was some question as to whether he would be back. The telephone switchboard lit up like a Christmas tree. The program director was upset, and the station manager was upset, not to mention the switchboard operator who had to field all the irate calls.

Years later, I asked General Manager Fred Mueller if he remembered the incident. He not only remembered it, he remembered the other managers coming to him, demanding that Burton be fired for embarrassing the station. I asked Fred if he considered firing Bob. He said he did, but with Burton's great popularity, it

Bob Burton, better known on WEEK-Radio as "Burton the Bounder."
(A Peoria Journal Star photo)

would be a difficult decision. He took the request under advisement, but after arriving home that night, he found a second reason that would make it even more difficult.

"What was that?," I asked. "Well," Fred said, "my wife Sally's mother was visiting us from Oklahoma, and she was a big Burton fan. I asked her if she'd heard the show. She had not only heard it, she thought it was the funniest thing he'd ever done. If I was to keep peace in the family, there was no way I could fire Bob Burton."

Needless to say, Bob, who died in 1959, wasn't fired. But, you have to admit..."Burton the Bounder" was not your average bear (or brass monkey, for that matter.)

...and it seems like only yesterday!

Famous Five return to BU tomorrow

"**A**nd now, ladies and gentlemen, the Bradley Braves!

"At forward, Carl Schunk and Chuck Orsborn. At center, Dar Hutchins, and at guard, Ted Panish and Les Getz. The officials for tonight's game, Jim Enright and Lyle Clarno."

"Thank you, Bob Leu. I'm Jack Brickhouse and we welcome you to our broadcast. Coach Robertson has told us we can expect to see a lot of service from Kenny Olson tonight. Even though the Famous Five is a durable group, the Bradley bench is one of the best, and since most are sophomores and juniors, the future looks bright indeed on the hilltop here in Peoria."

This excerpt from Jack Brickhouse's forward to Bob Leu's 1976 book, "Good Evening, Bradley Basketball Fans" is the best and quickest way to take you back 50 years to the way it was, with the team that first put Bradley Polytechnic Institute on the national map in college sports.

The man most responsible for it all, of course, was athletic director and coach A.J. "Robbie" Robertson. He and his assistant, John I. "Dutch" Meinen, the freshman coach, are legendary in Bradley sports history.

I remember those great "Famous Five" games well as a youngster, because my dad held season tickets for seats in the second row in the balcony in the Peoria Armory, where the home games were played. There were only three or four rows in that balcony, as I recall, but it was a great place to have a bird's-eye view of my heroes in action. I can still see Ted Panish, sitting on the ball, playing "come and get it" with the elite of college basketball.

Three of the soon-to-become "Famous Five" hit Bradley campus at the same time and on practically the same day in 1935. In September, a young man who later became president of Bradley held a part-time position as executive secretary and was an English instructor at Peoria Central High School. His name was David B. Owen.

He knew Carl Schunk was a great outside shooter at Central who had played twice in the "Sweet Sixteen" tournament in Champaign. In 1934, as a junior, his team was beaten in the first round by Urbana. In 1935, his Central team beat Danville, but was then defeated by Thornton of Harvey's "Flying Cloud" team.

Schunk was a Farmington native who had lived in Peoria since age ten. He and Joe Batchelder were honorary captains of Central's 1934-35 team. Schunk, strangely, had made no commitment to attend college, but a few minutes after a conversation with Owen, he found himself in Robertson's office.

Lyle M. "Dutch" Clarno, a sports official and former Bradley athlete, out of loyalty, kept a lookout for potential talent. His recommendation to Robbie was Ted Panish. Varsity player Bob Sayles was hustled off to Kankakee to meet Panish at McBroom's Cafe. Ted was an athlete at Morris High. He had signed to go to St. Viator College on a $62.50 scholarship, but they insisted he play football, in addition to basketball and baseball. Ted had broken his leg playing football at Morris, which nearly ended his career, and he had no desire to risk it further. Classes hadn't started yet, so he hopped in Dutch Meinen's car with Sayles and came to Peoria.

These six Bradley basketball players made up the Famous Five over three seasons, from 1936 to 1939. From left are Ken Olson, Carl Schunk, Dar Hutchins, Chuck Orsborn, Ted Panish and Les Getz. A Lee Roten photo. *(Photo courtesy of Special Collections Center, Bradley University Library)*

That same day, an unknown, tall, slender young man was walking around Bradley campus, looking things over. After awhile, Chuck Orsborn headed for college president Frederic R. Hamilton's office. He explained that his father, a Presbyterian minister, had passed away six years before, so Hamilton allowed him half off on tuition, and Ozzie decided to come to Bradley. (He not only became a member of the Famous Five, he became an outstanding coach and athletic director, and coached Bradley to three NIT tournament titles.)

As the day wore on, three of the future Famous Five...Schunk, Panish and Orsborn, were sitting before the fire place, as guests in the Sigma Phi fraternity house. But Les Getz was already an underclassman. Getz was a sophomore on the 1935-36 varsity, while Schunk, Panish and Orsborn played freshman ball. Freshmen couldn't play varsity ball then.

Les was from Goshen, Ind., and entered Bradley on Feb. 1, 1934. Surprisingly, he had not played high school ball. For his second semester, he signed up to play intramural basketball. He soon tried out for the freshman team and made it. He didn't know it then, but he was getting experience to join an elite group in his junior year.

Now all the building blocks were in place except one. Amazingly, 6-foot-4 Dar Hutchins, a two-year, all-state guard on that Thornton of Harvey "Flying Cloud" championship team, had not been taken by a big school. Two of his Thornton teammates went on to become captains at Illinois. Tom Nisbet and a fella by the name of Lou Boudreau.

So Dar, downheartedly, stayed home and played for Thornton Junior College. Dutch Clarno, again, got Robbie's attention, and this time Robertson personally went to Harvey to talk to Hutchins. (By the way, current athletic director Ron Ferguson is old enough to remember the "Flying Cloud" team. He knew all about Dar Hutchins, but back then Fergy had never heard of Bradley.)

Could Bradley be fortunate enough to land a two-time all-stater? Dar liked Robbie at first glance. He liked his calm bearing, no pressure approach. Although St. Ambrose had contacted him, Clarno was talking to Dar about Bradley. Robbie assured him, if he proved himself, he'd be eligible to play at once. There was a junior college ruling allowing this.

After coach told Hutch there were four Big Ten games coming up and about the good players he expected to have, Dar joined the group. This, then, rounded out what would be the original Famous Five.

The honor of naming them that goes to a young man by the name of Joe Hession, who is still prominent in the legal world around Peoria. Sportswriter Russ Perry of the Peoria Journal dubbed them the "All Mighty Five," but Hession, a Bradley freshman, writing for the Peoria Star, regarded them as "a forthcoming Famous Five," and it stuck. Hession and Art Szold were classmates and fraternity brothers of the Famous Five. Joe had a Peoria Star column called "Tech Talk," while Szold's Journal Star column was titled "Braves Briefs."

Jack Brickhouse, then broadcasting for Peoria's only radio station, WMBD, covered the Big Ten games and the Little 19 Conference games. The home games were sold out. The 1936-37 team went 15-4, after the previous year's losing record of 6-10. The 1937-38 team really turned things on with a 8-0 conference mark and 18-1 overall. It ranked Bradley as a premier national college team.

The National Invitational Tournament, the first national college tournament in the history of basketball, was formed that year, pitting the best Eastern teams against the best from the rest of the country. Bradley was invited, but lost to Temple 53-40. Temple went on to win the tourney.

The next season, 1938-39, was without graduated captain Les Getz. There were a number of possible starters, but previous college transfer, Kenny Olson, soon became the choice to take over Getz's starting slot. The tough schedule included Louisville, Pittsburgh, Nebraska, New Mexico, California, Oregon, SMU, and Yale, plus the Little 19 Conference schools. This Famous Five team, however, rose to the challenge, ending with an 18-2 season. The Famous Five compiled a 52-9 overall record in three years of varsity competition.

The first NCAA tourney was played that last year, after witnessing the popularity of the previous year's NIT. Bradley was invited to both. Robbie put it to a team vote and the players decided to pass up the NCAA bid and return to the NIT in New York. They lost to unbeaten Long Island U. but beat St. John's to take third place. Ironically, the first winner of the NCAA tourney was Oregon, a team the Braves beat in the regular season, 52-39.

Tomorrow, the memories will be relived when those who are still with us come back to the 50th Anniversary Celebration of the Famous Five. The "B" Club, Chief's Club, and Central Illinois Bradley Alumni Club are sponsoring a public noon luncheon, to be held on the basketball court in Robertson Memorial Field House. Former player Bill Ridgley has put together the event and will be M.C. Scheduled to be on hand are Chuck Orsborn, Carl Schunk, Ted Panish, Les Getz and Ken Olson. If he were still with us, I know Dar Hutchins would be there, too. But he'll be there in spirit, and in the hearts of that stellar group.

Other players of that time who plan to be on hand, in addition to Bill Ridgley, are Meyer Jacobs, Dale Engelhorn, Don Miller, Bob Leu, Phil O'Connell, Deane Richardson and Irv Wason. Old friend and Baseball Hall of Fame broadcaster, Jack Brickhouse, and Coach Stan Albeck will be featured speakers. That evening, Jack Brickhouse and Bob Leu will introduce the Famous Five and other players at half-time of the Bradley-DePaul game in the Civic Center.

Fifty exciting years ago

...and it seems like only yesterday!

Most of the information for this column was from "Good Evening, Bradley Basketball Fans," with permission from its author, Bob Leu. Bob was Bradley's first public address sports announcer, and handled the basketball duties at both the armory, and later, the field house. His book, published in 1976, is available at the Peoria Public Library. I heartily recommend it to every Bradley basketball fan. - B.A.

The "Famous Five" and their coach in a huddle. (Clockwise from Coach Robbie Robertson) Les Getz, Ted Panish, Carl Schunk, Chuck Orsborn, and Dar Hutchins.

(Photo courtesy of Charles Anderson)

Early radio fondly remembered as "theater of the mind"

When I was a kid I became hooked on radio at a very early age. Being an only child, when I came home from school or play I didn't have brothers or sisters to play (or fight) with, so my companion was this medium that we now fondly remember as "the theater of the mind." It was actually "do-it-yourself television." You had to listen and provide your own mental image which, I'm afraid, is something not done today unless pictures and laugh tracks are provided.

But what great adventures there were. Every day you could take an imaginary trip to nearly anywhere in the world with Jack Armstrong, or Little Orphan Annie (who said it's a man's world?), or the Lone Ranger.

I became such an avid fan I even got hooked on the soap operas of the day, especially in the summer when school was out. I remember listening with my mother or an aunt to their favorites. I vividly recall listening one day in August of 1935 with my Aunt Rilla Nelson when the network announcer interrupted one such soap with a bulletin that Will Rogers and Wiley Post were missing in a plane somewhere in Alaska.

So, let's go back to one specific week and take a "look" at what was happening on radio from Sunday, Nov. 14 through Saturday, Nov. 20, 1937. There were four basic networks: NBC-Red, NBC-Blue, CBS and Mutual. WMBD, a CBS affiliate, was the only local station. I was 12 years old. (You don't have to tell your age unless you want to.)

We'll start with daytime adult programs, Monday through Friday... Sponsors are listed where possible.

Mornings: Breakfast Club with Don McNeill; Linda's First Love; Stella Dallas; Bachelor's Children (Old Dutch Cleanser); Pretty Kitty Kelly (Wonder Bread); Story of Mary Marlin (Ivory Snow); Mrs. Wiggs of the Cabbage Patch (Old English Wax); Oxydol's Own Ma Perkins; Myrt and Marge (Super Suds); John's Other Wife; Just Plain Bill (Anacin); Pepper Young's Family (Camay); Betty and Bob; Today's Children (Pillsbury); David Harum (Bab-O); The O'Neill's (Ivory Flakes); Road of Life (Chipso); Mary Noble, Backstage Wife (Dr. Lyons); Big Sister (Rinso); Vic and Sade (Crisco); Aunt Jenny's Real Life Stories (Spry); The Goldbergs (Oxydol); Girl Alone (Kelloggs); Romance of Helen Trent; and Our Gal Sunday. Some morning shows were repeated in the afternoon, even on another network.

Afternoons: National Farm and Home Hour; Arnold Grimm's Daughter (Gold Medal); Kitty Keene, Inc.; Voice of Experience; Meet the Missus; Romance of Hope Arden; Young Widder Jones (Widder Brown didn't start until 1938); Club Matinee; Lorenso Jones (Phillips); The Guiding Light (White Naptha); Life of Mary Sothern (Hinds); Hilltop House (Palmolive).

Evenings: Lowell Thomas, commentator & Ed Thorgersen, sports (Sun Oil); Amos and Andy (Pepsodent); Uncle Ezra's Radio Station (Alka Seltzer); Whispering Jack Smith; Lum and Abner (Horlick's); Easy Aces; Boake Carter, commentator (Philco).

The kid's shows started after school and ran through early evening, but I'm told some adults listened, too: Terry and the Pirates (Dari-Rich); Don Winslow of the Navy; Jack Armstrong, the All-American Boy (Wheaties); Kellogg's Singing Lady; Adventures of Jimmie Allen; Charlie Chan; Tom Mix's Ralston Straight-Shooters; Little Orphan Annie (Ovaltine); Adventures of Speed Gibson; Uncle Don; The Lone Ranger (Silvercup Bread).

This particular week was the beginning of the new fall season for prime time radio in 1937. So, here's a look at these seven nights in November. All times listed are Central Standard Time.

Sunday, Nov. 14 - 6 p.m., Jell-O Program, Jack Benny; 6:30 p.m., Baker's Program with Ozzie Nelson Orchestra and Harriet Hilliard; Phil Baker Program (Gulf Oil); 7 p.m., Chase & Sanborn Hour, Edgar Bergan & Charlie McCarthy; Columbia Workshop; 8 p.m., Hollywood Playhouse, with Tyrone Power & Gail Patrick; 8:30 p.m., Walter Winchell; 9:30 p.m., President Roosevelt, Fireside Chat (on all four networks).

Monday, Nov. 15 - 7 p.m., Burns & Allen (Grape Nuts); Horace Heidt Program (Alemite); 7:30 p.m., Voice of Firestone; Pick & Pat, comedy team (Model Smoking Tobacco); Grand Hotel (Campana); 8 p.m., Fibber McGee & Molly (Johnson's Wax); Lux Radio Theater, Edward Arnold in "She Loves Me Not"; Hour of Charm, Phil Spitalny's All-Girl Orchestra (General Electric); 9 p.m., Carnation Contented Hour; Famous Jury Trials (Mennens); Lady Esther Serenade, with Wayne King's Orchestra.

Tuesday, Nov. 16 - 7p.m., Johnny Presents, Russ Morgan Orchestra (Phillip Morris); Big Town, Edward G. Robinson, Claire Trevor (Rinso); 7:30 p.m.; Al Jolson Show with Martha Ray (Lifebuoy);

George Burns and Gracie Allen on their radio show. *(A CBS photo)*

8 p.m., Watch the Fun Go By, Al Pearce's Gang (Ford); Vox Pop (Molle Shave); 8:30 p.m., Hollywood Mardi Gras, Lanny Ross (Packard); Jack Oakie College (Camel's); 9 p.m., Swing School, with Benny Goodman & Orchestra (Camel's); 9:30 p.m., Jimmy Fidler's Hollywood (Drene).

Wednesday, Nov. 17 - 6:15 p.m., Hobby Lobby (Hudson Motors); Mr. Keen, Tracer of Lost Persons (American

Home); 7 p.m., One Man's Family (Tenderleaf Tea); Cavalcade of America (DuPont); 7:30 p.m., Texaco Town, Eddie Cantor; 8 p.m., Town Hall Tonight, Fred Allen (Sal Hepatica); 9 p.m., Lucky Strike Hit Parade, Buddy Clark & Leo Reisman's Orchestra; Gang Busters (Palmolive Shave Cream); 11:30 p.m., Lights Out.

Thursday, Nov. 18 - 7 p.m., Rudy Vallee's Variety Hour (Royal Gelatin); Kate Smith Hour, with Henny Youngman; 7:30 p.m., March of Time (Time, Inc.); 8 p.m., Major Bowes' Amateur Hour (Chrysler); Good News of 1938 (Maxwell House); 8:30 p.m., America's Town Hall Meeting of the Air; 9 p.m., Kraft Music Hall with Bing Crosby, Bob Burns.

Friday, Nov. 19 - 7 p.m., Grand Central Station (Listerine); 7:30 p.m., Music from Hollywood, Alice Faye, Hal Kemp Orchestra (Chesterfield); Death Valley Days (Borax); Hollywood Hotel, Ken Murray (Campbell Soup); 9 p.m., Campana's First Nighter.

Saturday, Nov. 20 - 7 p.m., Ripley's Believe It or Not (Huskies); Jack Haley's Log Cabin; 8 p.m., National Barn Dance (Alka Seltzer); Professor Quiz, Bob Trout (Nash Motors); 8:30 p.m., Saturday Night Party (Pet Milk).

All those programs and sponsors.

...and it seems like only yesterday!

WMBD Radio relied heavily on local talent

Last week's column was about old radio and the programs carried during the week of Nov. 14-20, 1937. Since it covered the national network programs of soap operas, kid's shows and prime time, it seems only fair to give Peoria's (then) only radio station, WMBD, equal time this week.

As we said, there were four major networks, but WMBD was even then a CBS affiliate. So, many of the programs, by necessity, were heard on out-of-town stations. Most national shows were carried on Chicago stations and other major cities within the range of our "super-hetrodyne" sets. The ones I listened to most were WMAQ, WLS, WENR, and WBBM, and even though WMBD had no local competition, it sure had plenty nearby.

But there was another reason that many of the shows weren't carried locally. It was because WMBD had a big staff of announcers, musicians, and entertainers and these talented, local people kept the home folks busy with live entertainment a major part of the broadcast day. Believe it or not, the total WMBD staff in the mid- to late 1930's was nearly 200 people.

During that one week, WMBD carried just five CBS soap operas: "Myrt & Marge," "Linda's First Love," "Big Sister," "Aunt Jenny's Real Life Stories" and "Hilltop House." The only network show carried for kids was "Speed Gibson," and that was just Monday, Wednesday and Friday. But they did carry a local show for the kiddies five days a week at 5 p.m. It was called "Happy Train" and featured the singing and playing of Irene Kircher as "Cousin Rennie."

News was always an important part of radio then, as it is today. It was available every day, in one form or other, beginning at 6:15 a.m., then at 7:45, 9:45 and noon. Afternoon coverage was at 4:30 p.m., 6:15 and 10. News coverage was ably handled by one of the greats in early radio, Brooks Watson. Brooks became synonymous with broadcast news, as did another commentator, who was also versatile in other duties, Gomer Bath.

Sports, of course, was in the capable hands of a tall, skinny kid from the South End by the name of Jack Brickhouse. As we all know, he went on to big things in Chicago, handling the play-by-play of Cubs and White Sox baseball and winding up in the Baseball Hall of Fame.

Other local programs I recall were "The Musical Clock," hosted every morning at 7:15 by Milton Budd. Then at 1 p.m. it was time for "The Man on the Street." Gomer Bath was credited with its creation while Milton Budd was credited with creating the program which followed at 1:15, "His Majesty, the Baby," dedicated to the babies born at our local hospitals each day.

But of all the local programs presented throughout the broadcast day, one of the most entertaining was the one that put the station on the air each day at 6 a.m. As a rule it was a group of musicians who were a part of the huge WMBD musical staff. This particular week in 1937, it was "The Prairie Sodbusters" on Monday and Wednesday. Tuesday it was "Dot and Mayne" (Dorothy Ludwig and Maynard Meyer, who were married on the air, that coming Saturday night), and Thursday, Friday and Saturday, the program featured "The Peoria Ramblers."

The Peoria Ramblers were four very talented local musicians who could play all the popular music of the day, but their specialty was what we would term country-western today, and they dressed the part. The group consisted of Delbert and Delmar, the Kelly twins, plus Elmer Coulter and Henry Routt. Delbert played mandolin and Delmar, guitar. Elmer was on bass, with Henry on violin.

Delbert Kelly formed the Ramblers about 1933 after the Kellys had played in a high school foursome. The Peoria Ramblers played dates all over the area and on the road for many years. They joined the WMBD family of entertainers in 1934. This was when the studios were still in the Orpheum Theater building. Then in 1935 WMBD moved to the Alliance Life Building (now the First National Bank). From time to time, they provided musical accompaniment for some of the kids on Juvenile Theater.

There's an interesting personal story about the Kelly twins. In 1941, Delbert married May Kerr, and five years later Delmar married May's sister, Carolyn Kerr. Each couple had one child, a son. Delbert and May's son is, of course, Delbert, Jr., while Delmar and Carolyn named their son (you guessed it), Delmar, Jr. But if you think that's interesting, listen to "the rest of the story." Several years later, May and Carolyn's younger sister married a son of their husbands' oldest brother. This made the Kelly's nephew their brother-in-law as well. (Don't ask me to repeat that. I'm not sure what I said as it is).

I recently had the opportunity to visit with both Kelly couples and talk about those Peoria Rambler days. (They made it easy. They live just three or four doors from one another). As it turns out , I knew Carolyn Kerr Kelly when I returned to the Madison Theater after the Navy. She was cashier across the street at the Père Marquette from 1945 to 1947.

The Peoria Ramblers. (Left to right) Delbert Kelly, mandolin; Elmer Coulter, bass; Henry Routt, violin; Delmar Kelly, guitar. *(Photo courtesy of Mrs. Delbert Kelly)*

While looking at old pictures and memorabilia, they showed me an old, undated poster advertising a Sunday dance featuring "Del Kelly and his Peoria Ramblers," held at the Green Palace, at Illinois routes 88 and 90, at Edelstein.

That one had me stumped. Anyway, it's fun to go back in time with some of the folks who made it so enjoyable.

...and it seems like only yesterday!

Apollo opened with spectacular epic in 1914

About a month ago in the Music & Arts section of the Sunday paper, Jerry Klein did an interesting piece on the old Apollo Theater at 313 Main Street. Klein pointed out that the balcony of the beautiful old building still exists. This brought back a flood of memories to me because, although I never managed the theater, I was closely associated with it for many years.

During my time, it was one of four towntown theaters owned and operated by Publix Great States Theaters. They were the Madison, Palace, Rialto and Apollo. The Apollo opened as a silent motion picture theater on Monday, May 11, 1914. The opening picture was George Kleine's production of "Anthony and Cleopatra," an eight-reel spectacular epic of its day. The price was a whopping 15¢ matinee and 25¢ evening. Seriously, this was a big price in 1914, since the brand new, beautiful theater would establish a price policy of just 10 cents all day after this grand opening.

But the Apollo was preceded by another silent movie house in that location, the Crescent Theater. It was first listed in the City Directory of 1908-09.

It burned a few years later, and the Apollo was built on its site. Will Robinson, a brother to Dee Robinson (the man who built the Madison), died as a result of the Crescent Theater fire. Then, in 1914, Dee built the Apollo there.

Klein also mentioned canaries in cages placed on the walls throughout the Apollo auditorium that would sing along with the organ as it played mood music for the silent star's actions on the silver screen. That innovation was the brainchild of Dee Robinson.

There have been many managers of the Apollo over the years. In a previous column I mentioned that Len Worley hired Ralph Lawler as its manager, which was Ralph's first managerial assignment in a long theatrical career. But the first one I recall in my association was one James B. McDermott. "Mac," as everyone called him, was Apollo manager for many years. Even Henry Stickelmaier, who went on to become executive vice president of the Publix Theaters chain, broke in as an usher under him.

McDermott was quite a character. He had a big office back behind the last tier of seats in the balcony. It had a hardwood floor and there was an old brass spittoon a few feet away from his desk. Mac was always chewing tobacco. I'll give him credit. He always aimed for the spittoon, but his batting average was far less than .500, and there was a big, dark brown ring around that receptical to prove it.

When I went into the Navy in 1944, Chet Miller was my assistant manager at the Madison. When I returned in 1946, he was assistant to McDermott at the Apollo.

A short time later Mac retired and Chet became manager, and remained there until the mid-'50's.

The other day Chet gave me some pictures of the Apollo during his tenure. Some of them brought back memories of what crowds downtown were like back then, and how times have changed in just a few years.

In October, 1950, the Apollo played a controversial movie called "Because of Eve." It wasn't a very good movie. In fact, it was a very bad movie. But it broke house records with a full house at every show. Why? Well, for one thing it showed the actual birth of a baby. For another thing, the Catholic Church banned it so, naturally, everyone wanted to see it.

It was advertised "for adults only" and, believe it or not, even as late as 1950, it was felt that it would be in bad taste to show it to a mixed audience. (I also believe a little show business went into this thinking, too). In any case, the show ran just three times a day. It ran for

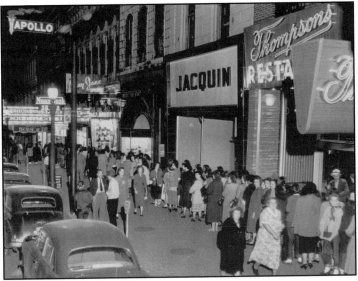

(Left) Women line up in the 300 block Main Street waiting to buy tickets to see "Because of Eve." This was just before the 7 p.m. showing for women only. The movie played the Apollo in October 1950. *(Photo by George W. Sommer, courtesy of Chet Miller)* (Right) Chet Miller, manager of the Apollo Theater at the time of the showing of "Because of Eve." *(Photo from Bill Adams' personal collection)*

women *only* at 2 p.m. and 7 p.m. Then at 9 p.m. it ran for men *only*. The opposite sex was strictly prohibited from going with their mates, even if they were married!

After Miller, a young manager from our Kewanee theaters, Ivan Cooper, was transferred to the Apollo. Then, the last manager of the beautiful old Apollo was Jack Beaird, another of my assistant managers. (It seems I was always breaking in assistants). After the theater closed with the final showing of "Peyton Place" starring Lana Turner on Saturday, May 31, 1958, Beaird moved up the street to the Palace as assistant to Merle Eagle.

But the Apollo had many good, successful programs during its 44-year history and here's one with a very local flavor:

On Sunday, October 24, 1920, (eight days after the Madison opened), the Apollo began a one-week run of a historic silent motion picture. It was locally produced for, and sponsored by, the Peoria Evening Star. The title was "Romance of Peoria," and the plot had something to do with a wedding. It played with a Hollywood feature, "The Yellow Typhoon."

While the Star praised it, the Peoria Journal, then a fierce competitor,

remember, played it down, indicating that the film-making should be left to the professionals, not amateurs.

But the Star said, "This will be a revelation to Peorians. It is the first professionally made Peoria picture in which Peoria scenes, beauty spots, exteriors, interiors are used. The characters are all Peoria people. Scores, perhaps hundreds, you know. See the wedding, the theater exterior, Main and Adams Streets, etc.

"The story is an absorbing one enacted in familiar scenes and among those taking part are Mayor E.N. Woodruff, Mrs. Charles Naffsiger, Miss Louise Strange, little Virginia Merkle, H. Paul Conrad, Eddie Clements, William Skinner, little Joseph Wilhelm, O. W. Hill, Evelyn Barnette, Margaret Burbridge, Garrett Lange, Ernest Ashley, L. B. Ague, baby Helen Winona Pierce, baby Marion Franklin, baby Geraldine Sturm and hundreds of Peorians in the wedding scene, the theater scene, the corner of Main and Adams Streets. It is the event of the amusement week."

We can't help wondering what ever became of this historic piece of film. Wouldn't it be fun to see today? Maybe once again in the old Apollo balcony theater, if it were to ever reopen.

The Apollo Theater, a most interesting segment of our entertainment history and part of it, at least

...seems like only yesterday!

Tiny Hill & Co. made a big splash in Midwest

By now you may have the impression that the Tiny Hill Orchestra was high on my list of all-time favorites from those good old yester days...and you're right. Although Tiny didn't achieve the national recognition others did, he toured the country but was most popular in ballrooms and theaters throughout the Midwest.

We've covered some of the band's activity and growth while previously featuring Ozzie Osborne and Dick Coffeen in this column. But we've not featured the big man, himself, or the rest of his great swinging organization.

Harry L. "Tiny" Hill was born in Sullivan, Illinois on July 19, 1906. He attended Illinois State Normal College, and while there he formed a three-piece band, playing country and what might be considered cornball music. By 1933, he had formed another band called "Hill's Heavyweights of Harmony," with no member weighing under 220 pounds.

As mentioned before, Hill was a drummer and, while in the Decatur area, he played in a five-piece group called "The Five Jacks," which came out of a bigger 11 or 12-piece band headed by Byron Dunbar. Tiny eventually fronted for the group and, in 1935, decided to move to Peoria because there wasn't enough work in and around Decatur. He felt they could get more bookings in our area.

The Tiny Hill band played its first engagement in Peoria on Halloween night in 1935, at the Inglaterra Ballroom, and it had its headquarters there for three seasons. The orchestra played various other places around the area, too, including the Père Marquette, the Jefferson Hotel, The Hub in Edelstein, and the Palace Theater.

In those early days I wasn't into dancing. We were married for ten years before Flossie got me out on a dance floor. But while working at the Madison from the early to mid '40's, I spent a good part of my "hard-earned" money at Jay's Radio and Adams Music on those old 78's, many of which I still have. I've found I can eliminate some of the scratchy noise by taping them. (As a matter of fact, I have an hour cassette of Tiny Hill and Dick Jergens in my car right now).

It must have been around 1941 when I first saw the Tiny Hill big band on stage at the Palace. I'd sit down front on Aisle Four. I'd be so close I could hear the banter going on between the performers and musicians.

On one occasion Tiny came out in a beautiful gray tuxedo. A half-hour later, he had perspired so, his gray tux turned to black. I don't know how much he weighed then. At one time he was said to have tipped the scales at 385 pounds, and was billed as "America's Biggest Band Leader." All I know is, he had to have lost several pounds a show, under those hot Palace Theater lights.

Tiny enjoyed doing new, innovative things with the band. One occasion in 1937 is an example. In April of that year, the Hill orchestra was the first to broadcast from a railroad train. (I've heard of "moving experiences" but....)

The Hill organization was an excellent swing band and featured good Dixieland at times but, over the years, it developed an "easy to listen and dance to" shuffling rhythm. His motto was, "If you can't dance to Hill, you can't dance."

Over the years, in addition to Ozzie Osborne on Vibraharp, guitar and banjo and Dick Coffeen on trumpet, many other fine musicians played in the band. With the help of names written on the back of photos, we'll list some of them, but this was, by no means, everyone. Many came from this area. Also on

Tiny Hill - America's Biggest Band Leader

(A Maurice Seymour Photo)

The Tiny Hill Orchestra with the engineer and locomotive when the band did a radio broadcast from the train. The picture was taken April 30, 1937, near Tuscola. Hill is at engineer's left.

(Photo from Ozzie Osborne's collection)

trumpet, there was Harold King, who also sang. Then there was Sterling Bose, Jack Alexander and Bob Anderson. Norman Maxwell and a man named Leuthard (I believe from Pekin) on sax and clarinet, along with "Nook" Schrier on tenor sax. Benny Garrels played string bass. Mel Montjoy was on drums and Don Fairchild on piano.

Others listed (but not their instruments) were: a man named Taylor, along with Bob Walters, Bob Kramer, Jim Shields and Reno Corrington. There was even a husband and wife in the group at one time, Harold Blackwell and Isa Foster. Vocalists on some of the band's records include Allan DeWitt, Erwin Bendel and Al Larson.

"Angry" was Hill's biggest hit recording and it became his, sometimes, theme song. Over a span of several years, the band recorded on the "Vocalion," "Okeh," and "Mercury" labels. I'm aware of 21 Tiny Hill records and here's a few of those 42 songs you may remember. "Angry"; "Skirts"; "Yes Sir, That's My Baby"; "Heartaches"; "Ain'tcha Comin' Out?"; "Every Little Movement"; "You Gotta See Momma Every Night"; "Please Don't Talk About Me When I'm Gone"; "Five-Foot-Two"; "When You Wore A Tulip"; "Sioux City Sue"; "I Need Lovin'"; "Pretty Baby"; and "If You Knew Susie."

Tiny's orchestra was featured on the "All-Time Hit Parade" radio show in 1943-44, and continued to record and tour through the '50's and '60's. In October, 1965, he returned to The Hub Ballroom to celebrate 30 years in the business.

Sadly, Harry L. Hill died, after a lingering illness, on December 13, 1971, in Denver. He lived there with his mother, Mrs. Osa Hill Ault, after his wife, Catherine, was killed in a Colorado car crash in November, 1958.

Tiny Hill...he contributed in a big way (in more ways than one) to those swinging big band years.

...and it seems like only yesterday!

Peoria's first radio station went on the air in 1922

Let's have a quiz regarding Peoria's first radio station.

1. WMBD was Peoria's first radio station. True or False.

(If you answered false, you are correct and you may proceed.)

2. WMBD was Peoria's first commercial radio station. True or False.

(If you answered false again, you are correct and may proceed.)

3. WMBD was: A. Peoria's second radio station. B. Peoria's third radio station. C. Peoria's fourth radio station.

(If you answered C, we'll give you a "qualified" correct answer.)

Now that we have you thoroughly confused, let's try to explain. WMBD-Radio went on the air for the first time on February 14, 1927. It was owned and operated by the late Enos Kahler. The living room of Mr. Kahler's home at 107 E. Glen Avenue, Peoria Heights, was the first WMBD studio. His garage housed the transmitting equipment. Early Peoria radio enthusiasts were his staff.

But Peoria's first radio station was experimental and went on the air a little over five years before that, in January, 1922. It was not only Peoria's first, but also one of Illinois' first radio stations. Its call letters were 9YAN, and it was the brainchild of a Bradley Polytechnic Institute professor by the name of Eric G. Shalkhauser.

Shalkhauser's experimental work actually began at Bradley in the summer of 1921, but the government license for the station, as well as the operator, was obtained on January 4, 1922. The station consisted of component parts, some purchased and many hand fabricated. It was built and assembled in the physics laboratory at Bradley's Main Hall. The transmitting equipment and the receiver were located on one of the lecture tables in the basement, and the first broadcasts took place there "under very primitive conditions." The antenna consisted of a wire stretched between one tower of Bradley Hall and the chimney of the power house across Glenwood Avenue.

Station licenses and renewals were issued on a three-month basis in those early experimental days so, as April approached, it was necessary to make a new application with the Secretary of Commerce (before the FCC), which was done on March 18, 1922. While waiting for the approval, the transmitter and receiver were moved to another part of the Bradley Hall basement, allowing more space.

On April 23, 1922, the license renewal was received, but it carried new call letters. At this point 9YAN became WBAE, and this license was good until July 20, 1922. When the school year terminated in June, however, no more regular broadcasts were aired, since much of the programming had been talks by the faculty and music programs from Bradley's music department.

It was at this time that the Peoria Star newspaper had been expressing an interest in radio broadcasting. Their interest was due to the fact that many people were paying attention to the market and weather reports which had become daily features on WBAE. So a new application was made dated July 18, 1922, by the Peoria Star-Peoria Radio Sales Co.

That March, Peoria Radio Sales Co. was re-established as a partnership between Shalkhauser and Lyle H. Gift. The new station was put on the air in August, 1922 under the call letters of WJAN. It was located on the third floor of the new Peoria Star building at 125 S.

Standing, Dr. Theodore Burgess, president of Bradley Polytechnic Institute and seated, E.G. Shalkhauser at Radio Station 9YAN in the basement of Bradley Hall.

(Photo courtesy of Peoria Public Library)

Radio Station WJAN, operated by the Peoria Evening Star in 1922.

(Photo courtesy of Peoria Public Library)

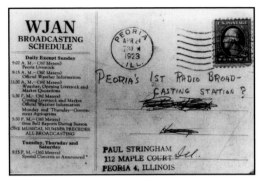

WJAN broadcast schedule in 1923.

(Photo courtesy of Peoria Public Library)

Madison Street. The antenna was mounted between two 40-foot poles on the roof. This station was also built in Bradley's Physics Department by Shalkhauser and much of the equipment was from the former WBAE station. WJAN was on the air for three years until operations were discontinued in the early fall of 1925.

In that same summer of 1922 that WJAN went on the air in association with the Star, Shalkhauser was also contacted by Brown's Business College, then located on the second floor at 327 S. Jefferson. They were interested in a radio class to be conducted there, and the professor built and licensed another radio station for that purpose. It also began operation in the summer of 1922 as WFAP. (He is not specific as to which station aired first). WFAP was in operation for approximately one year, in cooperation with the

Peoria Journal. It was under Shalkhauser's supervision and control during the first months of its existence, until another licensed operator was secured.

So the genius and energy of one man at Bradley Polytechnic Institute is responsible for at least three radio stations that transmitted from Peoria over five years before Mr. Kahler began his "World's Most Beautiful Drive" station. I say "at least" because the first station operated under two different sets of call letters, which brings us back to the "qualified" answer to question No. 3 in our quiz.

In one sense, WMBD would have to be considered Peoria's fourth station behind Bradley's, the Star's and the Journal's stations. But, if you go by call letters, then WMBD would be our town's fifth station.

The story of Eric G. Shalkhauser is certainly a fascinating one and after reading it, I wondered if the original equipment might still be around. Eric died five years ago, at the age of 90, but I talked to his widow, Emma, and their daughter, June Combs, about it.

It seems that a few years ago the equipment that was last used as WJAN was donated to the Harold Warp Pioneer Village in Minden, Nebraska, and may still be a part of their collection. Wouldn't it be interesting to bring it back some day, and display it here in Peoria, the scene where it all began, way back in 1922?

I'll admit it. This was a little before my time, but to some out there

...it still might seem like only yesterday!

Outstanding screenwriter was Peoria native

One of the things that continues to amaze us over the years is the number of Peorians who have made it big in the entertainment world. I'm sure by now almost everyone is aware of Marian and Jim Jordan, who made Fibber McGee and Molly household names for nearly 25 years. And you're probably equally aware of Charles Correll, who was a big name star of radio, stage and motion pictures since 1928 with his characterization of Andy of "Amos 'n' Andy." There are many other Peorians from the past as well.

And the trend is still alive and well today. Richard Pryor is currently enjoying star status in comedy and motion pictures. Dan Fogelberg is a big name in contemporary music as both a composer and performer. And, although you wouldn't readily recognize his name, David Ogden Stiers portrayed one of the most interesting characters on one of TV's most successful series, "M.A.S.H."

But a man who made it as big in show business as anyone (Peoria or not), was one you never saw or heard. His name is Frank Wilbur Wead.

Frank Wead was an author, a playwright and a Hollywood screenwriter of exceptional ability, and his life story is absolutely fascinating. So fascinating, in fact, that after his death a major movie was based on it.

Frank was the second son of Judge and Mrs. Samuel D. Wead of 109 Callender Avenue, Peoria. He grew up in our town and attended Peoria schools. He attended Whittier School, Peoria High School and Bradley Polytechnic Institute, and later the U.S. Naval Academy at Annapolis. He was a U. S. Navy officer in World War I and saw active duty, laying mines in the North Sea. After the war he became interested in naval aviation, so he became an aviator. Frank served in the West Indies and then flew seaplanes for seven or eight years.

Wead married and had two children, then tragedy struck. While home on leave in San Diego visiting the family, he fell down the stairs and suffered a broken neck. It paralyzed him from the neck down and he spent two years in the hospital.

This sort of trauma might end the career, or even the life, of others but not Mr. Wead. It certainly changed his career, but in a way it forced him to use a talent that might otherwise have never surfaced.

While lying in the hospital, he decided to write about what he knew best, even though he was so paralyzed he could only type with one finger. His first novel was titled "Security." Then, since he had an extensive background in the military, MGM hired him as technical director on their upcoming movie, "Gold Braid," starring Ramon Navaro.

Out of the hospital, Frank moved his family to Los Angeles. He soon was able to walk with two canes, slowly gained use of some muscles and regained some sense of touch.

Wead became very prolific as a writer. He turned out dozens of action — adventure stories, books and screenplays, mostly dealing with the military and flying. His tragic fall impaired him physically, but it never dulled his creative imagination.

Former Peorian, Frank "Spig" Wead, author, playwright, and Hollywood screenwriter.
(Photo courtesy of Peoria Public Library)

His first big success didn't come as a novel or screenplay. It came as a three-act stage play titled "Ceiling Zero." The play opened at the Music Box Theater in April, 1935. It was also made into a movie later that year, starring James Cagney, Pat O'Brien, June Travis, Stuart Erwin and Barton Maclane, and was directed by Howard Hawkes.

"Ceiling Zero" also has a Peoria connection. Peoria Players presented it here November 15-19, 1937, with a local cast totaling 21 people. It was directed and staged by Helen Wallace Younge.

By the way, the movie was remade and retitled "International Squadron" in 1941. This time a future president of the United States, Ronald Reagan, had a starring role.

Frank "Spig" Wead had many other early, better-known Hollywood efforts, including "Test Pilot" starring Clark Gable, Myrna Loy and Spencer Tracy; "Tell it to the Marines" starring Robert Taylor; and "Submarine D-1" with Wayne Morris, Pat O'Brien and George Brent. But, before you think all Wead's efforts were made for men in action, he also wrote "Tail Spin" (1939) starring non-singing Alice Faye, Constance Bennett, Nancy Kelly and Jane Wyman, a saga of female fliers.

Frank's forte was action-packed adventure as the titles imply: "Wings for Men," "Hell Divers," "The Flying Fleet," "Air Mail," "Dirigible," "West Point of the Air" and dozens more.

One of his best World War II screenplay efforts was "They Were Expendable" (1945) starring John Wayne, Robert Montgomery, Donna Reed, Jack Holt, Ward Bond, and another Peoria native, Marshall Thompson.

In addition to all this, another amazing occurrence happened to Frank during World War II. His Navy background and knowledge was so extensive that, even with his physical handicap, the U.S. Navy invited him back to duty, where he gained the rank of Commander and is credited with planning the battle of the Marianas in the South Pacific. He died shortly after the war of an intestinal disorder on November 16, 1947. He was 53 years old.

During his lifetime, Frank Wead would never allow his life story to be told. But in 1956, it was written for the screen and titled "Wings of Eagles." Frank "Spig" Wead was portrayed in the film by his personal friend, John Wayne. You might also remember some of its other stars. Maureen O'Hara, Dan Daily, Ward Bond, Ken Curtis and Edmund Lowe. Another friend and ex-Navy man, John Ford directed.

Well, the next time you feel depressed and a little sorry for yourself, think about fellow Peorian Frank Wilbur Wead. A real storybook life, but one he wouldn't write.

...and it seems like only yesterday!

Peorian helped develop gasoline-powered car

First of Four Parts

There has been a controversy for years as to whether America's first gasoline-powered automobile, the one that cleared the way for Ford, Olds and all the other auto pioneers, was built here in Peoria. The conclusion today is that the first car was completed, road-tested, and announced to the world in Springfield, Massachusetts, in 1893.

But it would also have to be concluded that the main contributor to the car, and its co-developer, was a man who lived here in Peoria at various times. His name was Charles Edgar Duryea. Later, he also built Duryea automobiles here and *may* have begun work on that first car here, before moving east.

The only fair statement, however, would be that Charles, along with his younger brother, J. Frank Duryea, were the car's co-builders, although the original idea was Charles' and the major part of the development was his. Ironically, he was living in Peoria at the time of the first car's completion by his brother, Frank, in Massachusetts.

This very complex story was put together in a 1973 book by George W. May. It is titled "Charles E. Duryea, Automaker." May is a former Peoria public school teacher, a Bradley graduate, past president of the Peoria Historical Society and, at the time of the book, was vice president of the Illinois Historical Society. We believe him to be well qualified as a historian on the subject and much of the following information came from his book.

Charles E. Duryea, the oldest of seven children, was born December 15, 1861, on a farm four miles southeast of Canton, in Banner Township. The big brick Turner (his mother's family name) farmhouse was dismantled in 1955.

His second year was spent in Peoria. The family returned to the Canton area farm in 1863. In 1865, his father, George Duryea, moved the family to a farm four miles southeast of Washburn in Woodford County. They lived there eight years, where brother James Frank was born October 8, 1869.

In January 1873, the family moved to Stark County, four miles east of Wyoming, Illinois. Charles attended a country school there but soon transferred to South Side School in Wyoming. It was here he was taught by Professor W.R. Sandham, who stimulated him to "turn toward mechanical thought and work." It was also at this time that a buggy, standing idle in a barn with no horse to pull it, started Charles thinking about a motor for it.

He graduated from the high school department of South Side School. Here he met schoolmate and farm neighbor, Rachel Steer, his future wife.

In 1879, his attention went to the bicycle. He couldn't afford one, so he decided to make one after seeing the Pope Manufacturing Co. catalog. He worked the farm all day but between 9 and 10 every night, by lantern light, he began making a bike. Charles took a 42-inch wheel from a corn cultivator for the front wheel, and a small wheel from a boy's wagon for the back one, and used a curved sapling for the frame. Oak strips were used for the fork and handlebars, and a block of wood covered with old carpet made the seat. He eventually rode his high-wheeler around a half-mile track at the local fair.

When Charles was approaching 20, he felt the need for college. In the fall of 1880, with tuition help from teaching a bookkeeping class, he enrolled in Gittings Seminary at LaHarpe. In order to cut expenses, he took two, full, three-year courses in two years, and graduated with honors.

Charles' visionary mind showed through in his graduating thesis titled "Rapid Transit," which was an oration delivered in June 1882. In it he stated, "...and the time will come when the humming of flying machines will be music over the lands; when Europe will be distant by a half-day's journey...." The Wright Brothers might be fortunate he didn't decide to put his mind to flying machines rather than automobiles.

During his second year at Gittings, the family moved to LaHarpe where they became grocers. A short time later, his father bought an interest in a store at St. David, near Canton, and Charles became a clerk and janitor there.

Then a Canton mill was being refitted by St. Louis millwrights, and they hired him as a carpenter at $2 per day. When they went back to St. Louis, they asked him to go with them, which he did. There, his carpenter wages enabled him to purchase a second-hand "Columbia" bicycle for $80.

In St. Louis, young Duryea found that boys were adding thick soles to their shoes to reach the pedals of big-wheeled bicycles. He thought a lower saddle would be better, and he began to make and patent the first hammock saddle in the U.S. Then he did some bicycle repairing during a two-week vacation and answered an ad for a cycle repairer in Washington D.C. He borrowed $25 on his bicycle for railroad fare, and arrived there almost broke.

Charles E. Duryea
(Photo courtesy of George W. May)

One week after his father's death in 1883, his mother gave birth to a daughter. Mom wrote Charles, asking him to return home and help her and brother Frank, which he did in the spring of 1884. Busy on the farm by day, Charles found time to "go sparking" at night. The girl was Rachel Steer, the youngest of nine children of Thomas and Grace Mitchell Steer. The family had come to Peoria County in 1854, in Limestone Township, where Thomas operated a lime kiln. They

moved to a big farm in Stark County in 1872 near the Duryea farm. While Charles was at LaHarpe, Rachel attended an academy in Dunlap and served as neighborhood reporter for the Wyoming Post newspaper. They were married on August 13, 1884, and a short time later moved to the Canton farm.

After a delayed honeymoon trip to New Orleans, Charles decided to sell out and go back to St. Louis, where he got a job repairing bicycles. In the summer of 1885, he developed a safety bicycle which could be ridden with skirts. It was generally accepted as the first step toward bicycles for women.

The Duryeas moved to Peoria in the fall of 1885, taking up residence on Knoxville Avenue, and he took another bicycle-repairing job. Here he developed a cycle called "the sociable." Two could ride side-by-side and hold hands. It was a second step toward ladies' safety and met with considerable favor. While in Peoria, Charles also developed a new and better shoveling board for corn-picking wagons and sold the patents for a few hundred dollars.

After awhile the ever restless Charles decided it would be advantageous to live in Washington D.C., where patents were granted. Baby Rhae Edna was born here on November 11, 1885, and in early 1886, the Duryeas moved to the capitol.

He was hired by Herbert S. Owens, Washington's leading cycle maker and importer, and was put in charge of the repair and construction shop. He also spent much time at the Patent Office. Charles asked brother Frank to join him in Washington. Frank, too, was hired by Owens, and also became interested in the Patent Office.

While working for Owens, Charles designed a bicycle for women, utilizing the principle of the "U" tube, allowing skirts to drop into the curve. This launched the safety cycle for women. He also improved the comfort of bicycling by developing a frame hinged at the crankshaft with long springs, taking the shock out of riding the hard-tired cycles.

His next attention went to bicycle tires. In the late 1880's he developed a cushion tire, wider than its rim, with an open base leading to the hollow center.

It only needed an air tube to become pneumatic. The Gormuller and Jeffery Co. (later American Motors) supplied the air tube to complete his idea. Pneumatic tires were introduced in 1890.

Duryea also realized that elastic rubber and non-stretching fabric were wrong combinations for tires. He experimented with fish-net and knitted fabrics, allowing the rubber to stretch freely but not beyond its limit. He also claimed the first patent on a gummy liquid used inside the air tire to stop small punctures. It was later sold under the trade name of "Neverleak."

In these early days, Charles also experimented with flying kites and hot-air balloons. When still a boy he told himself that if the problem of flight was not solved in 25 years, he felt he should undertake it.

About August, 1887, Mrs. Duryea left Washington D.C. to go back home to Illinois. Charles went as far as Columbus, Ohio, where he wanted to view a device at the Ohio State Fair. It was here he first saw an electrically ignited gasoline engine. It was as big as a table and must have weighed a ton, but it gave no great power.

At this same fair, a toy steam engine was displayed. He thought it could give enough power for what he had in mind. He decided his job would be to reduce the gas engine to the size of the steam engine. He later stated, "Then and there I selected the internal combustion engine as the coming power."

(Next week we'll follow Charles and Frank Duryea as they develop and perfect America's first gasoline-powered automobile.)

Duryea began planning gasoline engine in 1891

Second of Four Parts

Last week we followed the life of Charles E. Duryea from his birth near Canton in 1861 up to 1887, when he decided that the internal combustion engine was the coming power. Now we'll follow his and his brother Frank's development of a gasoline engine and the designing and building of America's first gasoline-powered automobile. It is described in George W. May's 1973 book, "Charles E. Duryea, Automaker."

Charles Duryea returned to Washington D.C., from visiting the state fair in Columbus, Ohio, in 1887, where he first saw an electrically ignited gasoline engine. In 1888, he organized the Duryea Manufacturing Co. to produce his "Sylph" bicycle. It utilized his own inventions of the spring-frame "knee action" cushion fork, plus his first hammock saddle and the "U" frame women's safety cycle features.

With his improved bicycle and a little money he'd saved, he contracted for 120 cycles to be built at a sewing machine shop in Rockaway, N.J. Then in 1880, the Duryea family moved to Rockaway and

lived there for 1-1/2 years. Charles invited Frank there, too. Charles next interested Harry G. Rouse of Peoria in his cycle. He gave Rouse a major interest and the two went to Ames Manufacturing Co. in Chicopee, Mass., to build the cycles. Later, Charles moved the family there. Frank also moved and resumed work in tool-making and mechanical drawing at the Ames Co.

Duryea and Rouse contracted with Ames for 300 cycles but the order was shelved for a bigger order that came in. So the next order was placed with Rouse in Peoria, under Charles' close supervision.

In 1891, Charles began planning a compact gasoline engine. In August, during the Ames Co. annual two-week shutdown, he and Frank made various experiments in the nearly empty plant. He thought the motor vehicle would be the coming trend in cycles and that Springfield might well be the start. So he bought a house at 339 Bay Street and the Duryeas settled in.

In January 1892, he began looking for shop space and money. In March he bought a used lady's phaeton (or buggy)

The first American gasoline-powered automobile, built in Springfield, Mass., and completed in 1893. It was designed and built by Charles E. Duryea and his brother J. Frank Duryea.

(Photo courtesy of the Smithsonian Institution, Peoria Public Library, and George W. May)

for $70 and a balance gear off of a tricycle for $3.88. On March 28th, he met Erwin F. Markham (a male nurse) who agreed to put up $1,000 in return for one-half interest. (Markham eventually invested about $3,000.) That same day, Charles rented an 85-by-35-foot space on the second floor of the John W. Russell & Sons Co. at 47 Taylor Street. With money and space now obtained, he turned to brother Frank as his mechanic. Frank reluctantly came after Charles offered him ten percent more than he was getting at Ames.

Frank's work was excellent and could be depended on. This was important, because Charles expected to be busy with his bicycle work in Peoria and he needed someone in charge. Frank started the last of March and construction began on April 4th.

The phaeton body was dismantled and laid aside. Work on the running gear advanced and engine construction began. Castings were poured. The "free-piston" cylinders (one inside the other) were built. An ignition system was not yet provided. A heating tube was devised with an alcohol burner to start ignition. Yet to be designed was a carburetor, a transmission, and a way to control the engine. The brothers toiled through the spring and summer of 1892.

Many years later, Charles stated that on April 19, 1892, a power test was made and some rides taken on the shop's second floor. Frank always disputed this and it became a heated controversy between the brothers. Charles also stated that the car was completely finished by September 12th and a pulling test was made on the floor. Frank also disputed this statement.

In July or August, the brothers did attempt to start the engine by using a perfume atomizer as a carburetor, which sprayed gasoline through the intake valve. They spun the flywheel by hand, but the engine failed to start.

At this point Charles had to have a salary. Since he had contracted with a Peoria firm to have bicycle parts made and was a partner in that Rouse-Duryea Co., he prepared to leave for Peoria. Another daughter, Grace Louise, was born and three weeks later, on September 22, 1892, the Duryea family left Springfield, Mass.

It's reasonable to assume that Charles was disappointed that he had to leave at this critical time, but he had a family to support. He had his health and a good bicycle business back in Peoria, and he could rely on Frank to continue the work. At first, he wanted Frank and William Deats, a close friend and his bicycle model maker at Russell's, to come with him to Peoria. Had they done so, the first car undoubtedly would have been completed in our town.

It appears that the further designs and construction of the car was done by Frank, including a four-cycle, water cooled motor. He also installed the electric ignition, spray carburetor, governor, muffler, engine framework and transmission, and heavier wheels.

Frank continued to work on a belt shifter and a burner for heating the ignition tube. In October he developed a severe headache, which he thought was from working in the fumes. It was later determined to be typhoid fever and he was rushed to the hospital, where he remained from October 5 to November 5.

As soon as he could travel, Frank came back to visit his mother in Wyoming, Illinois, and probably visited Charles about the car. Frank returned to Springfield in

Charles E. Duryea
(Photo courtesy of the Peoria Public Library and George W. May)

January 1893. He experimented with a carburetor, and a new heating tube that finally brought explosions, but the engine would not operate continuously.

Markham was threatening to withdraw financial support after all the test failures. Finally a test was made with Frank rotating the flywheel by hand, and it started. Work on the friction transmission followed and on February

J. Frank Duryea
(Photo courtesy of the Peoria Public Library and George W. May)

9th the "horseless buggy," without a body, got a pull test in the second floor assembly room. The vehicle moved! Unable to stop it, Frank grabbed the rear axle and slowed it down. It hit the wall with no damage done. (In a 1937 letter to Frank, Charles described this as the second pull test.)

The engine needed improvement. Frank drew up plans for a new one. Charles Marshall on Taylor Street made the patterns and turned them over to the foundry where the castings were to be done. This was a four-cycle engine, larger than the other.

In April, Frank took a short vacation to visit his fiancée in Groten, Connecticut. After his return to Springfield, he and Clara Root were married on May 17th. The work of making and assembling parts continued through the spring and summer. On August 28th Frank wrote Charles that the machine was almost ready for a road test.

On September 21, 1893, the car was rolled onto the Russell's shop elevator, stood up on end, and taken down to the area between the Russell and Stacy buildings until nightfall. A harnessed horse pulled it to Will Bemis' barn on Spruce Street. At Spruce and Florence Streets, the car was cranked...and it ran! First 25 feet, then 200. America's first running gasoline-fueled automobile! History was made that night in Springfield, Mass., but Charles Duryea was not there to see his dream come true. He was in Peoria and the next day Frank wrote him, relating the night's experience.

Charles exhibited bicycles and parts at the World's Fair in Chicago in 1893. He had entered their horseless carriage, but having nothing to sell, he withdrew it. He later regretted not having shown it, because there were only two cars shown and he thought the Duryea was far better. One of the two was the Sturgis Electric, which was built with money furnished by J.B. Bartholomew, later associated with the Avery and Glide automobiles of Peoria.

Frank decided to see the Chicago fair in October, and Charles came up again from Peoria. The brothers visited the fair for a week and discussed their vehicle fully. According to Charles, they decided to build a car of much better quality. He assured Frank that if the work was carried out and a company organized, he would give him an interest. (Up to now Frank had been an employee to Charles and Markham.)

Frank went back and reworked the car. On January 18, 1894, about 9 o'clock at night, he and another young man test drove along level streets to Markham's home. The water was boiling. They got water and drove along Central, Maple, State and Dwight Streets and finally to a shed, where they garaged it for the night. It had gone about six miles at a speed of eight mph. Demonstration rides followed and Markham also rode in it. A little more work was done on it but it was used little more. Its total mileage was probably less than 100. It was stored in the Bemis barn for a short time, then in a barn of D.A. Reed. In 1920, Ingis M. Uppercue, a former St. Louis neighbor of Charles, obtained the old vehicle and presented it to the Smithsonian Institution in Washington, D.C.

(Next week - Charles Duryea's career in Peoria and the building of the Duryea "Peoria Trap" automobile.)

Duryea's dream remained elusive

Third of Four Parts

America's first gasoline-powered automobile was the dream of former Peorian Charles E. Duryea. He also planned and designed it until he moved from Springfield Mass., back to Peoria in September, 1892. Then his younger brother, Frank, continued to perfect it until its first road test in September, 1893.

It's all described in George W. May's 1973 book, "Charles E. Duryea, Automaker."

While the two brothers visited for a week at the 1893 Chicago World's Fair, they began discussing and planning another, improved car. Frank returned to Massachusetts and work began in April 1894. It became operative in December. Frank improved the engine during January and February 1895, and it was road-tested in March. This was later called "The Chicago Car," because it is the one Frank drove in winning the first American automobile race, held in Chicago on November 28, 1895.

As mentioned in last week's column, Charles Duryea had first lived in Peoria when he was two years old. Then in the fall of 1885, a little over a year after his marriage to Rachel Steer, the young couple moved to Peoria, taking up residence on Knoxville Avenue. Charles got a job repairing bicycles. Here, he developed a cycle called "The Sociable," and he also developed a new, better shoveling board for cornpicking wagons. Also, their first daughter, Rhae Edna, was born here November 11, 1885, just before the Duryeas moved to Washington D.C.

In 1888 Charles organized the Duryea Manufacturing Co. to produce his "Sylph" bicycle. He later interested Harry G. Rouse of Peoria in his cycle. After attempting to produce them in Rockaway, N.J., and Chicopee, Mass., he placed the business with Rouse and formed the Rouse-Duryea Co. here in Peoria. As stated, Charles and family moved back here in September 1892 to oversee his bicycle business.

Charles was disappointed that he had to leave Springfield before their car was perfected, but he took comfort that brother Frank would continue the work. The brothers also corresponded regularly. In December 1894, he visited Springfield, sold his house and got his first ride in the car then under construction. Then in February 1895, Charles and Rachel went back to Springfield, and he and Frank took their wives for a ride. They were probably the first women to ride in an American gasoline-powered car.

Back home in Peoria, a son, Merle Junius Duryea, was born on June 22, 1895, at their residence at 208 Barker Avenue (now 1512 W. Barker). Then in July, Charles, again, went to Springfield to help organize the Duryea Motor Wagon Co.

In November, he journeyed to Chicago to see Frank win America's first automobile race. During that winter he brought the Duryea "Chicago Car" back to drive around Peoria. He also drove it to Wyoming to show around his old hometown.

Duryea's partner, Harry Rouse, was in business with Samuel B. Hazard. They operated the Rouse-Hazard Co. at 328-30 S. Adams, dealing in farm machinery, seeds, carriages, buggies, bicycles and typewriters. Duryea's bicycle was made at this location.

It was the golden age of the bicycle and Peoria was the cycle manufacturing hub. In addition to Duryea's Sylph bike, Peoria also produced the Ide, Patee, Cupid, Elfin, Rambler, Favorite and Aurora brands. But the automobile would soon change all that.

In 1896, Rouse and Hazard built a bicycle factory in Prospect Heights (now Peoria Heights). It still stands just south of the railroad tracks and east of Prospect Road. Charles tried to interest them in building his car but they thought the idea too farfetched.

This same year, Charles closed his Peoria bicycle interests and spent a year with the Canda Co. of Cateret, N.Y. The family resided in nearby Elizabeth. This venture was a virtual failure but he did get further experience making motorized wagons and buses.

The Duryeas moved back to Peoria in August 1897. A thriving industrial city of 50,000, Peoria had "electric lights and street cars; over 33 miles of hard-surfaced streets and over 100 miles of paved sidewalks; two free bridges; already "a city of parks"; three regular packet lines running the "Bald Eagle," "City of Peoria," and "Borealis Rex"; 12 passenger-carrying railways; two large hospitals; and almost every trade and profession represented — the city was the epitome of progress."

The family returned to the Barker Avenue address. Daughter Rhae later said it was here she spent six happy years attending Franklin, Columbia and Whittier schools. When she was 14, she marched in the parade when President William McKinley dedicated the Soldiers' and Sailors' Monument on the Courthouse Square.

Charles E. Duryea and his first Peoria trap automobile, with the trailer attached. Boys are said to be neighborhood children from Barker Avenue. The first Peoria cars were built in a barn in the rear of 208 Barker (now 1512 W. Barker).   *(Photo courtesy of the Peoria Public Library)*

About this time, Duryea asked J.B. Bartholomew to help make some patterns for a single-cylinder engine. Production shortly changed from one-cylinder to a three-cylinder engine, which became the first multi-cylinder machine ever built. Robert D. Andrew, an Avery Co. engineer, drew up the plans for the engine. The wooden patterns were made by Ernest A. Havens in a shop behind his home at 321 Jackson Street.

On February 19, 1898, Charles incorporated the Duryea Manufacturing Co., with Deloss S. Brown, president; Charles E. Duryea, vice president; and C.M. Wheeler, secretary-treasurer. The office was in the Niagara Building on S. Jefferson Street.

In 1959, Mr. E.B. Hazen, chairman of the Brass Foundry, 713 S. Adams wrote: "Between 1896 and 1899, he (Duryea) manufactured a three-wheel automobile with a three-cylinder gasoline engine. Our machine shop manufactured the first 18 of these engines for him." (Former Brass Foundry vice president, Bob Dickison, recently told me it appears the company was never paid for them.)

Duryea bought scrap sewing machines for their good steel. To save time and truckage, he carried the scrap home on his bicycle, then down to the foundry, and finally back home again with each finished block.

The first Peoria automobiles were built in a barn in the rear of the 208 Barker home. Mr. Andrew, the Avery Co. engineer, worked with Duryea in the barn, helping him build the first car.

Duryea traveled to Jonesboro, Indiana, in connection with work on his bicycle tire, where he met Monroe Seiberling of Kokomo. He encouraged him to come to Peoria and build a factory on a new city addition which Duryea would lay out, and Seiberling agreed. Charles came back and laid out "the Duryea subdivision" (now Peoria Heights).

Mr. Seiberling built a factory called the Peoria Rubber Manufacturing Co., on what later became the Pabst plant at (now) Seiberling near Prospect. It manufactured the Patee bicycle and bicycle tires.

The building of the Peoria Duryea trap automobile was transferred from Barker Avenue to the Seiberling company. Duryea raised $8,000 (maybe from Seiberling) to build the new car. He licensed Seiberling to go into production, but by doing so, lost control of the car's production. Previously pledged financing by local merchants never materialized. The lack of money and a "falling out" between Duryea and Seiberling caused its demise. Only a dozen or so automobiles were built.

But while still in Peoria, Duryea also experimented with an armored car, due to the Spanish-American War. Col. Royal P. Davidson of the Illinois National Guard commissioned him to design and make the first gasoline- powered armored car in 1899. Duryea had the Peoria Rubber Co. make a three-wheeled, one-cycle cycle with a front steel plate and a mounted Colt automatic gun that stuck out through a slot. It could carry a driver, a gunner, and two other men. It had a windlass attachment and rope to pull itself out of holes or up steep grades. After a brief test it was converted into a four-wheel with a three-cylinder engine.

About 1900, Henry Sturmey, a British editor and inventor, visited Duryea in Peoria. He later took a Duryea agency in Britain and made English Duryeas for several years.

Charles Duryea left Peoria for the last time in 1900. He moved the family to Reading, Pennsylvania, where he formed the Duryea Power Co. He manufactured cars there until March, 1908. (There is also a mention of a Waterloo-Duryea Co., in Waterloo, Iowa in 1904-05 but no detail on it.)

Then the nomadic Charles moved the family to Saginaw, Michigan, where he built cars in 1911-12. But, again, not many cars were made there.

Charles Duryea's final move was to Philadelphia in the fall of 1913, where he built cars, including the Duryea Gem, from 1917 to 1920. He also produced the Model B Truck there. These were the last cars he ever produced. It seems that he was chasing rainbows all his life but, although he always provided well for his family and raised and educated his children, he never found the elusive pot of gold.

His last years were spent writing and editing automobile publications. He also wrote numerous magazine articles, including pieces for the Saturday Evening Post.

Charles Edgar Duryea died of heart disease complications in Philadelphia on September 28, 1938, at age 76. He's buried in Ivy Hill Cemetery there, "where multitudes of schoolchildren and others have paused to pay him honor." His wife, Rachel, also died there in 1942.

(Next week we'll cover the current effort to "Bring Home the Duryea.")

Efforts under way to bring home the Duryea

Fourth of Four Parts

Following the life and legend of native Illinoisan and former Peorian Charles Duryea, the past three weeks, magnifies all the great moments of rich, historic tradition of our Peoria area.

We've covered the dreaming, planning and building of America's first gasoline-powered automobile by Charles and his brother, J. Frank Duryea, and then Charles Duryea's development of his Peoria Trap Duryea car.

Now there's an opportunity to purchase a refurbished Peoria-built Duryea of great historic significance. It's the only one that runs and is one of only two known to exist. The other one is incomplete and is in the Henry Ford Museum in Dearborn, Michigan.

I'm sure by now everyone in Central Illinois is familiar with the outstanding historic artwork of Elmer King. His local street scenes are unique artistically as well as in their exactness of detail. But what you might not know is that King and his art have played a key role in this effort to bring home the Duryea.

Several years ago, C. Clayton Andrew and his son, Robert C. Andrew, showed King some plans of Duryea's first Peoria car, which was built in a barn behind the Duryea home at 208 Barker Avenue. Clayton's father, Roy D. Andrew, had made plans and later worked with Duryea in building the first Peoria car.

Suddenly King was bitten with the bug and started painting the Duryea cars and other Peoria-built cars that came later, including the Glide and St. Louis car.

King wants to know all he can about his subjects. He found a book about Duryea, written by George W. May in 1973. After reading it, he was traveling near May's home in Metropolis, Illinois and decided to pay him a visit. This was in 1983.

May told him it was too bad he hadn't come a day sooner, because a man who owned a Peoria Duryea had been there seeking information on Duryea. He was L. Scott Bailey, an author, editor and publisher of automobile publications, in addition to being a collector of vintage cars. May gave King Mr. Bailey's New Jersey address.

King wrote and soon the two were corresponding. King also sent lithographs of his paintings. In one letter, Bailey indicated he was moving to England. He would take some of his cars with him but was thinking of selling others, including the Duryea. He said he had two previous offers to sell it, one from a California university for $125,000, but had declined.

Another letter from Bailey indicated he had space for the Duryea in England plus an offer from the British National Museum. (The Duryea Trap has special interest in England since it was the first American automobile to be licensed and built in England.)

But Bailey wanted to see the car remain in America and suggested that the car should really go back to the place it was built, Peoria.

King began talking to interested people around town. In 1987, he and John Parks of the Wheel's of Time and the Peoria Regional Museum Society, along with Mike Rucker of the Museum Society, sat down and began brainstorming the idea. The Museum Society became interested and they contacted Tom Leiter, president of the Peoria Historical Society.

These two organizations formed the "Bring Home the Duryea" Committee. An agreement was drawn up between Bailey, the seller, and Leiter and Rucker, representing the committee as buyers.

The committee is made up of seven trustees and 15 advisors. Rucker flew to New Jersey, met with Mr. Bailey and completed the signing of the agreement on February 20, 1988, in the amount of $125,000.

Like most fund-raising events, things have started slowly. A local campaign geared to the general public and corporations was begun and to date about $20,000 has been collected. A brochure and pledge forms were made available and an offer of a color picture of the car was made for donors of $50 or more.

To date, the Bielfeldt Foundation has donated $5,000 and Caterpillar has given $3,000 plus a promise to match gifts from Cat employees. Eight $1,000 donations have also been received.

A new offer is currently in the works to stimulate $100 donations from the general public. A limited edition of lithograph prints of King's painting of the Peoria Duryea, individually signed by King, will be offered.

Rucker also says that a plaque with the names of donors of $100, will be part of the permanent display of the car. Also planned in the display are building blocks with gold name plates for $10,000 donations, $5,000 in silver and $1,000 in brass.

More and more local people and firms are donating their services without charge. Ross Advertising designed the brochure and Edward Hine Co. printed it. Bill Haas did the color separation of King's prints, C & H Company is doing the printing, and the paper is being donated by Bob Coker of the Tobey-Peoria Paper Company. The Brass Foundry is providing brass replicas of the foot-step on the car, and Adams Outdoor has offered free billboard space for the promotion.

Another promotion under way is an automobile auction to be held Saturday, April 29th, on the riverfront, downtown. It's hoped that over 100 classic, sports, vintage and specialty automobiles will be auctioned off, with a percentage going to the purchase of the Duryea. Jack Seamon is chairman of the event and Jumer's Castle Lodge is cooperating on reservations. Other efforts are in planning, including area automobile dealers and other businesses.

As you can see, this is not a small undertaking and everyone involved should be congratulated for taking up the challenge. I know our town's pride and generosity will see it to a successful conclusion, but there is a deadline and time is growing short.

$125,000 is a lot of money, but there is a bonus from Bailey which is written into the agreement. Upon full payment of the purchase price on the Duryea by November, 1990, he will also include, as a gift, an additional antique (unrestored) automobile, known as a 1915 Duryea Gem. It was one of Duryea's last cars, built in Philadelphia shortly before he retired from automaking.

There are plenty of incentives to raise the money, but the most important one is the one pointed out by Bailey to King. The Duryea should go back home, to the place it was built, Peoria, Illinois.

"Bring Home the Duryea!"

Elmer M.King
33/125

ELMER M.KING PTL 88

Elmer King's painting of the 1898 Duryea Peoria Motor Trap, one of only two traps in existence and the only one in running condition. It was one of the first cars Duryea made in Peoria.

(Photo courtesy of Peoria Public Library)

"Fibber McGee and Molly" left legacy in radio

First of Two Parts

It was just about a year ago (April 1 to be exact) that Jim Jordan passed away. His wife, Marian Driscoll Jordan, died in 1961. For the one or two who don't know, thus husband and wife team made radio history as "Fibber McGee and Molly" and were native Peorians. We did a short profile on them before, but maybe now would be the time to do a more detailed account of their entertaining lives.

James Edward Jordan was born the evening of November 16, 1896, in a brick farmhouse about five miles out Farmington Road. The next time you drive west past Norwood School, look for the big tree standing in an open field between the school and the Second Baptist Church. It's all that remains of Jim's birthplace. He attended the original Norwood School.

The next event of note was that "heavenly day" 1 1/2 years later, April 5, 1898, when Marian Driscoll was born into what was to become a large Driscoll family of four girls and nine boys. The family still refers to the boys as "the baseball team." Mr. Driscoll was a hardy coal miner, (very hardy, obviously). Marian was born in a little house in Dutch Hill, in the "south end" of Peoria.

Jim's family consisted of four boys and three girls. By no means a small family, but just a little more than half the size of Marian's. When he was 12, the Jordans moved to the city, in a house at then 601 Bradley Avenue. It's just a Bradley University parking lot now, two doors from Glenwood and just three doors from Bradley's Library.

Jim was enrolled in St. Mark's Grade School. After graduation, he attended Spalding Institute. One of his basketball buddies was "Spike" Sheen, better known later as Archbishop Fulton J. Sheen who, incidentally, had his own top-rated prime-time TV program, "Life is Worth Living," in the 1950's.

While Jim attended Spalding, Marian was one grade behind, across the street at the Academy of Our Lady. But they didn't meet there. They met formally at Christmas choir practice at St. John's Catholic Church on Antoinette Street, in December 1915.

Jim and a partner were there to entertain. Marian, a choir member, danced an Irish jig, which caught Jim's eye. He asked his friend Johnny McGann to introduce him. Bashful Jim couldn't work up the nerve to walk her home, but they had their first date on New Year's Eve.

In January 1916, Marian invited him to a piano recital. He gave her red roses with a card. He wrote, "Roses are red, violets are blue. Red really means I love you."

In 1917, Jordan organized the Templeton Quartet, consisting of Paul Mehlenbeck, Ed Ellis, John Hanson and himself. In September, he landed a job as top tenor with a Chicago quartet, singing in vaudeville. They were billed as "A Night with the Poets."

They toured the U.S. and Canada for 39 weeks, but Jim was homesick for Marian. He left the act in April 1918, and returned home...to become a mail carrier.

Marian had been saving her money from teaching piano. Soon they had a nest-egg big enough to get their parent's permission to wed on August 31, 1918. After a St. Louis honeymoon, Uncle Sam invited Jim to enter the Army, to help win the "war to end all wars."

Back home in 1919, the Jordans bought a modest, four-room house in the 900 block of First Street, and Jim went to work in a machine shop. Not being much of a machinist, he quit before the boss fired him. Then he sold washing machines, vacuum cleaners and life insurance, with little success.

The two talked it over and decided to give show business a try. They sold their old car, remortgaged their home and Jim borrowed the rest from his beloved Aunt Kate Doubet. He hired some musicians and formed a troupe called "The Metropolitan Entertainers." The act was a huge success, one year earning $25,000.

The Jordans found great happiness in their work and added to it when daughter Kathryn was born on June 18, 1920. They continued to tour until just before son Jim Jr. was born, on August 13, 1923. Marian and the kids returned to Peoria while dad continued on the road.

At times, Marian would leave the children with relatives and join Jim in an act called "Marian and Jim — Harmony Team." Finances played out though. They went broke in Lincoln, Illinois and wired home for car fare. But they didn't quit. In 1925, a Kewanee appearance paid them $50. Jim headed for Chicago to work in a musical act with top-singer-songwriter Egbert VanAlstyne and baritone Clem Dancy. Marian would visit him

Native Peorians Jim and Marian Driscoll Jordan, who began in vaudeville and created "Fibber McGee and Molly" in 1935. They played the roles on NBC Radio for over 24 years, until 1959. *(An NBC photo)*

occasionally in Chicago. Jim's brother, Byron, had a home in Rogers Park. In 1925, Marian and Jim were listening to the radio. Jim remarked that they could sing better than what they were hearing. Byron bet him $10 they couldn't get a job at the station. They hurried down to WIBO, auditioned, and were hired for six months at $10 a week.

They were then billed in vaudeville as "Marian and Jim — In a Cycle of Songs." They were playing Chicago's Palace Theater, and about to go to New York, when an old Peoria friend and radio executive, Howard Neumiller, told them about an opening at WENR, Chicago. They landed the job. Three days a week, at no pay!

The Jordans were first heard on WENR's "Air Scouts," a 15-minute kid show, on October 3, 1927, for $50 a week. Here, Marian first experimented with her "Teeny" voice. The idea came from chatting with her daughter, Kathryn. Jim experimented with an "old man" voice. By 1928, the two were portraying a rural couple, "Luke and Mirandy."

Marian and Jim were on "The Smith Family," debuting on June 9, 1928. It is credited as being the first soap opera. It aired twice a week until April 3, 1932.

While at WENR, they met Don Quinn, an unemployed cartoonist and gagwriter. Here they also met E.W. Rusk in 1931, and appeared on his "Farmer Rusk" program, which moved over to WMAQ, and them with it.

...and it seems like only yesterday!

(Next week - The program that became No. 1 in radio, "Fibber McGee and Molly.")

"Fibber McGee & Molly" got started in 1935

Second of Two Parts

Last week we followed the lives of Jim and Marian Jordan from birth, through their Peoria days, early vaudeville and radio careers, until 1934. Now, let's see them as they were transformed into America's favorite radio couple, "Fibber McGee and Molly."

In 1934, Johnson's Wax was sponsoring "The Tony Wons" radio program, which was going off the air. Henrietta Johnson Louis was the wife of Jack Louis of a Chicago advertising agency, Needham, Louis and Brorby. She was also, not so incidentally, the daughter of H. F. Johnson, the head of Johnson's Wax. She was an avid "Smackout" fan, the program the Jordans were doing on NBC, and she got her husband interested.

Jack Louis knew Johnson's would be looking for a new show to sponsor, so he pitched an idea featuring the Jordans. He contracted Don Quinn to write the show. Jim had done an "old man" character, Luke Gray, who told tall tales, so it was decided the new character should be similar. At a staff meeting, Don Quinn wrote "Fibber McGee" on a slip of paper and that became his name.

Marian and Jim thought the name "Molly" would be a good character name if Marian ever did another Irish dialect, as she had done on the "Smith Family" soap opera. So the two became "Fibber McGee and Molly."

The agency wanted the main characters to be a married couple, touring the country by car. Why? So Johnson's Wax could sell their line of auto-polishing products.

So the Jordans went to New York and on April 16, 1935, they stepped to the microphone in NBC Studio 8-H, in costume for the benefit of the studio audience, and "Fibber McGee and Molly" premiered. That first studio audience, by the way, included many of their old radio friends, two of whom were George Burns and Gracie Allen.

In the fall of 1935 the show underwent a major change because the Johnson company decided to switch from Car-Nu products to their new line of floor wax products. So they created a fictitious mid-American town of Wistful Vista (Why not Peoria?), and the roaming tourists of Highway No. 79 (a number Don Quinn came up with by blindly hitting two keys on his typewriter) became residents in a house at No. 79 on a street of the same name, Wistful Vista.

For many years 79 Wistfull Vista opened its doors to a parade of radio characters, including the original announcer, Harlow Wilcox. "Waxy," as Fibber nicknamed him, was one of the first announcers to, not only plug the sponsor's product, but to do it within the plot of the program.

One of the best characters on the show was Throckmorton P. Gildersleeve, created by Harold Peary. "Gildy" was Fibber's next door neighbor, who joined the show in 1937, and continued until 1941, when Peary left to become radio's first spin-off series, with his own show, "The Great Gildersleeve." (I wonder if he might have been named after the man who ran Throckmorton's Drug Store in Peoria.)

Isabel Randolph portrayed Mrs. Abigale Uppington on the show from 1936 until 1943. "Uppie" was the McGees' rich neighbor who became flustered over McGee's antics.

One of the most versatile actors on the program was a young man by the name of Bill Thompson. He not only portrayed The Old Timer, ("That ain't the way I heered it") but also the W. C. Fields sound alike, Horatio K. Boomer ("...and a check for a short beer"), plus that wimp character, Wallace Wimple, who was continually harassed by his "big old wife," Sweetie Face. She was never heard. Cliff Arquette, who later gained fame as Charley Weaver on the Jack Paar TV show, first created The Old Timer on the McGee show, and the role was later taken over by Bill Thompson.

Arthur Q. Bryan took the part of the irascible Doc Gamble from 1943 until the end of the program's regular run. (Bryan also did the Elmer Fudd voice in the "Bugs Bunny" cartoons.)

A real show-stopper on the program was Beulah, the maid, especially for the studio audience. The reason was, the one who did her voice was the very handsome male actor, Marlin Hurt. Every time he stepped to the microphone and Beulah's high-pitched voice came out, the audience went into convulsions. Hurt left the show in 1945 to be another spin-off with his own "Beulah" series for CBS. His show was on for less than a year when he died of a heart attack at the age of 40.

Mayor La Trivia could get more flustered over Fibber's antics than all the others combined, with the possible exception of Gildersleeve. In real life he was the incomparable Gale Gordan. He joined Fibber and Molly in 1939 and was on the show for 13 years, except for three years in the Coast Guard during World War II.

One of the characters to appear regularly was done by Marian. It was little neighbor girl, Teeny, who invariably exasperated Fibber instead of the other way around. A Christmas segment became an annual tradition with Teeny joining the singing quartet, The King's Men and Billy Mills' Orchestra in "The Night Before Christmas."

Expressions from the show's characters became national catch-phrases. The public quickly picked up on Molly's "Tain't Funny, McGee," Gildersleeve's "McGee-e-e-e," Beulah's "Love that man!" and practically everyone borrowed Molly's "Heavenly days!"

Jim was a master at tongue-twisters, using words beginning with the same letter in a machine-gun delivery that would invariably leave him and the audience breathless. The amazing thing is, he would do this twice a week. Once for the first broadcast, and repeating it later for the West Coast. (Programs were done live on those days.) He rarely, if ever, flubbed a line.

I met Jim Jordan for the first time in 1950, while managing the Madison Theater. He and Marian were back in Peoria visiting relatives and friends, and Look magazine was doing a story on them. The magazine called me and asked if I would open the old, closed Orpheum Theater. They wanted to photograph Jim in the theater where they used to appear in vaudeville. For some reason Marian wasn't with him that day.

I went over and opened the Orpheum and met Jim and the photographer. As we were leaving, the photographer walked on up the street and Jim started laughing. I asked what was so funny. He said they never played the Orpheum. He pointed to the Palace and said, "When ever we came in vaudeville, we played over there." If that was so, I asked, why let Look magazine take the pictures? He said, "It's their story, let 'em tell it any way they want." There was always a "bit of the Dickens" in Jim Jordan.

Then in 1984, I had the privilege of meeting him a second time. Marian died in 1961 and he was remarried and living in Beverly Hills. Flossie and I met a TV camera crew at his home, and I interviewed him for a special program on WEEK-TV. He was 87 at the time.

After the interview, he took us into his library and showed us all the leather-bound scripts of his radio programs. He has every "Fibber McGee and Molly" radio script, over 700 of them, plus several of their old "Smackout" scripts. Jim passed away April 1, 1988, on Good Friday, and ironically, April Fool's Day, too. He was 91 years old.

Jim and Marian Driscoll Jordan, two great Peorians.

...and it seems like only yesterday!

(Some of the information on the Jordans came from the book, "Heavenly Days," by Charles Stumpf and Tom Price.)

Seneca Hotel fire left entertainers on street

Being an eyewitness to a disaster leaves an indelible imprint on your mind, especially when you're a mere child at the time. Such was the case with me the day the Seneca Hotel burned.

It was the afternoon of Tuesday, February 11, 1936. I was ten years old and we lived "up the river" in Holmes Center, north of Mossville. My dad was deputy county recorder and worked in the "old" courthouse. Mom and I came to town with him that day. (I must have been celebrating Lincoln's Birthday early.)

In any event, we were downtown. Mom was shopping and paying bills, maybe to save the 3¢ postage. We stopped in CILCO's office, then located in the 300 block of Southwest Jefferson, where the Commercial Bank parking deck is now located.

Someone noticed smoke rolling out of a building across Franklin Street (now Kumpf Boulevard). The Seneca Hotel was on fire. It was readily visible out of CILCO's big front windows. Soon fire trucks began arriving with their sirens screaming and bells clanging.

We stayed and watched all the excitement for quite some time. There was plenty of smoke and flames billowing out of the hotel, and firemen were rescuing people with their big hook-and-ladders, and at least one person jumped into a net held by the firemen. To me, this beat shopping any old day, and we had a great view of everything in the nice, warm CILCO office.

Maybe some of you remember this hotel fire. Crowds estimated between 3,000 and 4,000 braved the cold that day. If you were there, you'll remember the big red neon "Gipps Amberlain Beer" sign that stood on top of the hotel roof. After the fire ate through the top of the hotel, the heat became so intense it began to melt the steel frame of the sign. The huge sign began to slowly lean over, a little at a time, until it finally collapsed into the flames. I can still see it in my mind's eye.

The building was constructed in 1904 as the Hotchkiss Apartments. In 1920, G. H. Sommer leased it and ran it as a hotel until 1926. Then the lease was taken over by George C. Brosios, who operated hotels in several other towns. About 40 percent of its 90 rooms were occupied by resident guests, and there was a popular nightspot in the basement called "The Tia Juana Tavern."

Back then, the Seneca was a popular place to stay for traveling orchestras and vaudeville entertainers. The night before the fire, Horace Heidt and his Brigadiers were playing a Caterpillar Girl's Club Charity Ball at the Inglaterra Ballroom.

For three days, the Palace Theater was featuring a stage show called "Ed Lowry and his Company of Stars." It featured Lowry, Helen Compton (former Peoria and Chillicothe girl) and her all-girl orchestra, Rita Joyce and the Reece Brothers, the Joyce Brothers and Dean, Lillian Dawson and Elaine Arden. The Horace Heidt band and the Palace stage troupe were all staying at the Seneca.

The fire broke out shortly after noon on Tuesday. It was said to have started in Room 307, which was occupied by R. Bott and J. Hanson of the Horace Heidt band. There were about 25 people in the hotel, including guests and employees, when the fire started. Three suffered minor injuries: Marietta Gift, a vaudeville actress; Mrs. Lina Galvin, a hotel house-keeper; and an unidentified orchestra member.

The big tragedy for this vaudeville troupe was that they lost all of their personal belongings. We've talked before about Len Worley's generosity when friends and show people are in need, and this occasion was no exception. But it wasn't just theater management that took part this time.

Right after the last regular show at the Palace on Wednesday night, a benefit stage show was presented at 11:45 p.m. It was one performance only, with all seats 50¢. All the proceeds went to the performers who lost their belongings in the fire.

In addition to Ed Lowry, Helen Compton's band and all the show's regular performers, and all the entertainers appearing at Peoria's nightclubs joined in the festivities. Publix Great States Co. donated the theater, while the stagehands, musicians, motion-picture operators, cashiers, and ushers donated their time for the benefit. Even the streetcar company provided special transportation service, and several hundred people braved the sleet and cold that night to attend.

But there's a somewhat humorous sequel to this story. For many years after the Seneca fire, the Horace Heidt orchestra didn't play in Peoria. During my Madison Theater days I can remember hearing the rumor that Horace Heidt was afraid to book our town for fear of repercussions over the Seneca fire.

Finally, in the early '50's, he did play the Shrine Mosque. When the curtain opened, Horace Heidt stepped to the

The Seneca Hotel fire on Feb. 11, 1936. *(Photo from the Grassell File, Peoria Public Library)*

microphone and said, "I don't care what they say, I never burned down the Seneca Hotel!"

I told this story the other day to a Shrine Seniors' luncheon. After I finished, Neil Skow told the group that he remembered that appearance because he and Jerry Conlogue were responsible for bringing Horace Heidt to the Shrine.

He said it was very bad weather that night, which kept the crowd down. As a matter of fact, they lost money on it. But he added that while they were visiting with Mr. Heidt after the show, someone mentioned their loss. Horace Heidt took out his checkbook and wrote a check to cover the loss.

Yes, it has been said that positives often come out of negatives, and it would seem the Seneca Hotel fire is one such example.

...and it seems like only yesterday!

Three Peoria entertainers got early start at WMBD

It's truly amazing how many people who were prominent in music around our town back in the early radio days, got their start on WMBD. Three young ladies who did just that are Mary Jane Doebler LeMaster, Margie Burling Karagianis and Phyllis Hunt Fabry.

Phyl Fabry's maiden name is Hunt and she and her sister, Shirley, along with a neighbor girl, Kay Blew, formed a trio. They began on Juvenile Theater when their ages ranged from 7 to 10.

The Hunt sisters got their talent naturally. Their mother originally sang with them. Mom played piano by ear, and at one time played for the silent movies. She also played banjo. Phyl started playing piano at age 4 and first took lessons from her Aunt Gladys Pierce.

The young trio auditioned for Wayne West around 1937, and he put them on the show. He later named them "The Victory Trio." When Phyl was 12, she was a prize winner on Chicago's Morris B. Sach's Amateur Hour program, and at 14, she started accompanying for the other kids on Juvenile Theater. Phyl began playing the organ at WMBD. She knew so little about it she actually had to call Charley Adams at Adams Music to find out how to turn on the warmup switch. While still in high school, she also performed on WSIV-Radio in Pekin. A young announcer there by the name of Bill Houlihan would pick her up at the Peoria bus station and drive her to the radio studio.

Phyllis married Bob Fabry at 19, and in 1953 she did the first live show on the new WTVH-TV, Channel 19. Husband Bob of the Commercial Bank later joined her on the show and it became "At Home with the Fabry's." She also hosted one of the earliest TV kid shows, "Kartoon Korner" on 19.

A few years later, Phyl moved over to WEEK-TV and hosted "Coffee Time" in the afternoons, after Bev and Dick Vance left the show. Harry Cool, the former great vocalist with Dick Jurgens' Orchestra, later joined her on this show. She also hosted "Melody Lane," on then Channel 43.

In later years, Phyllis Fabry has entertained everywhere from Frank's Place in Galesburg (with Harry Cool), to the Père Marquette, D'Amico's Supper Club, The Mecca Supper Club on Farmington Road, to the Gold Lion Restaurant.

The Fabrys have recently retired to Wyoming, Illinois. They have six children, and Phyl and Bob now operate the "Another Tyme" antique shop. Say, that sounds like a good title for a newspaper column.

Another young lady who had quite a career singing began as a child dancer. Her name is Margie Burling Karagianis. Margie Burling started at age 10 on Juvenile Theater. She took dancing lessons from Betty Washburn. One day Ms. Washburn had her sing a song. It went over even better than the dancing, and that's how it began. The song? "The Hawaiian War Chant." Milton Budd saw one of her recitals and had her audition for the show. Jack Lyon was her on-air accompanist.

In 1939-40, Margie was female vocalist for Verle Bogue's house orchestra at the Inglaterra. She was 13 years old, and her feature number? "The Hawaiian War Chant," of course.

Bogue's band ("music in Vogue by Bogue") played on Thursday, Saturday and Sunday at the Ing but they also played other dates, too, including Macomb and Kewanee, and a lot of Bradley dances. So much so that Margie received an honorary Bradley "B" letter, compliments of the B Club.

Mary Jane Doebler LeMaster as she appeared at the WMBD microphone.

(Photo courtesy of WMBD.)

left the band and returned home. But Margie holds the distinction of being Eddy Howard's first, and only, female vocalist.

Burling went back to WMBD, and in 1942 she appeared on a 15-minute afternoon show for Nabisco. She also did a show with Wayne West, on location from the Induction Center.

In 1943, Margie was singing in local clubs. She sang for six months with Ozzie Osborne's orchestra in "The Tropics" nightclub in the Jefferson Hotel. Angelo Karagianis played sax and clarinet in Ozzie's band at WMBD and The Tropics. Margie and Angelo were married in 1944. The Karagianises had five children, and Margie says after the second child she changed from singing professionally to singing lullabies. To talk to her today, she is still singing "The Lullaby of Peoria." Margie Burling. One of Peoria's brightest juvenile stars.

Mary Jane Doebler LeMaster is our third young lady who began on WMBD, but she was a little older than the required "under 16" age limit for Juvenile Theater. She was 18 when she joined the WMBD radio family of entertainers. She began singing when she was 15 and took lessons from Mrs. Cooper on Northeast Monroe Street.

Mary Jane Doebler became a LeMaster after her marriage to Steve LeMaster. He was a salesman for Chris Hoerr and Son Co.

She was appearing in Bloomington one night with Bogue, when a Chicago booker from MCA heard her sing. Eddy Howard, vocalist with Dick Jurgens band was forming his own orchestra and they were looking for a female vocalist. He talked to Margie's mother, and Margie landed the job. She was 15 years old. Margie's older sister, Imogene, couldn't continue to travel as her chaperon, so after eight weeks, the homesick Margie

Phyllis Fabry as she is best remembered, singing and playing in supper clubs.

(Photo courtesy of Phyllis Fabry.)

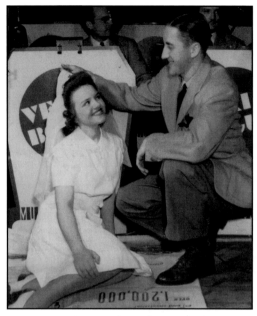

Margie Burling with orchestra leader Verle Bogue during the Inglaterra days.

(Photo courtesy of Margie Burling.)

When she first began on the station, she remembers that one of her piano accompanists was Hod Hyatt, and she worked with many talented people over the years, including Milton Budd, Wayne West and Jimmy Carragher. She and Wayne had a weekday afternoon half-hour program. Then on Sunday afternoons, she shared honors with the very talented Sarah Murdock.

And what a time to be in radio. You had to be good to stand before the microphone and sing with such outstanding musicians as Ozzie Osborne on vibra-harp, organ and guitar; Dick Coffeen on trumpet; Dick Raymond on violin; Warren Doss on bass fiddle; Angelo Karagianis on sax and clarinet, and Zeke Sanders on piano.

In 1941, Mary Jane auditioned for the opportunity to appear on a network radio program. She won a trip to Hollywood where she appeared on "Al Pearce and His Gang," on CBS as guest vocalist. You'll remember Pearce as a comedian who developed a character by the name of Elmer Blurt, a bashful door-to-door salesman. Music played a major role on the show, too, and Mary Jane fondly remembers the experience.

She had a long radio career and even after her "over-the-air" days, she stayed on at WMBD doing behind the scenes work until 1959. She is now widowed, but she and Steve had three children. A son lives in Wisconsin and twin daughters live in Peoria. Unfortunately, Mary Jane's health has deteriorated the past few years. She is now living at Bel-Wood Nursing Home where she is under oxygen 24 hours a day. Even though she's bedfast, she still maintains that pleasant attitude we remember so well. She does beautiful embroidery work to pass the time.

Her 50th Woodruff High School class reunion is coming up in June. She won't be able to attend, and visitations are difficult, but I know she'd love to hear from all her fans and friends. Drop her a card or note of "thanks for the memories." Margie, Mary Jane and Phyllis, three gals who entertained us so well.

...and it seems like only yesterday!

Old menu has a unique story

One day last fall I received a call from Mrs. Charlotte Wright of Wright's Furniture Store in Canton. Something I'd mentioned about Block & Kuhl's "Big White Store" had brought back a flood of memories to her and some of her friends about a wonderful dining room on the store's seventh (top) floor..."The Skyline Restaurant."

She specifically wanted to know if a menu from the restaurant might still be in existence. I mentioned this to a friend and former Block & Kuhl executive, Gaylord Zellmer. He called me sometime later and said a man he used to work with at Block's, and later Carson Pirie Scott, had one. His name is Walter Kraps.

Walter not only had an old menu, it was autographed by himself and several other B&K employees. Walter and his wife, Shirley, are both former Block & Kuhl employees. Not only that, his first job was bus boy for this same dining room and the lunch counter on the main floor, in 1938. Shirley also has a spoon from the dining room with a scrolled "B&K" engraved on the handle.

But there is an interesting story connected with this particular menu. On Thursday, July 2, 1959, new carpeting was being laid in the restaurant. Someone decided (fortunately) to have a menu of that day signed by the carpet layers and the dining room manager and cashier, and put under the new rug. 15 years later, long after Carson Pirie Scott had taken over the store, the carpet was taken up and there was the menu.

The autographs were signed and dated 7-2-59 at 4:30 p.m. and the temperature was stated at 80°. The crew consisted of Walter Kraps, Pat Hughes, Del Caughey, Dick Vickey, George Cobb, Herb Brown, Donald Douglas and C.F. Schertz. It was also signed by Myra Shaner, manager, and Priscilla Siebel.

What is also interesting is the menu's wide variety and prices. The permanent ala carte menu featured appetizers from Fresh shrimp cocktail, 85¢ and $1.25, down to homemade soup, 15¢ and 25¢. Pastries featured homemade pie 25¢ and cake 20¢, "Prepared in our own kitchen."

A cup of coffee was 10¢ and a pot of tea, 15¢. The fountain listed ice cream, any flavor, 20¢; sodas and sundaes, 25¢; hot fudge or crushed fruit sundaes, 45¢; milk shakes 30¢; malteds, 35¢ and parfait, 35¢.

The Blue Plate Special (remember those?) was $1.60. There were nine salad or cold plates, from crab meat or fresh shrimp plate at $1.75 down to tropical fruit or combination salad at $1.35.

I showed the menu to Phyllis Springer Evans the other day. You'll remember her as the record nine-time Peoria women's golf champion. Her eye went immediately to her favorite at this restaurant — tomato rarebit on toast, broiled to a golden brown, chef's salad, hot roll and muffin, sherbet or ice cream, coffee or tea, $1.25.

Orders from the grill and broiler offered six choices. The highest prices were $1.85 for T-bone steak or filet mignon. Two pork chops or whole boneless trout were the cheapest at $1.45. The shrimp? $1.75. And if you weren't that hungry, there were 14 sandwich choices in addition.

That was just the permanent menu, but two daily menus were also offered, one for the luncheonette and one for the dining room. The luncheonette, by the way, was a soda fountain-type bar with stools, to your left, just before entering the main room.

Its menu printed for Thursday, July 2, 1959, featured five choices, from Kentucky fried chicken with giblet gravy at 85¢ down to breaded veal cutlet on a bun with lettuce and pickles for 50¢. Your choice of pie or cake from this menu was only 15¢.

That same day's dining room menu featured homemade vegetable soup or New Orleans ham gumbo — cup, 15¢, bowl 25¢. The Skyline Shopper's Special was cold baked hickory-smoked ham with pineapple slices — $1.25.

The other, more expensive dishes ranged from a low calorie special at $1.50, up to roast choice sirloin of beef au jus at $1.75. The less-expensive lobster tidbits was only $1.65. There was also a "Little Customer's Menu Served to Children Under 8," at apparently no charge, except that milk with dinner was 5¢ extra.

You must admit that the wide range of choices in this beautiful restaurant was truly amazing. What's more amazing is that on most days, except when the store was open at night, maybe once a week, this fabulous Skyline Restaurant was open just three hours and fifteen minutes a day, from 11 a.m. to 2:15 p.m.

Walter Kraps began with Block & Kuhl's at the age of 18 in 1938. His wife, Shirley, began in 1940, in the distributing building on South Washington at Oak. She later moved to the store's general auditing department on the fifth floor.

The front cover of Block & Kuhl's Skyline Restaurant menu as it appeared in 1959.
(Menu for photo courtesy of Mr. & Mrs. Walter Kraps)

She worked on and off for B&K and then for Carson's after they bought the company. She last worked in the mall store about a year before they sold to Famous Barr.

After Walter's bus boy job, he went to work for James "Bud" Wade in the delivery/receiving department. Then he worked for Richard Iben, the store's planning director, and was working on B&K's new Kewanee store before entering the Army in 1942.

He spent over 4½ years as an army combat engineer. Walter and his 1st Amphibious Brigade actually landed on the beach a little before H-Hour on D-Day and set explosives to destroy the barb-wire defenses before the first waves of the attack. Talking to him now, he seems more impressed with the fact that Block & Kuhl's sent him a $25 check and a carton of cigarettes every month he was in service.

When his Army duty ended in 1945, he came back to B&K. They sent him to night school at Bradley and he stayed with them and then with Carson's when they took over. Walter became property manager, and when Carson's combined their Chicago and downstate's two buying departments, he was put in charge of maintenance of all their stores. He maintained his office in Peoria and commuted to Chicago for ten years, where he had another office, plus another in Normal. He worked on developing new stores as well as overseeing the closing of old ones.

Walter retired this past March 17th, after 51 years of service with Block & Kuhl's and Carson Pirie Scott. Not a bad record for an 18-year-old kid who started as bus boy.

Thanks, Walter, for preserving the "Skyline Restaurant" menu. Thanks, also to Mrs. Wright for remembering.

...and it seems like only yesterday!

SKYLINE RESTAURANT, BLOCK AND KUHL COMPANY, PEORIA, ILLINOIS

Block & Kuhl's Skyline Restaurant as it appeared in this postcard supplied by the Peoria Public Library.

Glen Gray had roots in Peoria

Just about everyone old enough to be nostalgic about "Yester Days" (let's say 50 and over) remember the great music of one of the biggest names in big bands — Glen Gray and his Casa Loma Orchestra. But did you know Glen was a local boy? If you didn't, it may be because that wasn't his real name.

Oh, the Glen was real enough, although when he was eight years old, he signed his name Glenn (two n's) Rudy Knoblauch. He assumed his mother's maiden name when he decided on a professional musical career.

Glen was born June 7, 1900, in Metamora, but when he was still an infant his family moved to Roanoke, where he went to school. He graduated from Roanoke High in 1917. Because of his tall, slender build, he acquired the nickname "Spike" while playing high school basketball. Glen's father, Lurdie Knoblauch, died when Glen was two years old. Later his mother, Agnes Gray Knoblauch, married a man by the name of DeWilde. After high school graduation he attended Illinois Wesleyan College for awhile and then went to work for the Sante Fe Railroad as a freight handler.

One day, Glen picked up an old piccolo that was lying around the house and learned to play it. Then he taught himself how to play the flute, piano, clarinet and saxophone.

In 1921, he went to Chicago. He studied at the American Conservatory of Music for six months, then was called back to Peoria to play for George Haschert's orchestra, where he got his professional start.

Young Knoblauch played with several bands around the Peoria area and I've been told he also played in theater pit orchestras, including the Apollo Theater.

He wasn't satisfied playing for others, so he formed his own five-piece group and called it "Spike's Jazz Orchestra." He was the director. The other four members were his sister, Mable Herbst, on piano; Mable's husband, E. L. "Nick" Herbst, Jr., on sax; John F. Hubbell, trombone; and Glen Hornbeck (from Washington) on drums. At other times, W. H. Small played cornet and H. J. Dourlain played drums. Spike did his best to sound like the Original Dixieland Jazz Band, the white New Orleans outfit that was inspiring young record fans in those days.

A few months ago, I called Frank Bussone, knowing that he was from Roanoke, and asked him if any of Glen Gray's relatives were still around. He called me back later and said he'd talked to Roger Herbst, who was a nephew. Roger and his wife, Sandy, and family, live in Roanoke and, as luck would have it, they had some old pictures and memorabilia. Roger is the son of Nick and Mable Herbst, who played in Spike's Jazz Orchestra. There was also a picture of Nick and Mable with Nick's brother, Frank Herbst, in a Roanoke orchestra called "The Merrymakers."

In 1924, the young Glen went to Detroit where he caught on with Jean Goldkette's Orange Blossom Band. In 1928, they played the Casa Loma Hotel, a palatial building in Toronto, Canada. It was originally built to accommodate England's king and queen on a visit.

The band was well received but the hotel folded. The orchestra later adopted the Casa Loma name for jobs in and around Detroit. In addition to Glen, early members included Pee Wee Hunt, trombone; Billy Rauch, trombone; Joe Hall, piano; Gene Gifford, guitar and arranger; Pat Davis, tenor sax; and Henry Biagini fronted the band.

The orchestra reorganized as a corporation in 1929, with Glen as president and leader, but for years Gray preferred to sit in the sax section and let violinist Mel Jenssen front the band. Gray finally began leading the group in 1937.

Vocalist and saxman Kenny Sargent joined the band in 1931 and became a top romantic singer through the '30's and early '40's. Pee Wee Hunt handled the novelty and rhythm vocals and jazz trombone. Other key jazzmen were Clarence Hutchenrider, clarinet; Grady Watts, trumpet; and Sonny Dunham, trumpet. Pat Davis was the hot tenor sax soloist and Billy Rauch's trombone was featured on lead and sweet solos.

The band played New York in late 1929 and began attracting attention recording hot numbers for Okeh Records. They changed to Brunswick in the early '30's. Gene Gifford was the chief arranger from 1930 to '35 and was responsible for the orchestra's style. His jazz compositions helped usher in the swing era (sorry, Mr. Goodman). They included "Casa Loma Stomp," "Black Jazz," "White Jazz," "Dance of the Lame Duck," and "Maniac's Ball." (Who said today's rock kids invented weird titles?) The orchestra required much rehearsing because of Gifford's intricate writing and fast tempos. He also wrote their beautiful theme song, "Smoke Rings." They switched to Decca in 1934.

In 1934 to 1936 Glen Gray's Casa Loma Orchestra was featured on the popular radio program, Camel Caravan, with Walter O'Keefe, host. In 1938, they were with the Burns and Allen radio show and, like all major orchestras of that era, they did hundreds of radio remote broadcasts.

(left to right) Pee Wee Hunt, Glen Gray, Bing Crosby and Kenny Sargent at the racetrack. Pee Wee and Glen look like they bet on a winner. Kenny looks as though he bet on Bing's horse.
(Photo courtesy of Mr. & Mrs. Roger Herbst)

Later arrangers for the band were Larry Clinton, Dick Jones, and Larry Wagner. Murray McEachern starred on trombone and alto sax. Eugene Baird was vocalist in the early '40's and Red Nichols and Bobby Hackett joined during the wartime. Two big hits about then were "Sunrise Serenade" (1939) and "No Name Jive" (1940). They appeared in two Hollywood movies, "Time Out for Rhythm" (1941) and Gals, Inc. (1953).

Glen and his wife Marion (Douglas), had one son, Douglas Gray. The Grays retired in Plymouth, Mass., in 1950. Glen made a comeback in 1956 and launched a series of LP records, using all-star sidemen to recreate the big band sound. The musicianship was outstanding and the records were acclaimed by fans and critics, alike. Glen died in Plymouth on August 23, 1963, at age 63. His ashes are buried there, although there is a tombstone with his name on it in the Roanoke cemetery.

Well, that's the story of Glenn Rudy "Spike" Gray (DeWilde) Knoblauch. From Metamora, to Roanoke, to Peoria, to Chicago, to Detroit, to Toronto, to New York, to the world...the world of great big band music! Not a bad trip for a tall, skinny kid who picked up a piccolo in Roanoke one day, and decided to learn to play it.

...and it seems like only yesterday!

Original TV anchors still in business

Local television came to Central Illinois for the first time on Sunday, February 1, 1953. That's the evening that WEEK-TV, Channel 43 (remember?) first went on the air in "living" black and white.

Three young men had the distinction of being the first news, weather and sports anchors, and one is still with us at the same old stand. They were Bob Arthur, news; Bill Houlihan, weather; and Chick Hearn, sports.

Chick and Bob left for bigger markets many years ago, and both are still very prominent in Los Angeles broadcasting. Houli had opportunities elsewhere, too, but being a local boy, he chose to stay in his home town. He told me years ago he'd rather be a big fish in a little pond here, than go to a major market and be a little fish in a big pond.

Bill did leave the TV business for awhile, though. When fast food was becoming the rage back in 1964, he left WEEK to take a fling in the franchise business, but it didn't work out. He came back in 1966 as backup news, weather and sports.

He left again in 1969 when he bought a partnership in Waddell Airport near Manito. He managed it and taught flying there until 1975. In July of that year he became general manager of Mount Hawley Airport. He returned to WEEK-TV as weather director on December 1, 1976, the same day a young lady by the name of Chris Zak joined the staff.

Bill is an excellent pilot, but he holds one rather dubious honor. He took me up in a plane for my first time ever. It was a Mooney airplane owned by John McGinnis, whom I worked for at TV TimeTab for a short time. (McGinnis later forgot to lower the landing gear and "bellied it in").

Chick Hearn was a native of Aurora. He was a good athlete and later became an excellent basketball official. That's why, when doing Bradley basketball radio broadcasts, he was able to call the foul on the air before the official blew the whistle.

Fred Mueller brought Chick to Peoria primarily to compete with WMBD and WIRL radio on Bradley basketball. He was also grooming him for the future

TV sports spot. Chick was a tall, handsome guy with a machine-gun delivery who soon built a big radio audience. But one night he really put his foot in his mouth.

His Bradley broadcasts were sponsored by Staat's Appliances who, among other things, sold refrigerators. Chick would look for ways to tie in the sponsor in his play-by-play. He came up with a perfect gimmick. Whenever Bradley would have a comfortable lead near the end of the game, he'd say, "This one's in the refrigerator."

One night in 1951, Bradley was playing St. Louis University at St Louis. As I recall, Bradley was leading by about 15 points with less than three minutes to play. Hearn was comfortable with that and gave it his "its in the refrigerator" call. Suddenly St. Louis began whittling away, and before the buzzer sounded, they overcame Bradley's lead and beat them 72 to 69. Chick was dumbfounded. A game had finally jumped back out of the refrigerator on him. Chick left WEEK on August 25, 1956, for the West Coast, but he never lived down his blunder. I'm told he still hears about it on occasion.

Chick went to KNX in Los Angeles to do the broadcasts of all University of Southern California sports events. He then became the voice of the L.A. Lakers, which he still is, and has been credited as a major contributor to their phenomenal success.

The original three WEEK-TV anchors were guest speakers at the Downtown Rotary Club in 1955. Standing, left, Chick Hearn; right, Bob Arthur. Bill Houlihan is the short guy in the middle with the crew cut. Vice president and general manager of WEEK-TV, Fred Mueller, is seated at left. Seated at right is J. Forrest Bennett, Rotary president.
(Photo courtesy of WEEK-TV.)

Bob Arthur left the station in 1960. I remember it well, because I became promotion manager for WEEK-TV on September 1 of that year, just one month after a young man by the name of Chuck Harrison moved over from WMBD to replace Arthur.

Bob moved out to Albuquerque before settling in Los Angeles. He's been doing news on radio and TV for many years. He's also half of one of the most popular morning drive-time radio shows on the West Coast. He's the Bob of KABC-Radio's "Ken and Bob Show" and it's the No. 2 morning show in the Los Angeles area.

But there's a lot more Peoria representation in the Golden State than Chick Hearn and Bob Arthur. Sportscasting in LA sounds like Peoria reincarnated.

Ralph Lawler, formerly with WEEK and WAAP, is the voice of the L.A. Clippers pro-basketball team on radio and TV.

Bill King, formerly with WIRL, does the L.A. Raiders Football play-by-play.

Tom Kelly of WMBD fame handles sports on cable TV and play-by-play of Southern California University football.

Bob Starr, also from WMBD, covers pro baseball on the coast.

And Bob Steinbrink, formerly with WAAP, covers UCLA football and news in L.A.

But they had fun both on and off camera back in those early TV days. Bill Houlihan's weather was being sponsored by Pabst Beer when they came out with a new "snap cap, full-quart can." It was a beer can with a bottle-type cap on it. Bill had to do the commercial live, showing how easy it was to open it by prying the cap off with the cap from another can. One night, just before the news block, Chick had the engineers solder the cap on the can. When Houli tried to open the "so easy to open" can, it wouldn't budge.

Chick was down on his hands and knees behind the camera laughing, when Bill finally got the can opened. He pointed the can at Chick as the hot beer came out like a gusher, all over Hearn's $200 cashmere sports jacket.

Houlihan had the last laugh a few nights later, too. Chick had to demonstrate the great flexibility of a fishing rod for George Murray's Sporting Goods on his show. Bill went into the studio early, took the rod apart and just barely put the handle back on. When Chick whipped the rod, it fell to the floor in pieces. George Murray called to say it was the funniest thing he'd ever seen, but Les Williams, his store manager, strongly suggested they not do it anymore.

Live commercials and black-and-white TV were fun times back in the '50's and '60's, and the viewers would tune in to see what would happen next.

...and it seems like only yesterday!

1940's "golden era" of Hollywood pictures

...and the Hippodrome became the Rialto

My early years at the Madison Theater were great times in the history of that grand old theater. I still consider the 1940's the "golden era" of Hollywood motion pictures.

In those days, our company, Publix Great States Theaters, owned and operated Peoria's four leading downtown theaters — the Madison, Palace, Rialto and Apollo. Ed Harris was our only loop competition. He owned and operated the two other remaining movie houses, the Princess and Columbia, both on South Adams Street.

There were two closed houses, the Orpheum, across from the Madison's side doors, and the Majestic, across Jefferson from the Rialto. They were both owned by the Leisy Brewery estate, but Publix held the leases on them in order to control downtown business.

Young and old alike remember the Rialto as the theater that lost the battle to build the Civic Center but, like a few other old theaters, it began under another name, decor and format.

The Hippodrome, at 207 SW Jefferson, was built by a corporation under the direction of Mr. C. J. Off. It opened on Monday, October 20, 1913, under the management of Mr. E.P. Churchill, who had formerly managed the Main Street Theater on Main near Jefferson. Mr. Churchill was also the father of a famous stage and motion picture actress of the '20's and '30's, Marguerite Churchill.

The building and theater were designed by local architect Frederic J. Klein. In 1920 Mr. Klein also designed the Madison Theater, and in 1927 he designed the Coronado Theater in downtown Rockford.

The feature attraction for the Hippodrome's grand opening was most appropriate. It was "Powers' Elephants" — five live elephants, put through their paces by George, Jeannette and Julia Powers. They had been featured for eight seasons at New York's famous Hippodrome Theater, and this was their first western trip. The opening performance also included seven other acts plus the orchestra and silent motion pictures.

The new theater's decor was definitely "early pachyderm." The proscenium arch featured a frieze of performing elephants, and a large elephant head was displayed on each side of the stage. On the outside of the building, light bulbs outlined an elephant sign. His trunk appeared to move up and down as the lights switched on and off. Its bright animation could be seen for many blocks up and down Jefferson Street.

The elephant decor has always been a mystery to me though because, over the years, elephants and parrots have been signs of "bad luck" in the theater. So much so that when the Palace was remodeled in 1936, city manager Len Worley nearly had convulsions because the artist had used parrots on the new wall murals. He shrieked, "Take 'em out," and they were replaced by birds of paradise. Actors and others in the business were superstitious and shunned parrots and elephants, even pictures of them. By 1926, the Hippodrome's short history came to an end. Movies and radio were taking their toll on vaudeville and talkies were on the way. Publix Great States took over the lease. The closed theater was renamed the Rialto and on Christmas Day 1926, it reopened as a motion picture theater. The silent motion picture for its grand opening was "War Paint," a western starring Tim McCoy with Pauline Starke "and a cast of thousands" (of Indians, I'll bet!). Admission for adults was 25¢ and "kiddies" 10¢. Community singing, with the organ soloist leading the audience, was to be a regular feature. The Rialto closed in 1930, and its future was in doubt, but it opened again in 1931 and was used by visiting speakers, politicians running for office and many local events, including the "Golden Gloves."

The Rialto Theater was remodeled in 1934. Its new look, using black glass on the front and modernizing the interior, was an effort to "improve" its looks and bring it up to date. I always felt these modernizing attempts with the Rialto in 1934, the Palace in 1936, and the Madison in 1937, were big mistakes that took away much of the original beauty of these wonderful old theaters.

During this remodeling, the elephants in the front auditorium wall were chiseled out of the plaster, and Peoria's first escalator, the only one in a local theater, was taken out, but the old Barton pipe organ remained. The Rialto reopened with W. C. Fields in "You're Telling Me." The theater was now equipped with sound but, when the sound track failed, the popular Madison organist, Russell Fielder, ran to the rescue and played the organ until the sound was restored.

Several Great States managers were assigned to the Rialto over the years. Merle Eagle was brought to town to manage it. In 1935 he was replaced by Richard Rodems while Eagle went to the Madison for a short time before being reassigned to the newly remodeled Palace in 1936. John Brady was brought in from the Lyric Theater in Blue Island in the early '40's. He managed the Rialto until shortly before it was sold to Kerasotes Theaters in 1951.

Great States had used the Rialto as a second-run, double-feature house over the years, and would close it when down-

The Hippodrome - which later became the Rialto Theater.
(A Bert Powers photo, courtesy of Peoria Public Library)

town theater business was slow, especially in the summer. But it received a new lease on life when Kerasotes took over.

Frank Larkin came in to manage until Howard Young was named the permanent Rialto manager. Howie remained manager until around 1960 when he left to go with the Foster-Gallagher Co. Larkin then moved his district office into the building and remained there until its final closing in 1979.

Kerasotes' first program started Saturday, September 1, 1951, with "Jim Thorpe, All American," starring Burt Lancaster. "Quo Vadis" followed in March, 1952, setting new house records. Then Peoria's first cinemascope movie, "The Robe," shattered the "Quo Vadis" records. These were followed by Elvis Presley, The Beatles (kids lined up at 5 a.m. to be first in line), and James Bond movies. The Rialto box office was humming.

The Rialto Theater being razed in February, 1979.
(Courtesy of R. W. Deller from Lee Roten's Historic Peoria Photo File)

But by the mid-'70's things downtown had changed and the Civic Center Commission was looking at the Rialto Theater location, among others. Many Peorians became concerned, including Frank Larkin and architect Les Kenyon. A "Save the Rialto" campaign was launched, but it was too little, too late. The Rialto finally closed on January 20, 1979, with the showing of Clint Eastwood's "Every Which Way But Loose." The grand old building soon shuddered to the pounding of the wrecking ball.

If you stand on the site of the old Hippodrome and Rialto today, you might still hear applause. But if you do, it's the "occasional applause" from the nearby Civic Center Theater or Arena. Well, that's progress. Anyway

...it seems like only yesterday!

"Chief" Coy also an unforgettable character

A man who had to be near the top of our town's "unforgettable characters" list was Robert Merle "Chief" Coy. If you ever met Chief, it would be impossible for you to forget him, for a number of reasons.

First, his face was very distorted. The right side was paralyzed, allowing the eye and mouth to droop down on that side. Most people thought his distorted face was from his being a professional wrestler and boxer, and that he was punch drunk. This was not the case. His interests and mental and physical feats weren't what most of us would consider normal, but he was far from punchy. The paralysis caused him to lisp when he talked, and he drooled at times. But if you started talking to him about history, you had to be careful.

He was a self-taught student with much information. When he was a small boy he knew he was different from other kids, and he asked his mother how he became scarred. She told him that when he was just two or three weeks old, he cried for three days and nights without stopping. Finally, his father got out of bed, went over to the crib and hit him in the mouth with his fist. She said he was unconscious for three days and nights.

Robert Coy was born February 22, 1902, in Holden, Missouri, and came to Peoria about 1913. He wrote an essay when he was in the eighth grade at Tyng School in which he portrayed himself as the chief of a band of bandits. He was reciting it to the class when principal, William G. Russell, walked in. Russell called him "Chief" and that was his name from then on.

Chief claimed that his disfigurement was responsible for many of his physical and mental accomplishments. His difference made him strive to be better than most people at many things. He became a good welterweight boxer. He defeated the likes of Cyclone Miller, the Texas Bull Dog, and Knockout Brown (whom he knocked out in three rounds). It was said he knocked out 17 consecutive opponents. In 1929 the readers of the National Police Gazette named him the most popular welterweight in the country, and he was given an engraved silver watch by them. He retired in 1931.

The Chief was also hailed as the world's lightweight wrestling champion in the 1920's. He took on all comers professionally and also in traveling show exhibition matches. He retired undefeated.

Coy developed and performed a strongman act. One of his feats was bending a six-foot piece of machine steel, 1¼ by ⅜ inches, into a three-leaf clover. He'd also tear a tin tobacco can in two with his bare hands, and bend a 15-inch machine bolt double.

Marathons were very big back then and here are some interesting Chief Coy records:

- Most holes of golf played in daylight hours, 302 (covering 61 miles, 6-17-31).
- Most holes of golf in 24 hours, 314 (with the aid of flashlights, 6- 21-34).
- Most consecutive holes on championship course, 476 (39-1/2 hours, 1- 35).
- Most holes without stopping, 1,000 (51 hours, 31 minutes, covering 155 miles, 1935).
- Playing pocket billiards, 120 hours, 17 minutes (3-30).
- Playing piano without stopping, 118 hours (in Janssen and Joosten Music window, 1932).
- Ran 23.6 miles in pouring rain (3 hours, 11 minutes, 10-27).
- Ran 2 hours, 45 minutes with first 20 minutes ahead of world record (1932).
- Ran barefoot for 3 hours, 11 minutes (Peoria to Pekin and return, 1933).

• Visited all 48 state capitols, securing each governor's autograph (1937-38).

• Only person in the world to recite, in less than four minutes, the 50 states and capitols, presidents of the United States, the books of the Bible in order, the first 50 Popes of the Catholic Church, name 15 ancient historical events in order, recite the alphabet, and the months in Hebrew.

When I first met Chief Coy he free-lanced for us at the Madison and other theaters. He'd put our advertising cards in store windows and pass out handbills of upcoming shows. He'd come into the office and visit with Len Worley and me. I must admit that in the beginning I saw him as just another street person. As time went by, however, I gained a lot of respect for him. He was a victim of his handicap and the brunt of jokes he didn't deserve.

He knew the passages of the Bible like the back of his hand and he had written books on the Bible and the history of the Catholic Mass.

The other day Joe Hession mentioned to me that his brother, Tom, who died a year ago in California, had written a beautiful poem about Chief Coy. His tribute was written at the time of Chief's passing. I'd like to share it with you.

A Parting Hail to the Chief!

Let us pause to think of old "Chief" Coy
Whom I recall since just a boy.
A man of kindness and strange repute
In the days of Dempsey and football's Knute

We thought him an Indian
    from the life he spent
Then found him of Irish and
    German descent.
He had great strength of the physical kind
And developed a most unusual mind.

While bending bars and untying ropes
He named off Presidents, States and Popes.
I recall how well he could hammer a nail
With only his fist and a little travail.

He could pull it out with tight bit teeth
With the poise of a President laying a wreath.
Many just laughed when he sought to amaze
Like playing a piano for more than five days.

Folks never could fathom his purpose or aim
Till they learned of all of the
    records he'd claim.
While he chose Peoria for his home
He frequently would widely roam.

He covered the states and met their leaders
As he matched memory with the
    best of readers.
He is a man to remember among God's sons
Who ran his race as none other runs.

I'm sure the angels with joy now hark
For the "Chief" who uniquely made his mark.

By Tom Hession

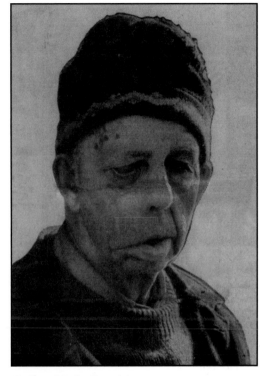

Robert Merle Coy, 73
(A Journal Star file photo)

Chief Coy died on October 2, 1980. I hope, somehow, he is aware of Tom Hession's remembrance. He would have been so proud that he finally gained the respect that he so earnestly sought and earned the hard way.

...and it seems like only yesterday!

Brewing up memories of Peoria's Leisy family

A few weeks ago the Journal Star ran a story about a young man named David L. "Harry" Puterbaugh who's in the real estate business in Texas, and who just last week made a bid for the Peoria Rivermen hockey team. He's a former Peorian and has an idea, if not a plan, to build a sports complex on our riverfront. The only problem is that it would take the Taft Homes property to make it work.

The story reminded me of the old Leisy Brewery. Harry is the son of Walter Puterbaugh and the great-grandson of Edward Leisy of the family that established the brewery in our town many years ago. This is the same Leisy Brewing Co. that later became known locally as a real estate and building firm.

As I've mentioned in previous columns, the Leisy estate was the landlord of the Orpheum and Majestic theaters during my days of managing the Madison Theater. Our company, Publix Great States Theaters, held leases on both of these theaters until the Majestic lease was taken over by WMBD in 1948 and the Orpheum was torn down in 1952.

The Leisy Co. began in our town in 1884. The family came from Keokuk, where they operated one of the largest breweries in Iowa. The brewery was incorporated by the family on March 1, 1889, as the Gus Leisy Brewing Co., with capital listed at $60,000. By 1892 the stock had increased to $250,000. In 1893 the corporate name changed to the Leisy Brewing Co. Its officers were brothers Edward, John and Albert.

During its tenure, Leisy was Peoria's largest brewery. It produced a quality beer at a time when some beers were known to be inferior and impure. Leisy beer was very popular. Demand outgrew the original structure which necessitated plant expansion. In 1900 more brick structures were built and equipped. It was one of the most modern breweries in America and was fully automatic. The company watchword was cleanliness, and visitors were amazed by its spotless condition.

Leisy's most popular beer was "Rochester." The firm also sold a specially brewed Pilsner and "Malt-Ease," a malt beverage named after the Leisy trademark — the Maltese cross. It was marketed as a "health tonic" because of the medicinal qualities of malt, and it was geared to the non-beer drinking public even though its label stated it contained less than 5 percent alcohol.

Soon the new plant was producing 100,000 barrels a year, which necessitated the hiring of 125 men. It eventually became the largest Illinois brewery outside Chicago. By 1904, 7,500,000 bottles of Rochester beer were sold and shipped to every state plus Cuba, Puerto Rico, Hawaii and the Phillipines.

Edward Leisy, as president, became the driving force of the brewery. Under his supervision it survived and flourished. Brothers John and Albert were vice president and secretary-treasurer, respectively. Edward also had other interests. He became involved in real estate, banking and building.

By 1914 prohibition efforts by the Women's Christian Temperance Union and the Anti-Saloon League were being felt by brewers and distillers. Beer sales plummeted nationally. The Leisy Co., aware of growing sentiment against alcoholic beverages, introduced "Temp-Brew," a non-alcoholic beverage. The Volstead Act, which outlawed the manufacture and sale of alcoholic beverages in the United States, was ratified in 1919. The Leisy Brewery was able to remain open by manufacturing soft drinks.

This artist's rendering of the old Leisy Brewery appears in the illustrated industrial Souvenir & Magazine of Greater Peoria, "Pearl of the Prairies." The 1904 publication can be found in the Peoria Public Library's Peoria and Illinois collection. *(Courtesy of Peoria Public Library)*

Edward expanded his real estate interests. Henry Sandmeyer opened the Majestic Theater at 212 S. Jefferson on December 21, 1906, and Leisy bought it a few years later. Leisy built the Jefferson Building at the corner of Fulton and Jefferson, added on to it, and joined it with the Majestic, for Peoria's first large office building.

In 1911 the Orpheum Theater, at 108 N. Madison, was built by Edward Leisy and his brother, Albert. The Leisy's owned other properties around Peoria and, at one time, the brewing company owned more than 200 "saloon" properties.

Edward Leisy died in 1929, and his widow, Emma Welte Leisy, succeeded him as company president. With no family member interested in continuing the soft drink business and no sign of Prohibition being repealed, the Leisy Brewery was sold in 1930 to the Premiere Malt Co. Two years later Pabst moved into town and they merged. For years Pabst used the old Leisy building as its corn-grits mill for its Peoria Heights plant.

The tavern properties were gradually liquidated and other real estate was obtained. In later years the extensive holdings of the Leisy estate were controlled by Edward's daughters, Florence Blanchard, Lucille Cashin and Mildred Elliman.

The old Leisy building is still with us today, but things have changed a great deal. Leisy Beer and Malt-Ease are no longer brewed there, but fermentation still goes on. In 1985, a Japanese company, Fujisawa Pharmaceuticals, bought the Leisy building which houses its subsidiary, PMP Fermentation Products.

This company manufactures sodium gluconate, which, incidentally, was developed at our Northern Regional Research Center. Sodium gluconate is used by many industries for efficient cleaning, bottle washing and metal finishing, and in industrial cleaning products.

Many old-timers remember Leisy Beer and, to some at least

...it seems like only yesterday!

Gipps beer ads played well here

"Gimmee Gipps!" If you lived in this area after Prohibition, up to the 1950's, you had to be aware of one of the greatest local advertising catch phrases for Gipps Amberlain Beer. Since we talked about Leisy Beer last week, it only seems fair to give Gipps equal time.

The history of Gipps Brewery goes back many years in Peoria. As a matter of fact, it was indirectly associated with the first Peoria brewery, which wasn't Leisy, by the way.

The honor of Peoria's first brewery goes to Andrew Eitle, not later than 1837. On June 24, 1836, Eitle, a German, bought a lot from the Underhill and Bigelow Co. for $673 and on March 31, 1838, they conveyed lots 1, 11 and 12, block 49 of Underhill and Bigelow's addition to Eitle for $1,756. Title was warranted, except for French claims which were then awaiting settlement. It was on these lots at East Franklin Street and the Illinois River that Eitle built his brewery. It was known to be in operation on April 1, 1837.

Eitle operated it for a short time with Frederick Muller but Mr. Muller filed a suit against him on July 19, 1838, for "covenant broken." Muller claimed he leased the property from Eitle but the suit was still unsettled when Eitle died on September 16, 1838. He died with no apparent wife or relatives in Illinois. Claims against the estate included one from Jane D. Lindsay, asking $11 for board for three weeks and a day, and $1 for washing.

Eitle's brewery house was erected at a cost of $78.10, according to a claim of a carpenter, Rudolphus Amsler. Total claims against the estate amounted to $4,235.95, including an arbitrated settlement with Frederick Muller for $125 on account of brewery improvements. Muller bid $1,390 for Eitle's brewery and lots and received a deed from the administrator on March 3, 1840.

It appears that Muller then operated the brewery until he died on October 3, 1840. He was survived by five children but, somehow, only three were named in his will. He is buried in Springdale Cemetery.

John M. Gipps, a native of England, visited this area for the first time on a hunting trip. As many people still do today, he became attached to the area. He sold his property in England and settled on an estate in Tazewell County, between Morton and Washington.

He founded the Gipps Brewery in 1864 on Water Street near Bridge Street (East Franklin). It was a partnership with W. H. Hines, directly across the railroad tracks from the Muller Brewery. He then moved his residence to Peoria. Hines later sold his interest to H. Howe and the company name changed to Gipps, Howe and Co.

In 1869, Howe sold his interest to Nathaniel Shurtleff and the brewery became Gipps and Shurtleff. In 1871, Shurtleff's interest went to Thomas Cody and Willis H. Ballance and it became Gipps, Cody & Co. Cody retired in 1874 and Gipps acquired his interest. He then sold two-thirds back to Ballance and a lawyer and former Peoria mayor, Leslie Robison. Robison was also Ballance's brother-in-law. Gipps Brewery took over the Muller Brewery operation in 1881.

Gipps later sold out to Ballance and Robison, but they kept the Gipps company name. About 1911, Ballance bought out Robison. When Ballance died in 1913, his son, Willis H. Ballance, Jr. continued the operation until Prohibition closed them in 1919.

The Electrox Co. then produced hydrogen, nitrogen and acetylene gas on the property during the dry years.

But the "Gimmee Gipps" beer most of us remember is the one that reorganized after the 15-year hiatus, in October 1934. President was the same Willis H. Ballance, Jr. with his brother, Nevius, as vice president. The brewery was completely rebuilt and reequipped with modern, up-to-date equipment, with a 100,000-barrel annual capacity. At first it was only available in barrels. Bottling facilities were installed later. The new Gipps was also not the same old formula.

On July 17, 1941, a Gipps warehouse, at the foot of Franklin Street, suffered a spectacular fire; 40,000 beer bottle cases burned but, fortunately, they were empty at the time. In 1948, a new warehouse was built and in 1949 a completely new, larger, modern bottling machine was installed. But like many local beers, time caught up with Gipps and they sold out in 1957, bringing an end to one of our town's oldest industries.

Now, this might have been the end of the Gipps saga if it weren't for a copy of a 1952 beer ad I received the other day. If you've lived or worked in Peoria the past "few" years, you must know, or know of, Al and Hazel Kauffman. These two have worked in tandem in the printing business since they first installed a small press in their home basement at 715 N. St. Anthony in West Peoria in the early '50's.

In 1952, an artist's rendering of Al in his ever-present bow tie showed up in a Gipps advertisement. It's an interesting story but I promised his nephew, Judge Bob Kauffman, I wouldn't tell where I got it.

At the time Al was selling for Illinois Engraving. While calling on Kraft Brothers, commercial artists, Jack Kraft asked Kauffman if he'd be the subject of an ad. Always happy to oblige, Al gave him a photo of himself and Kraft did the art work. Kauffman didn't want payment but Kraft said it was an unwritten law that models had to be paid. So he paid him one whole dollar!

With this buck and a couple more Al and Hazel had laid aside, they rented half a building at 1213 W. Bradley. Soon they bought the building, expanded Kauffman printing and paid it off in eight years. A few years ago Channel 47 talked the Kauffmans into retiring and selling them the building. They moved into the Twin Towers downtown, and they also maintain a consultancy office there.

So the next time you see Al just say "Gimmee Gipps." He'll get the message. Word has it he still has the dollar, too.

...and it seems like only yesterday!

Al Kauffman in a 1952 advertisement for Gipps Beer. Artist's rendering was made by Jack Kraft. *(Courtesy of Bob Kauffman)*

Two class reunions double the pleasure

Woodruff High School, Class of 1944! All right, I confess. I was a member of that class, and we just had our 45th class reunion the weekend of June 9, 10 and 11. I also have another confession to make. Last year my wife and I also attended the 45th reunion of the Class of 1943.

Does that make me some kind of a reunion nut? Well nut maybe, but the fact is I was an in-between. I graduated in mid-year, January, 1944 instead of June, 1943, so we were invited to both great class celebrations. Not a bad deal either. Kind of like the Wrigley gum commercial, "Double Your Pleasure." We were able to visit with twice as many classmates and after 45 years, did we ever reminisce!

It didn't really occur to me then, but the '44 class was only the seventh of the new E. N. Woodruff High School, and just the fourth class to have served all four years there. It opened its doors for the first time on September 16, 1937. The new 627,000 facility had an enrollment of 1,039 students and a faculty of 46, headed by our beloved principal, Mr. L. R. McDonald, "Mr. Mac." It was Peoria's first new senior high school building since Peoria Central High was built in 1916.

The school was dedicated the evening of Friday, October 22, 1937, with Mr. Mac as MC. Those in attendance included Mr. R. B. Juerjens, president of the Board of Education; E. C. Fisher, superintendent of schools (Harry Whitaker was later in the Class of '45); former Peoria Mayor, E. N. Woodruff, for whom the school was named; and Dr. E. C. Melby, dean of the College of Education at Northwestern University, who dedicated the school.

Woodruff's 10,000-square-foot gymnasium was the largest playing floor in Peoria. Between the auditorium's 1,300 chair seats and the gym's 700 bleacher seats, it could accommodate 2,000 people. In December of that first year, Bradley's basketball team played the University of Nebraska at Woodruff. Another historic sports event took place that year, too. Woodruff's basketball team dealt Manual its first loss in 12 years.

The new school sported a model, modern cafeteria with a capacity of 360 and its library was described as ideal. Its auditorium, music rooms and industrial arts shops were so soundproof the students inside couldn't hear the fire alarm.

Woodruff offered the most progressive education in town. It was also the first school offering electricity classes and electric math. It pioneered an exploratory course in industrial arts, consisting of mechanical drawing, electricity, printing, machine shop and wood shop. I should know. I took this course as a streamlined way to a diploma.

I'll admit this didn't help much in my theater, broadcasting and writing careers, but being retired now, there isn't anything I can't fix around the house. (Well, Flossie says I'm not much of an electrician, but outside of that....) As for writing, thank God for Mrs. Pfander. She saw to it that I acquired some limited use of the "king's English."

The class of 1943-44 was geared toward the war effort. Many fellow students didn't graduate with us, having joined the armed forces before diploma time. One such was my best buddy, Gil Crotty. New added classes also reflected the war effort, such as Pre-Flight Aviation Science, Command Training, First Aid and Nursing...all helping to win the war.

A young friend of ours, Clay Johnson (Woodruff Class of 1987), was assigned to write about our '44 class in the 50th anniversary publication on Woodruff, two years ago. Describing us back then he said, "Impudence, make-up and gossip were frowned upon and absent from the halls of Woodruff. Teachers called all the shots. If one were corrected by a teacher, one stood corrected with no need for discussion."

The Woodruff senior class officers of 1944 were, from left, Clarence Bireline, treasurer; Robert Steimel, president; Alice Ann Keys, secretary; and Dean Spence, vice president.

(Photo from the 1944 Talisman yearbook)

king and queen that night were Bob Alberti and beautiful Barb Engstrom (now Bordeaux). And speaking of big bands, one of the best over the years has been our own classmate, Bill Hardesty, who played for us once again at our Mount Hawley Country Club reunion. Bill is currently playing first trumpet with the Guy Lombardo Royal Canadian orchestra. He's still one of the best.

But back in 1943, our homecoming was climaxed the following evening with a dance at the Inglaterra. "Pow Wow" chief and princess were Joe Trefzger (now my entry for world's greatest baker), and pretty Marjorie Lois Wilson.

Our 1943-44 student body president was Dan Wells and, old friend over these many years, Wayne Katus, was vice president. Senior class officers were Bob Steimel, president; Dean Spence, vice president; Alice Ann Keyes, secretary and Clarence Bireline, treasurer.

Well, that's at least part of the story of Woodruff High and the Class of '44, except for a personal note. I've mentioned in this column before that 1944 was a spectacular year for me. Not only did I graduate from Woodruff that year, I also joined the Navy. Well, I didn't exactly join the Navy, I received a letter from President Roosevelt that began, "Greetings:" But, most of all, I had the good fortune that year to marry Flossie Castle (even if she did go to Manual). And you know something?

...it seems like only yesterday!

I don't know, Clay. There may have been a need for discussion, but one-way "conversations" with teachers were not discussions, that's for sure. By the way, are you suggesting that things are different today?

Speaking of faculty, it was nice to see so many of our teachers at our dinner-dance. Our principal, L. R. McDonald; our dean of boys, T. C. Colgan; and teachers Harry Landis, Edwardine Sperling, Helen Nance, Orville Northdruft and Mildred Martens. And what fun to call them by their first names. I've been waiting 45 years to do that.

But sadly, some of our faculty and classmates are no longer with us. One such was our valedictorian who graduated with a near-perfect average, the unforgettable Mary Ellen Bramlet.

The 1943 Junior Prom, though, was the most important dance of our junior year. We danced to the big band music of Freddy Stevens' Orchestra. Our prom

"Captain Jinks" cornered the market in Central Illinois

The late 1950's, '60's and early '70's were not the greatest of times for kids growing up in America. But if the exercise was less painful in central Illinois, a major factor may have been a kids' program on WEEK-TV, "The Captain Jinks Show."

For most of its nearly 20-year reign, it was hosted by Stan Lonergan as Captain Jinks and George Baseleon as his first mate, Salty Sam. All the "high jinks" took place on the "high seas" aboard the S.S. Albatross. George Baseleon passed away in 1985, but Stan is still in Peoria, although retired from broadcasting.

I had the privilege of working with Stan and George for most of those years. I began at the station in 1960 as promotion manager, and the most fun was being involved with "The Captain Jinks Show."

Stanley Thomas Lonergan had a considerable radio career in Chicago, long before he came to Peoria. The son of George P. and Fay Oliver Lonergan, he was born and raised in Chicago. By the age of ten he was a radio buff and could recognize all the announcers' voices and played at radio announcing.

His Aunt Stella Ketchum saw his interest when he was 17. She suggested and financed his entry into the College of Radio and Drama in Chicago. That fall, it led to his joining the Chicago Junior League Radio Theater. This group would go to the NBC studios in the Merchandise Mart and work with professional directors.

When Stan was 19, the group was doing a show at WGN. Staff director Gene O'Connor asked him to do an Old Dutch Cleanser commercial and suggested he audition later. When Stan showed up, there were 60 or 70 guys waiting to audition for one job.

Through the process of elimination, Stan and Cliff Williams remained in the running. Because of Lonergan's lack of experience, Williams got the job, but they asked Stan back for summer relief announcing in 1940. He later did a little free-lance work and then took a six-month speech course at Loyola.

One day, on his own, he called the studios of WAAF in the Palmer House.

He auditioned and was hired. He did everything from record shows to commercials for glow-in-the-dark gardenias. It was here that Lonergan did his "famous" stock market report.

One morning he stated the number of cattle, hogs, sheep, etc., at the Union Stockyards, including EE-WEES. As soon as he was off the air the transmitter engineer called to ask what the h--- an ee-wee was. Stan said that's what the script said, "ewes." When the engineer quit laughing he told him "ewe" was pronounced "you." This is still considered one of Chicago radio's great all-time bloopers.

After a year, Stan went back to WGN for two years, 1944 to '46. He landed a few drama parts, including soap operas. He played a visiting nephew on "The Baxters." Other shows included "College Humor," and "Uncle Walter's Dog House." Stan also landed a famous commercial, "Whiz-z-z, the best nickel candy there iz-z-z." It was done live, $5 a spot, five nights a week.

It was 1944 when Stan married Jean Fisher. They were married eight years and had two daughters, Carol Lea and Susan. The marriage ended in divorce.

Lonergan went from WGN to WIND. Then, in 1948, he auditioned and was hired at WCFL, where he remained for six years. In 1955, while working at WJJD, he sent tapes of his work to Ed Cash at WEEK, and was hired to do radio news.

ADAMS

Continued from Page D1

lance work and then took a six-month speech course at Loyola.

One day, on his own, he called the studios of WAAF in the Palmer House. He auditioned and was hired. He did everything from record shows to commercials for glow-in-the-dark gardenias. It was here that Lonergan did his "famous" stock market report.

One morning he stated the number of cattle, hogs, sheep, etc., at the Union Stockyards, including EE-WEES. As soon as he was off the air the transmitter engineer called to ask what the h--- an ee-wee was. Stan said that's what the script said, "ewes." When the engineer quit laughing he told him "ewe" was pronounced "you." This is still considered one of Chicago radio's great all time bloopers.

WEEK-TV's reluctant "weatherman," Stan Lonergan, Oct. 18, 1969. His opening line was, "You are probably wondering why I'm standing here doing the weather. Well, you're not alone. I'm

…radio's great all-time bloopers.

After a year, Stan went back to WGN for two years, 1944 to '46. He landed a few drama parts, including soap operas. He played a visiting nephew on "The Baxters." Other shows included "College Humor," and "Uncle Walter's Dog House." Stan also landed a famous commercial, "Whiz-z-z, the best nickle candy there iz-z-z." It was done live, $5 a spot, five nights a week.

It was 1944 when Stan married Jean Fisher. They were married eight years and had two daughters, Carol Lea and Susan. The marriage ended in divorce.

Lonergran went from WGN to WIND. Then, in 1948, he auditioned and was hired at WCFL, where he remained for six years. In 1955, while working at WJJD, he sent tapes of his work to Ed Cash at WEEK, and was hired to do radio news.

"The Captain Jinks Show" started about the fall of 1956. The first Captain Jinks was Hal

"The Captain Jinks Show" started about the fall of 1956. The first Captain Jinks was Hal Searles, whose on-air disc-jockey name was Johnny Dark. A short time later, Hal took a job at WBBM. Stan took over as Captain Jinks in 1957.

He did the show alone until 1960, when George Baseleon put on the moustache and stocking cap and joined him as Salty Sam. The show became so popular, it was expanded from one to two-and-a-half hours a day, five days a week. It virtually cornered the afternoon TV audience, and not just kids. One East Peoria tavern actually formed a Captain Jinks fan club and Bradley students did the same.

Stories of the program are legion, but here's my favorite. Local kids (including all five of ours) would appear on the live show. They were booked months ahead, and each child would be interviewed. One day the captain asked a little boy where he lived. He said on a farm. Jinks asked if he had cows on the farm. When the lad nodded, Jinks asked, "How does a cow go?" The boy thought a second and then replied, "Oh, he just stands there and pees." Jinks, of course, was speechless and tried to throw it to Salty, but Sam was breaking up, too. Finally, with tears running into his beard, the captain said, "Salty, do you think this would be a good time for a commercial?" And they went to film.

But Stan Lonergan's most memorable performance out of costume has to be the evening of October 18, 1969, when he did

WEEK-TV's reluctant "weatherman," Stan Lonergan, Oct. 18, 1969.

(Photo courtesy of WEEK-TV)

Captain Jinks and Salty Sam aboard the S.S. Albatross on WEEK-TV.

(Photo courtesy of WEEK-TV)

his first weather show - without rehearsal. He was filling in on George Baseleon's weekend weather. George was out of town.

His opening line was, "You're probably wondering why I'm standing here doing the weather. Well, you're not alone. I'm wondering the same thing." Getting into the report he said, "You've heard that the rain in Spain falls mainly in the plain? Well, the rain may fall in Spain but today it fell in Peoria — in the plain — in the gutters — every place. Now, let's take a look at the weather map. Well, it's certainly there, isn't it?"

The switchboard lit up with calls and letters flooded in later, asking for more of Stan's refreshing weather reports. For years, a tape of the show was shown to visitors of WEEK-TV.

"The Captain Jinks Show" went off the air in 1972. A taped version came back from 1978 to '81. Stan continued as staff announcer and, for a brief time, announced on WSIV, Pekin.

Stan is retired now. Last September, a malignancy was found in his lung and abdomen. He's taking chemotherapy and is responding to treatment. His doctor gives him good reports. If any of his fan club would care to write the "old captain," he rooms with Mr. and Mrs. Larry Thorhaug (a former WEEK engineer) at 814 Cooper in Peoria.

Stanley Thomas Lonergan, one of a kind.

...and it seems like only yesterday!

This is a rewrite of the column that originally appeared on June 20, 1988.

Madison Theater's debut was a grand day for Peoria

Saturday, October 16, 1920...the grand opening of the Madison Theater.

Mother Nature was certainly cooperating to make this as grand a grand opening as possible, with absolutely perfect fall weather. The temperature the night before dropped to a mere 56° and by noon, when the box office opened for the first time, it had recovered to a delightful 72°. The forecast was for continued fair weather through Sunday. (Believe it or not, this was accomplished without the help of Bill Houlihan, Lee Ranson or Rollie Keith.)

The anticipation of success was already in the air. Long before noon, the crowds began to arrive and gathered in front of the Madison, being touted as a "shrine of the silent art." By 1:30, when the doors opened, the sidewalks, theater lobby and most of the intersection of Peoria's Main and Madison streets were jammed with people eager to be the first to see the glories of the new "theater palace" and its first showing of "Humoresque." More importantly, it was the first showing here of anything ever, truly a momentous historic event for "our town."

The new Madison seated a little over 2,000, and shortly after 1:30 every seat was filled. Throngs that would have to wait for the next performance at 4:15, were waiting in the outer lobby and in the street. The next day's newspapers estimated that more than 10,000 people attended on opening day. With five shows a day, that would indicate a capacity crowd at each show.

Although the theater was filled by 1:30, the first show wasn't scheduled to start until 2:30. The management, including managing director Dee Robinson and general manager Herbert McNally, arrived shortly for the opening ceremonies and musical concert on the mezzanine at 2.

Visiting guests included representatives of Paramount Pictures, Motion Picture News, Moving Picture Magazine, the Chicago Journal and New York Telegraph newspapers, and many others.

The 20-piece Madison Theater Concert Orchestra, conducted by its first musical director, Charles Wonnell, presented a short musical from the mezzanine, as advertised. The orchestra then had to move to the orchestra platform (not pit), in front of the stage, for the beginning of the first showing of the picture. The vocal solo by Miss Lou Eastman, a prima donna from Chicago, was also on the opening day program.

"Humoresque," a silent motion picture, was a poignant story of a violinist and leaned heavily on the musical ability of the 20-piece orchestra and lighting capability of the theater. The story, written by Fanny Hearst, first appeared in Cosmopolitan Magazine and later in Hearst newspapers.

The movie starred Alma Rubens and Gaston Glass, prominent silent actors of the day. There was such impact to this story that Vera Gordan, an unknown actress portraying the boy violinist's mother, became a star because of her powerful performance in this picture.

What a day! What a program! What a picture! What a theater! The thing that boggles my mind is that the Madison Theater building cost about a half-million dollars to build, furnish and decorate in 1920. That included the upstairs offices and Main Street store fronts.

A crowd begins to form on opening day, October 16, 1920.
(Photo courtesy of Peoria Public Library)

The Madison Theater inner lobby as it appeared on opening day.
(Photo courtesy of Peoria Public Library)

That was a lot of bucks 69 years ago. But the theater provided top-of-the-line Hollywood motion pictures, a 20-piece orchestra, beautiful varicolored electrical lighting effects, exquisite architecture and furnishings, and a huge service staff.

And the ticket prices? Matinee: adults 30¢ (loges 40¢), children 10¢. Evenings: adults 40¢ (loges 50¢), children 15¢.

Now I may be a little old-fashioned but, to me, one of the greatest features of all in those "Yester Days," was that you never had to worry about a movie rating. They were all "G" rated and G stood for good. To this day I don't understand how four-letter words and innuendo improve a good story, be it a book, a play, a movie, or (now) even a song.

Anyway, Saturday, October 16, 1920, was one spectacular day in Peoria's entertainment history...and, to some at least,

...it seems like only yesterday!

This is a rewrite of the column that originally appeared on June 27, 1988.

Yes, but will it play in Peoria?

Go just about anywhere in the world, certainly anywhere in America, and ask, "Will it play in Peoria?" You won't have to explain it. Everyone knows what it means and, if you tie a specific to the question, you'll probably get an immediate "yes" or "no" answer.

One of the few things for which I'm grateful to President Nixon is his perpetuation of the phrase. It is still used, occasionally, at the White House, or in Congress, but it's just as probable it will be used by anyone else, almost anywhere else.

Most everyone here in Central Illinois is aware that the legendary question began in show business. It had a very meaningful connotation.

When a new, live act or stage show was produced, it was soon booked into a Peoria theater. If it didn't receive a strong approval, one of two things usually happened. The production was either rewritten, recast, or otherwise improved, or it was cancelled altogether. It was truly believed in show business that, if a show could achieve the approval of the Peoria audience, it would be successful anywhere in the country, or even the world.

What some local folks don't realize is that this reputation is alive and well today. Not in show business so much any more but as a test market for advertisers of products in newspapers, or on television and radio. Many new products appear in Peoria-area stores before they are marketed nationally and internationally. On the other hand, some are never heard of again.

Peoria is certainly not the only market used for testing, but it's one of the better ones. Our cross-section of people seems to be ideal, and our market size is important, too.

Many actors and performers developed close friendships with the Peoria citizenry over the years. Also, many show business personalities were, either born, raised, or began here. Many more than you realize. We've covered some, and will cover many more in future columns.

My research tells me that the legend probably had its beginnings in the 1850's, when public halls came into vogue in our town. Newspaper accounts of that era indicate this:

- April 5, 1859 — "The Peoria Theater opened last night in Parmely's Hall," (200 block of NE Adams), "with Maggie Mitchell, the 'Minnehaha of the stage,' returned after an absence of two years from Peoria, to headline the grand opening...."

- March 10, 1867 — "Emma Abbott," (a native Peorian and, later, famous opera singer), "sang at a doings in Parmely's Hall today. She was unknown and the performance was only tolerably successful."

Another article dated the next day, March 11, 1867, states that Miss Abbott was, "...received with only slight enthusiasm by the home folks who well-remembered her as the little neighbor girl, who's father has a passion for music and not much else, still striving to reach the heights in the entertainment world. She vowed to come back some day, "and make them come hear me sing, not me run after them."

Fifteen years later, after gaining fame and fortune in grand opera, both in New York and abroad, she accepted an invitation to come back as the leading

The Grand Opera House and adjoining buildings in the 300 block of Hamilton Boulevard. This photograph was taken May 10, 1906, by F. H. Sykes. The building also housed the Journal offices, right.
Photo courtesy of the Peoria Public Library)

attraction at the opening of the Grand Opera House. She came and the box seats and orchestra circle patrons fought for the opportunity to pay $15 a seat to hear her.

These are the earliest examples I've found of the "critic-ability" of the Peoria audience. Miss Abbott obviously "honed her act" considerably between her 1867 appearance and 1882, when the Grand Opera House opened.

So, will it play in Peoria? You bet it will. And it did!

But it was a little before yesterday!

This is a rewrite of the column that originally appeared on July 11, 1988.

World premiere brought Peoria to standstill

The date was Tuesday, July 14, 1936. It was the day before the hottest day on record in Peoria. On Wednesday, July 15, 1936, the temperature reached an astronomical 113° but Tuesday only reached a mere 110°.

These were also the 10th and 11th days in a row of 100° or more. "Weather" or not, July 14th was a big day for another "hot" reason. The Madison Theater was the site of the world premiere of a Hollywood motion picture. It was a Warner Brothers comedy, "Earthworm Tractors," starring Joe E. Brown, one of filmdom's top comics of the 1930's and '40's.

His supporting cast included Guy Kibbee, June Travis and Carol Hughes and a Peoria "star," a Caterpillar Tractor.

"Earthworm Tractors" was based on very popular stories written by William Hazlett Upson, a former Caterpillar employee when he worked in the service department at Cat.

They were about a fictitious Earthworm Tractor company in Earthworm City, Illinois. A few years later, Saturday Evening Post bought his hilarious stories and they caught the fancy of the entire country.

So the Madison was the obvious theater for the world premiere of a movie built around the loosely disguised Caterpillar tractors.

When Joe Brown and his wife arrived by train in Chillicothe at 11 that morning, the temperature was already 108°. An entourage of Cat officials and local dignitaries (eat your heart out, Mayor Maloof) escorted him by automobile, with the help of 50 uniformed policemen and ten state troopers.

Joe E. seated himself on top of the backseat of a 1936 Cord (remember that?) convertible automobile. He waved to the fans who lined up along Illinois Route 29 from Chillicothe to Peoria in the 108° heat, just to get a glimpse of their hero.

A parade began at Jefferson and Fayette. The 40-piece Caterpillar Tractor Co. band joined the cars and police escort through the loop and then back up Main Street to the Hotel Père Marquette. WMBD-Radio (the only Peoria station at the time) had microphones at the Rialto and Apollo theaters, the Alliance Life Building, and in Mr. Brown's suite at the Père. Announcers described the big event all the way through downtown.

By now it must have been all of 110°. How do I know? I was a skinny 11-year-old kid, running alongside Joe E.'s brand new Cord, that's how. Yes, it was hot, but somehow I remember the excitement of the day, not the heat.

Joe E. Brown didn't let a little heat bother him, either. In the afternoon, after a scorching parade and a luncheon in his honor, he took a brief rest in his Père suite. Then he asked to be taken to the Home of the Friendless on Knoxville and, later, to the Guardian Angel orphanage on West Heading, where he visited, entertained and played with the orphan children. He explained that he was an orphan and lived in an orphanage until he was seven. Then he joined a circus at nine years of age.

Quite a guy, this Joe E. Brown, who came up a very hard way. He obviously never forgot it, or those less fortunate. The following Friday he arranged for all

Joe E. Brown — as he arrived for the World Premiere of "Earthworm Tractors."
(Photo courtesy of Peoria Public Library)

Crowd-pleaser — A traffic-stopping crowd masses in front of the Madison to see the festivities of a World Premiere of Joe E. Brown's "Earthworm Tractors" on July 14, 1936.
(Courtesy of R. W. Deller from Lee Roten's Historic Peoria Photo File)

the orphans at both homes (although he had already gone to New York) to be his guests to see his movie at the Madison.

(After reading this in last year's column, a good friend, John Ziegler, told me he remembers this very well. He was one of the orphans at the Guardian Angel Home at the time.)

Another member of the cast visited our town that hot day, too. He also had a Peoria connection in the form of a lookalike brother. Guy Kibbee was an outstanding comedy actor in his own right, and his brother, Jim Kibbee, was superintendent of Flemming-Potter Printing Company in Peoria.

According to Jim Logan, who was working in the third-floor embossing department at Flemming-Potter that day, Guy Kibbee visited the plant. He took a "cook's tour" of the place with brother Jim and co-founder Harley O. Potter.

The Kibbees were from Texas. Guy made a career in show business, but Jim was a printer, although he had also done some amateur acting before he moved to Peoria. Jim was also quite an after-dinner speaker.

The brothers weren't exact lookalikes, but enough so that, when seen separately, it was hard to tell which was which. They had the same hairline and bald head.

I remember seeing Jim around town for years and I'll tell you, the resemblance was striking.

The world premiere was held that night at the Madison. Crowds gathered, filling the street until traffic was blocked up and down Main Street. Streetcars were at a standstill. It seemed that all of Peoria came downtown to see the Hollywood celebrities as they arrived for the very first showing of "Earthworm Tractors."

One of our town's hottest days and warmest nights

...and it seems like only yesterday!

Peoria had major role in St. Jude Research Center

Next Saturday night, right after the 6 p.m. news on WEEK-TV, Mayor Jim Maloof and the Channel 25 news team will co-host the 12th Annual St. Jude Telethon. I need not tell you what an important part this six-hour telethon plays in this area's fight against childhood leukemia and other cancer-related catastrophic child-killers.

It may come as no surprise to many of you that this particular event is close to Flossie's heart and mine, as we were instrumental in bringing it to television back in 1978. I was general manager of the station at the time and we had not had a telethon on the air up until then, for a couple reasons.

First of all, the station felt that if we were to do one, it would have to tie in closely with our coverage area. Nothing we looked at did that until Jimmy Maloof approached me about St. Jude. The other problem was that our parent Kansas City firm, for some reason, had a "no telethon" policy.

Well, Jim began a "selling job" on me. That's a nice way of describing the continual bombardment from a man who wouldn't take "no" for an answer. But, with the help of my K.C. boss, Bill Bates, we finally sold the company on the importance of being involved with an organization whose primary function is helping sick kids in central Illinois. One of the major selling points was that no child or family need pay. I'm happy to say this still holds true.

If you took a map showing where the kids lived who were being treated at the St. Jude Mid-West Affiliate and laid a WEEK coverage map over it, it fit like a hand in a glove. How better can a TV station serve its viewers than by providing this annual fund-raising event?

But we went one step further. Not only did we decide to air the telethon, we also offered air time, production time, everything (including network and local revenue loss that night) at no charge. We wanted every dollar raised to go to helping sick kids get well. I'm happy to say that the station's new ownership still continues this policy we instituted back in 1978.

That first telethon raised around $50,000, as I recall. In 1988, after 11 years, it had grown to nearly $565,000. This year? $600,000 sounds like a nice round figure to me.

Bergner's department stores, then under the leadership of chairman Tom Liston and president Herb Glaser, soon joined us as co-sponsor, picking up other out-of-pocket costs such as telephone installations, line charges, signs, etc. Bergner employees soon became great contributors over the years, and still are.

The whole concept of the St. Jude Research Hospital in Memphis began with a prayer of a struggling young comedian from Toledo, Ohio, named Amos Jacobs. He prayed to St. Jude, the saint of hopeless and impossible causes. He promised him that if he were ever fortunate enough to make it in show business, he'd help St. Jude provide for afflicted people in some way.

The name you know him by today is Danny Thomas, and he sure made it big. He first made it in nightclubs, stage, radio and motion pictures. But his biggest success came in television, both as a star and a producer. He starred in the "All Star Revue" (1950-52) and "The Practice" (1976-77). His daughter, Marlo Thomas (now Mrs. Phil Donahue), also had a hit sit-com called "That Girl" 1966-71.

But Danny is best remembered for the 18-year reign of "The Danny Thomas Show," which, for its first three seasons, was called "Make Room for Daddy."

The St. Jude Children's Research Center in Memphis is the monument to Danny's promise to St. Jude. Many of his friends, including our, now, Mayor Maloof and his lovely wife, Trudy, were a part of this initial effort back in 1957.

Then the Maloofs, along with many other local people, including Sam George, Marj Crowl, Moris Adland, John Taraska, Bob Hart, Ron Hall, and so many more, opened the St. Jude Mid-West Affiliate office in Peoria in 1971.

In the early days, the "Teen March" was originated here in Peoria. Danny Thomas heard about its success and expanded the idea nationally. To date, the local affiliate has helped over 400 children in their battle against catastrophic childhood illnesses. Some have grown, married, and are now raising their own healthy families. They are living testimony of the hospital's success.

The first five telethons were held in the WEEK studios in East Peoria, which it soon outgrew. It moved to the Shrine Mosque in 1983, and in 1986 it moved to its present location, the Peoria Civic Center Theater.

Many events happen around central Illinois throughout the year that contribute greatly to the telethon's success, but none greater than the Memphis-to-Peoria run.

It was created in 1982 by Mike McCoy and Gene Pratt, the same two men who still co-direct it. The first year the run raised $22,000. Since then it has grown to $62,000, $92,000, $151,000 and last year it brought in $162,000.

Danny Thomas came and co-hosted our telethon with Jim Maloof in 1982. Then in 1984 his daughter, Marlo Thomas, co-hosted.

Bill and Flossie Adams with Danny Thomas at the WEEK-TV studios the night Danny co-hosted the local telethon with Jim Maloof.

Jim Maloof and his wife, Trudy, have been an important part of every telethon, with Jimmy as host. Many WEEK personalities have appeared over the years and this year's show includes Tom McIntyre, Chris Zak, Bill Houlihan, Lee Hall, Shelli Dankoff, and Mike Dimmick.

But one of the toughest jobs for ten years has been that of WEEK veteran Steve Shaw. He produces videos of the child patients. He shoots them alone because others usually can't handle the emotions. Steve's learned to deal with it, but there's one from last year that's especially hard for him to watch. It was a teen-ager who succumbed to her illness.

I can sympathize with Steve. Several years ago I ran into a mother and her daughter on two different occasions on Ozark flights coming back from

The official ribbon-cutting which opened the St. Jude Mid-West Affiliate in Peoria, in January, 1972. (left to right) Dr. Moris Adland, St. Jude board member; Danny Thomas; Clarence Yordy, chairman of Methodist Hospital board of trustees; and Jim Maloof. *(Photo courtesy of Jim Maloof)*

Memphis. Her mother kept a bonnet on her daughter's head because she was bald from the radiation treatments at the hospital. A few weeks later I picked up the paper. On the obituary page was a picture of this little girl in the same bonnet. She didn't make it, and I felt a terrible void. I didn't know her personally, but she was one of our kids. But, because of the St. Jude Hospital, more and more of our kids *are* making it. Remember that next Saturday night. Tune in and participate. With your donations, kids can someday beat the cancer rap.

Danny Thomas said it best. "If any child should die before its time, it is totally unacceptable!"

1978, the first St. Jude Telethon.

...it seems like only yesterday!

Cartwright Orchestra delighted Ing crowd

It's a Thursday night in the fall of 1938. The "house band" of the Inglaterra Ballroom is no longer Tiny Hill. He has just accepted a lengthy engagement at the Melody Mill Ballroom in Chicago.

Milton Budd steps to the microphone, waits for the cue from the WMBD radio engineer, and announces: "Another night with Charley Cartwright...Charley on trumpet and brother Bob with the baton."

Charley Cartwright and his 12-piece orchestra comes in with their theme song, "Scarlet," and "the society band for dancing" is playing once again to the delight of the Ing crowd and thousands listening in throughout Central Illinois.

But the Cartwright orchestra wasn't just Charley's, nor was it a brotherly affair. It was agreed from the outset that it would be cooperative, with each member sharing equally. George Simpson was named secretary-treasurer.

Charley was the elder of three brothers, Chuck, Bob and Tom. He was born in 1916. Bob was born in 1918 and brother Tom came four years later, in 1922; but Tom didn't pursue music.

Their parents, Victor H. and Mildred Barnes Cartwright, moved from Murphysboro to Lacon shortly after Charles was born. Victor managed the Sparland brick plant of the Hye-Tex Brick Co. His office moved to the Lehmann Building in 1926 and the family moved into the house on North University. Chuck and Bob entered Franklin School. About 1929 their dad built a home on Prospect Road and the boys transferred to Heights Grade School. Then the lads went to Central. Chuck graduated in 1934, and Bob in 1936.

Their first introduction to music came with the addition of a grand piano in their Prospect home. Mom enrolled them with an instructor at the Bradley College of Music.

Saturday morning lessons proved unpopular with both boys. It conflicted with their sandlot ballgames, YMCA basketball games and lunches at Block and Kuhl's soda fountain. Not to mention matinee movies, preferably at the Palace Theater, where stage shows were included.

At the beginning of Charley's eighth-grade term at Peoria Heights (1929), John O'Toole, a Byerly Music salesman, organized a school band. Instruments were on a rental-purchase basis. Chuck's choice of "weapon" was a Conn cornet, an improvement over the piano, except for their pet dog, Rex, who accompanied him by howling through practice.

The following year he joined Peoria High's band under the direction of Irving Bradley. He soon began leaning toward popular music. He listened to remote broadcasts of name bands and attempted to play cornet accompaniment.

In 1931, Chuck approached Peoria High band members to form a "Cartwright Orchestra." He believes the original band members were Carl Magnuson, Harold and Verne Phillips (sax); Tommy Moran and himself (trumpet); Don Elkins (trombone); Glen Palmer (drums); Walter Jameson (piano); Hank Borgen (guitar); and George Simpson (tuba).

In 1932, they landed their first public appearance...playing for their supper in the basement of the Heights Congregational Church.

After summer vacation the band reorganized, and 1933 brought on several personnel changes. Bob Huisman replaced Glen Palmer on drums. Walter Schaeffer replaced Carl Magnuson on sax, and Bob Lindig replaced Walter Jameson on piano.

In 1934 and 1935 several local orchestras were popular, including Chuck Barnes and his Seven Little Stables, Harry Jackson's Orchestra, Carl Engles and his Royal Aces, and the Kramm-Calkins Orchestra, made up of Bradley students.

The band's first "big break" came in May, 1934 with the "Sophomore Frolic" at the Central gym. It paid each member $2.50, and they later played dances at Bradley and Glen Oak Park pavilions, Al Fresco Beach, Lacon Country Club and Mt. Hawley Country Club.

By 1935 the group still took a backseat to Red Deames and his Orchestra, which was an outgrowth of the Kramm-Calkins band. But now Cartwright was playing the Peoria Country Club, Ivy Club, North Shore C.C. and such towns as Princeton, Mendota, Morris and Canton.

It was also in 1935 when brother Bob joined and began "fronting" the band. By 1936, Harold Garrels, by far the youngest member but an accomplished guitarist, joined the group.

The group experimented with female vocalists with only moderate success. A trio of Peoria High classmates were introduced on a two-night stand at Bill Jasper's Auditorium Ballroom in LaSalle. They were: Lois Miller, Lucille McClintock and Mary Jean Carey. The overnight hotel stay, road travel, low pay, etc., convinced the women that the glamour of orchestra life was not for them. They quickly and quietly bowed out with no further aspirations for stardom.

Charley Cartwright Orchestra in 1938. At left: Bob and Charley Cartwright. Back row: Harold Garrels, George Simpson, Verne Phillips, Tommy Moran, Walter Schaeffer. Front row: Don Elkins, Harold Phillips, Lorraine Parr, Bob Lindig, and Danny Burke.

(Photo courtesy of Walt Schaeffer)

The band's second female vocal venture came with the addition of Ann Day. Ann was an attractive girl and did a commendable job until the love bug bit her. She soon exchanged vocalizing for wedded bliss.

The third and final attempt to offer a female vocalist came in the form of an attractive redhead named Lorraine Parr. She preferred riding in the band's truck, which, naturally, led to the omission of "street language" conversations by the male members. Lorraine finally decided her association created adverse social conditions and she resigned. This was the band's final effort to feature a female vocalist.

(Next week we'll follow the Cartwright orchestra through its peak years of the late 1930's.)

Cartwright band's popularity took off in 1936

Last week's column covered the Charley Cartwright Orchestra from its beginning until 1936.

Early in '36 the group was approached to accompany WMBD Radio's "Juvenile Theater," under the direction of Jack Lyon. It aired every Saturday morning from the studios in the Alliance Life Building auditorium.

This program was difficult for the band. No arrangements were furnished by the youngsters and with no rehearsals, the orchestra couldn't ad-lib its "sound," which left much to be desired.

But the show's popularity increased and it moved to the Madison Theater stage to accommodate a larger live audience. But after three months, the show moved back to the radio studios and (with a sigh of relief) without the Cartwright Orchestra.

The band's popularity began to take hold in mid-1936. Along with Peoria club dances, they began regular engagements out of town, including Mackinaw Dells, Fernwood Pavilion, O'Neil's Park in Bloomington and Park Pavilion in Jacksonville.

Vocal renditions were assigned to various band members. Bob Lindig and Don Elkins handled up-tempo numbers. Walter Schaeffer handled the ballads, and Charley did several renditions, including "Basin Street Blues." And, from time to time, the entire band sang in unison.

During the 1936 Christmas holidays, Cartwright played for the majority of high school fraternity and sorority dances at the Hotel Père Marquette.

In 1937, circumstances forced a change in band personnel. Bob Huisman was asthmatic and had to leave for health reasons. In a "chance" meeting at the Hitching Post, Danny Burke showed an interest in joining on drums. Danny was jobbing out with various Peoria bands, including Harry Jackson's Orchestra. He also instituted comedy routines to the repertoire, including "Alice Where Art Thou Going?" This became one of their most remembered numbers.

In June 1937, Cartwright's band played 20 dates in Peoria, Fernwood, and the Silverleaf and Coliseum ballrooms in Davenport, Iowa. Others included the Fountain Amusement Park in Louisville, and the Lakeview Club in Paducah, Kentucky.

Bookings in 1938 continued for a wide variety of local and road engagements such as Ideal Beach at Monticello, Indiana, the Evansville Country Club, and Twin Lakes Park in Paris, Illinois, plus repeat engagements in the Quad Cities.

In March, the band played for the Spalding High Junior Prom. It was its initial appearance at Peoria's "mecca" for dancing, the Inglaterra Ballroom. They repeated in April for the Peoria Central Junior Prom.

In the spring of 1938 a farm show location in Edelstein became a popular area ballroom. Bert Potter and his son, Jim, farm implement dealers, built a building to house their implements on the lower level and, what became a dance floor, on the upper level. After a record crowd at the "grand opening" of the farm show, the Hub Ballroom was born. The Cartwright Orchestra played several dates at the Hub in the fall of 1938.

Charley and Bob both attended four years at Bradley College. Chuck graduated in 1938 and Bob two years later. After graduation, Charley decided to augment the orchestra income by opening a talent and booking agency, the Peoria Amusement Service.

Seasonal dances and functions often fell on dates their band was booked. This gave Charley the opportunity to book other area bands. Jack Davis of Peoria was probably the most booked, and he and Chuck became close friends over the years.

The Cartwright Orchestra's private bookings at the Inglaterra brought the band to the attention of Ing manager, Harold Newsam, and he hired them to replace Tiny Hill. At this time they added a fourth saxophonist, Bob Walters. He had formerly played with Hill but chose not to go on the road with Tiny. Bobby also wrote music. He wrote special arrangements which ultimately replaced the "stock" orchestrations previously used.

The group continued to thrive in 1939, but a time of decision arose in early 1940. Band members were engaged in other daytime occupations while still playing professionally. Several were graduating from Bradley.

January 1, 1940, the band ushered in the New Year with a doubleheader...a tea dance at Bloomington Club from 2 to 5 p.m. and their regular stint at the Ing from 8:30 p.m. until 2 a.m. This was followed by two engagements on New Year's Day.

On the following Sunday night, the Charley Cartwright Orchestra played its final big band engagement at O'Neil's Park in Bloomington, bringing to and end their musical contribution to the "Yester Days" experience by both, the band members, and their many friends of the late '30's.

But Chuck and Bob didn't stop completely. Later that year, Jerry Gordon, manager of the Père Marquette, talked

The Charley Cartwright Orchestra about 1936, the year the band's popularity took hold. From left, front row: Verne Phillips, Harold "Hal" Phillips, Walt Schaeffer, Harold Garrels, Bob Lindig, and Bob Cartwright at the microphone. Back row: Don Elkins, Tom Moran, Charley Cartwright, Bob Huisman, and George Simpson. *(Photo courtesy of Walt Schaeffer)*

them into forming a smaller, seven-piece band to open the new Peoria Room. They played there for two years. Charley left for the Navy in 1942, while brother Bob continued until 1943.

Charley married Josephine Peggy Sparks, a former schoolmate, in 1942. They have one daughter, Janet Lee Wilken, now of Seebrook, Texas. Janet and her husband have four children, three girls and a boy.

Bob married Betty McCaddon later in 1942. They had a son, Robert Bruce, who is now an attorney. He and his wife have two children, one boy and one girl.

As of this writing, Walter Schaeffer, Harold Garrels, Verne Phillips and Charley Cartwright reside in Peoria.

Danny Burke lives in Santa Barbara, California, and is still active in small combos and Jazz groups. Harold "Hal" Phillips, formerly of WMBD, resides in Ocean City, California. Bob Lindig is in San Diego, and Don Elkins lives in Atlanta, Georgia, and still plays in an organized dance orchestra. George Simpson is still musically active with the Springfield band.

Bob Cartwright passed away with a lingering illness two years ago. Tommy Moran, Bobby Walters and Bob Huisman have also passed away.

As Milton Budd said, "Another night with Charley Cartwright".

...and it seems like only yesterday!

Orient Express brings back memories of The Rocket

Flossie and I have recently returned from a fabulous vacation in Europe, celebrating our 45th Anniversary. We were with a couple long-standing Peoria friends, Bob and Dorothy McNamee. The four of us visited Brussels; Paris; Besancon, France (where our daughter, Kerry, went to college her junior year); Geneva; Zurich; Vienna; Salzburg; Innsbruck; Friedrichshafen, West Germany (our sister city); Basel; Amsterdam and all points in between.

We experienced two (among others) exciting modes of transportation. One was a beautiful five-day cruise on the Rhine River from Basel, Switzerland to Amsterdam, Holland. The other was a breath-taking trip through the Alps of Switzerland and Austria on the Venice Simplon Orient-Express. (We'll describe that experience and the history of the Orient-Express next week).

But riding on the Orient-Express reminded me of the days of my youth when railroad passenger service was very much in vogue in our town. There were many lines operating, earlier, in and out of

Peoria, but I'm referring specifically to the streamline train that began service in 1937 on the Rock Island Railroad between Peoria and Chicago, the "Peoria Rocket."

The Orient-Express didn't remind me of the Rocket because of their similarity. Far from it. But it did remind me of days when railroad passenger service was "the" mode of public transportation.

It might surprise you to know that this wasn't the first Rocket. As a matter of fact, the very first "iron horse" to arrive here at 10 p.m. on November 7, 1854, was also called "The Rocket." That was just 135 years ago and it was greeted with throngs of Peorians at a small, temporary wooden depot above Morton Street. The festivities included cheers, speeches, banquets, and booming cannon.

The crowds had a right to be jubilant. This was the golden age of the steamboat but the city was feeling a lack of railroad transportation. There was a great need for good connections with towns other than river communities.

As early as 1844 Peoria was attracting industry but it was feeling resistance to its location and the difficulty of getting here. (Sounds all too familiar, doesn't it?) The Frink and Company Stage Coach Lines maintained a 30-hour schedule between Peoria and Chicago.

The Peoria and Bureau Valley railway, later known as the Rock Island, had been surveyed in the fall of 1852. Peoria granted a construction charter in February, 1853. The Sheffield and Farnam Co. received a contract in August.

The rails for the new road came from England and were shipped from New York through the Hudson River, Erie Canal, and the Great Lakes to Chicago. The railroad ties were cut from the area where Evanston now stands. Some were brought down by canal boat through the Illinois and Michigan canal.

The first railroad pirated its crew from the steamboats. The Rocket rolled into town with former steamboat engineer James Lendabarger at the throttle.

In those times, freight was second to passenger service. The first load of rail freight actually left Peoria on November 15, 1854. It was a single carload of groceries weighing less than ten tons. It was shipped 40 miles up the new line at the amazing rate of 15¢ a hundredweight. Passenger fares were equal to 5¢ a mile.

But the Peoria Rocket I relate to is the streamlined version that began service between Peoria and Chicago in September, 1937. I was living in Holmes Center, north of Mossville, at the time.

A Ray Barclay Photo of the Peoria Rocket, in front of the Rock Island Depot.
(Courtesy of R. W. Deller from Lee Roten's Historic Peoria Photo File)

Being a 12-year-old boy, I became familiar with all the steam trains and their schedules. They went right past our house, and I made it my business to be at the fence waiting to see if they were on time. I had a responsibility to wave to the engineer or fireman.

The sleek, new Rocket was on display at the Peoria depot a few days before its first run. Mom and Dad took me down to look her over close up. That shiny red engine with stainless steel cars was something to behold.

The Lionel company soon came out with an electric toy train facsimile and I was probably one of the first to find it under the Christmas tree. As I recall, my dad enjoyed it almost as much as I did.

The first public run of the Peoria Rocket left the Peoria depot at 7 a.m. on Sunday, September 19, 1937. It was scheduled to make the 161-mile trip to Chicago's LaSalle Street station in 160 minutes. It would begin its return trip at 11 a.m., arriving here at 1:40 p.m. Then it would go to Chicago again at 3 p.m., arriving there in 2 hours, 40 minutes, and start back at 7 p.m., arriving here at 9:40 p.m. Two round trips a day would be the permanent schedule. It reduced the time of the run by nearly an hour over the fastest previous steam trains.

The Peoria passenger agent was Mr. A. Langfeldt. The four-car train, plus dinette car, accommodated 177 passengers, and he anticipated filling every seat, at least in the beginning. This represented over 700 passengers daily.

The Rocket maintained the same fares as the steam trains, $3.02 one way, and $5.44 round trip. Steam train service also remained in effect to give local service to other towns along the route.

In January 1956, the Rock Island unveiled a new Talgo-type 1200 horsepower diesel-electric streamliner called the "Jet Rocket." It was capable of speeds up to 120 miles per hour (although it was kept at 90 and below), and was able to take curves at 70, because of an exceptionally low center of gravity.

The Talgo was a highly touted train and the Rock Island had big plans for it, but it proved impractical. It rode so roughly it was impossible to even get a cup of coffee to your lips, let alone drink it. It was soon relegated to commuter service elsewhere.

The old Peoria Rocket served us well for 42 years, but air travel and the automobile finally did it in. Its last, sad run occurred on January 1, 1979.

It left the (again) Morton Street depot an hour late and without a single passenger. The once proud Peoria Rocket became just a memory. But what a memory, at least to me, and I'll bet to a lot of others, too.

...and it seems like only yesterday!

Queen of the European railways

As I mentioned last week, Flossie and I, along with our good friends Bob and Dorothy McNamee, recently returned from a fabulous European vacation. We traveled the continent for three weeks. We flew; we rented a car (twice); we cruised for five days on the Rhine River; and we rode the Orient Express from Zurich, Switzerland to Vienna, Austria. Since I wrote about the old Peoria Rocket last week, it only seems fitting to give the Orient Express equal time.

This column is dedicated to the history of the Peoria area, but I hope you'll forgive this week's deviation while we talk about the "queen of European railways."

If I must give it a local historic connection, I need only go as far away as Chicago (which, after all, is a suburb of Peoria). Because the man most responsible for luxury train travel in the first place was one George Mortimer Pullman (1831-97), the inventor of the Pullman sleeping car. He founded the Pullman Palace Car Company in 1867. Pullman attempted to make the company a "model town" but Pullman, Illinois, was annexed to Chicago in 1889.

Pullman first visualized luxury train travel when he built the "Pioneer" car in 1864. He was invited to England by James Allport of the Midland Railway, which eventually led to the Pullman Palace Car Co. there in 1882. Pullman built coaches in Illinois and shipped them to Britain. He also tried to infiltrate Europe's luxury train travel but Georges Nagelmackers, founder of the Wagon-Lits Company in 1876, had a virtual monopoly on it.

Sir Davidson Dalziel bought the British Pullman company in 1908 and started building Pullman cars in England. The company went public in 1915, and Dalziel remained chairman. He became a director of the Wagon-Lits Co., and his daughter married Georges Nagelmackers' son, René. He then became chairman of that firm in 1926.

The first Simplon-Orient-Express trip took place on April 15, 1919, shortly after World War I. The twenties and early thirties were the heyday of luxury train travel. Over the years this line connected various routes from London to Paris to Istanbul, where it connected with mideast trains.

But World War II began in September 1939, and the Night Ferry across the English Channel and England's Golden Arrow train stopped operating, and by the end of the war Calais and Boulogne were almost completely obliterated.

The Simplon Orient Express resumed in 1946, from Paris to Milan, Venice and Rome. But cheap air travel caused people to lose the habit of luxury train travel. Then in 1947 the Iron Curtain seriously curtailed the routes east. The train continued with much difficulty over the years, and it slowly became a mere shadow of its glory days. The Orient Express' last run left Paris May 19, 1977, made up of a shabby sleeping car, three scruffy day coaches and no restaurant car. It arrived in Istanbul five hours late.

The man responsible for reviving the train is Mr. James B. Sherwood of the Sea Containers Group firm. After the Orient-Express folded in 1977, Sotheby's auctioned off five of its 1920's carriages that had been used in the filming of "Murder on the Orient Express." Mr. Sherwood attended the sale in Monte Carlo and bought two of the cars.

In four and a half years he located other rolling stock, restored it, negotiated the routing, engaged a staff, and promoted the operation. Today's Venice Simplon Orient-Express left Victoria Station in London for the first time on May 25, 1982. It currently runs two routes from London through Paris. One to Venice, Italy, and the other (the one we rode) to Vienna, Austria. Our 12-hour trip was one breathtaking view after another through the Alps of Switzerland and Austria. I'm sure it was the most picturesque area on the route.

Before I describe our ride, though, I must tell a somewhat embarrassing story on the Adams' and McNamee's. We landed in Amsterdam and flew to Brussels. Then we rented a car and drove to Paris and, later, to Besancon, France, where our daughter Kerry, went to school. Then we drove to Geneva and Zurich, Switzerland, where we boarded the train.

Now if you're at all familiar with Europe you know that every major city has its central railroad station in the heart of town. So did Zurich, and Bob McNamee even arranged for us to stay at the delightful Kindli Hotel near the station.

We arrived at the station the next morning at 6 a.m. an hour before departure. When we presented our tickets, the agent looked at us and said, "What's the Orient-Express?". That's when we knew we had a major problem.

After much scrambling, the stationmaster informed us that another station had recently been built at the airport, and that's where our train was. He phoned and the Orient-Express was there waiting for us. They said if we could take the next commuter train which was leaving immediately, they'd wait. You never saw four people move luggage onto a train faster. We boarded the Orient Express a half-hour late and I think it moved the second our feet hit the step.

I don't know how popular we were, but the look in the conductor's eye indicated it wouldn't have taken much to have a repeat of "Murder on the Orient-Express." But from then on the experience was delightful. Both couples had private compartments with an adjoining door, which opened into a suite. We were

Bob and Dorothy McNamee enjoying the ride in the bar car on the Venice Simplon Orient-Express.

Flossie and Bill Adams enjoying a short stop at Innsbruck outside their #3309 car on the Venice Simplon Orient-Express.

in Sleeping Car No. 3309, the oldest of the lines cars. It consisted of eight single and four double compartments. It is one of the 18 Continental Rake carriages owned by VSO-E and was built in 1926 in Nivelles, Belgium. Its interior decoration is Floral Art Deco marquetry, and its designer was René Prou.

This particular car has an interesting history. It operated exclusively in the Orient-Express on various routes from 1928 to 1939. It operated from Paris to Bucharest or Munich, and also ran to Istanbul via Vienna and Budapest. It is associated with a number of dramatic events, including being marooned in snow for ten days in February 1929, sixty miles from Istanbul.

The Orient Express has three dining cars; #4095 (built in 1927); #4110 (1927); and Lalique Pullman #4141 (1929). The last one has beautiful glass wall panels designed by René Lalique. They are faintly blue opaque showing classical nude figures. Mr. Lalique is also responsible for the design of some of the Pullman chairs and the "tulip" light shades throughout the train.

The bar car #3674, was built in 1931 in France. It is created in Art Nouveau style. In addition to the bar and comfortable upholstered seating, it also has a grand piano, which is played by a musician who travels with the train. What a life!

So, if you've ever wondered how the other half lives, take a ride on the Orient-Express. But be sure to go to the correct station to catch it.

This didn't just seem like only yesterday...*it was!*

(Most of the factual material on the Orient-Express came from the official book, "Venice Simplon Orient-Express" by Shirley Sherwood, the wife of the originator of VSO-E.)

"Dusty" Rhodes was true genius

Genius is a word often misused to portray someone with great ability, but it's the only word I know that truly describes an old friend and former co-worker, Mr. C. J. "Dusty" Rhodes.

Dusty, as everyone called him, was a commercial artist who headed up the Publix Great States Theaters Art Department in Peoria from the mid-1920's until he left the theaters in the mid-'40's. If you lived around here in those years and didn't know Dusty personally, you most certainly knew of his work. He and his department developed all the false fronts, lobby displays, commercial tie-ins, special artwork and supporting advertising for the shows that played the Madison, Palace, Rialto and Apollo Theaters.

But he was much more than "just" an artist. He was an inventor with a very creative mind. He had to be to come up with all the moving, flashing, lighted displays that adorned these showplaces week after week.

C.J. Rhodes was born in Fremont, Nebraska and studied art at the University of Nebraska, taking post-graduate work at the Chicago Art Institute. He studied

Dusty Rhodes
(Courtesy of Carole Schlatter)

later with Gordon Bennet, a prominent Omaha designer, and also studied for six months with Lee Van Voorhis of Seattle, a foremost west coast artist.

Rhodes, by the way, went by the name Dusty or his initials, C.J., because of his aversion to his first name, Cecil. (His fellow worker Len Worley had a similar problem with his middle name, going by Leonard C., instead of Cecil.) Lord help you if you referred to either of them using this unmentionable name to their face.

Dusty started with the Balaban and Katz Theaters in Chicago about 1924. A year later he came to Peoria to head up their downstate company, Publix Great States Theaters' art department. He was an artist who constantly explored new color combinations, lighting effects and striking materials. He felt an artist must work toward the public's appreciation of what is good.

Well, if my experience is any indication, Dusty certainly reached his goal of public appreciation. His work was used so much that when a movie came and was not supported with one of his theater

fronts, the theater looked naked. At the time, I had the feeling that this conveyed to the public the impression that the movie was inferior, and wasn't worthy of Dusty's special art.

If you're old enough, maybe you remember just a few of the early movies and their stars that played the Madison and Palace and were worthy of the "Rhodes treatment":

Norma Shearer in "The Last of Mrs. Cheyney"; 30 Paramount Stars in "Paramount on Parade"; Lawrence Tibbett in "The Rogue Song"; Johnny Weissmuller in "Tarzan the Ape Man"; Al Jolson in "Mammy"; Richard Dix in "Cimarron"; Cecil B. DeMille's "The Crusades"; Dick Powell in "Shipmates Forever"; Maurice Chevalier in "One Hour With You"; Helen Hayes & Lewis Stone in "The Sin of Madelon Claudet"; Katharine Hepburn in "Little Women"; Irene Dunne in "Back Street"; Gary Cooper & Jean Arthur in "Mr. Deeds Goes to Town"

But his creativity went far beyond the special theater fronts. One of his most memorable displays was one that adorned the inner lobby of the Madison, between Aisles 2 and 3. It was a coming attraction for Charles Laughton and the "beautiful new Irish star, Maureen O'Hara," in "The Hunchback of Notre Dame." It was a 20-foot high replica of the Notre Dame Cathedral with its beautiful stained glass windows made of various colored transparent paper. A 10-foot high hunchback was standing to one side.

Dusty Rhodes' special front on the Madison Theater advertising the "The Sin of Madelon Claudet," starring Helen Hayes and Lewis Stone.
(Courtesy of Carole Schlatter)

Many other outlets for Dusty's work included store windows in record shops, book shops, clothing stores and department stores, especially Block and Kuhl's. Streetcars would travel all over town with huge billboards on their sides advertising Great States movies, with special lighting effects that Dusty would rig, since the streetcars were electric.

But Rhodes' crowning achievement came in 1936 when he designed and built the Palace Theatre's new, modern canopy. It was adorned with running lights, lights that changed colors and neon lights of various colors. It was one of several he designed for the company.

One of the most effective gimmicks I recall was one Rhodes came up with to promote a Palace picture, "The Son of Frankenstein," in 1939. It was a huge facsimile of the Frankenstein monster lying on a float built on a flatbed semi-trailer. It would rise up, turn its head from side to side and groan with a big roar, then lie back down again. I was fourteen at the time, and I still remember the shock when I first saw it.

I first knew Dusty when I began as an usher in 1941. Then we worked together after I became assistant manager, then manager of the Madison Theater, until I went into the service in 1944. He was not only talented, he was a great guy to be around, too. He always had time to explain his latest contraption, and he was always working on the next one.

Johnny Duncan, who was later a stagehand for me, was working for Dusty in the Art Department in the basement of the Orpheum Theater when I first met him. When I returned from the Navy in 1946, the Art Department was a thing of the past. Rising costs made it prohibitive, and Dusty left about 1945 to go into partnership with Charley Smith in the Rhodes-Smith Sign Company at 329 S.

Adams. Great States Theaters continued to have all their sign work done there.

A young man who joined Dusty and Smitty after his Air Force duty in 1946 was Art Reed. Art remembers those early days, too. Before entering the service in 1942, he worked in the display department of the Peoria Dry Goods Store and later for Sutliff and Case Drug Stores.

When Smith and Rhodes parted company, Art went with Dusty who formed a new company called Rhodes Displays. They made displays and models of tractors for Caterpillar and eventually moved to East Peoria, across from Cat.

Dusty Rhodes retired in 1966 at the age of 65 and moved to Apache Wells (Mesa), Arizona, where he ran an art department, taught art classes and played golf until he "retired" again at 75. He and his wife, Marion, then moved to Roswell, New Mexico, but he still was painting elaborate scenery for the Roswell Community Little Theatre. He finally really retired at 85 when he couldn't hold a paintbrush steady.

Dusty passed away in January 1988 at age 87. Marion is at the Sunset Villa rest home in Roswell. Their son, Steve, and daughter, Carole Schlatter are both married and live in Roswell. They each have two children.

You could call him C.J. or you could call him Dusty, but never, never call him Cecil, at least not to his face.

...and it seems like only yesterday!

Kresge fire a spectacular experience

We've had our share of spectacular fires in "our town" over the years. The Hiram Walker Distillery, Gipps Brewery, The Grand Opera House, The Corning Distillery, The National Hotel, and The Pascal Hotel, just to name a few. I'm old enough to remember a couple of those and others. Last April, I described one I happened to see first hand, the Seneca Hotel fire on Franklin Street. But there's another one that stands out in my mind because I was there, also.

It was the Kresge 5 and 10¢ store in the 100 block of South Adams. An explosion and fire gutted the store on Wednesday, December 21, 1932. I was seven years old at the time. Not only was I an eye-witness to the tragedy, but if it hadn't been for an ironic twist of fate, my mother, my cousin and I would have surely been in the store when it happened.

It was about 7 p.m. that Wednesday evening in 1932 at the height of the Christmas shopping season. My Mother and I had taken a streetcar from our home on North Jefferson Street. Mom had phoned my cousin, Betty Nelson, who lived on Ravine, and invited her to meet us at the corner entrance of Clarke's Department Store at Adams and Main. This is where our two streetcars would intersect. The streetcar she was to be on came and went, but no Betty. Mom said she may have missed it, but another one was due shortly. So we'd wait for it where we were.

She mentioned in passing that as soon as Betty arrived, we'd stop first at Kresge's 5 and 10 (on Adams between Clarke's and Block and Kuhl's). It seems that she had no more than mentioned it when we heard a huge explosion.

We turned and looked down Adams in time to see broken glass being blown out into the middle of the street and black smoke billowing from the gaping hole that had been the front window of the Kresge's store. Then I remember a woman in a white uniform running from the store with her hair on fire.

I have thought many times since that, if Betty had been on that first streetcar, there is little doubt we would have been in the store or, maybe worse, walking in front of it, when the explosion blew out the front windows.

The next day's Peoria Journal said a girl was missing and 16 were injured in the fire. The Peoria Star's headline was: "FEAR GIRL TRAPPED IN FIRE." To see pictures of the store, you'd wonder how anyone survived. It was a tangled mass of charred debris.

The Peoria Evening Star said a store clerk, Miss Genevieve Arter, age 20, was missing and at least 19 persons were burned and injured in the spectacular blaze. The fire broke out in the holiday-crowded store at 7:15 p.m. and it spread with lightning-like rapidity. A dozen or more clerks and employees were trapped in a third-floor rest room, and were forced to leap into firemen's life nets.

The worst fears for Miss Arter were not unfounded. Her body was found partially buried in the debris of the fireswept ruins of the store the next day. She had decided to remain in the store during her lunch period rather than accompany Mary Folich, with whom she lived at 603 N. Jefferson, on a shopping trip outside the store.

She apparently had attempted to reach the front door on the store's south aisle, which took her directly into the most intense part of the blaze.

Most of the survivors were injured by burns, inhaling flames, or by jumping into life nets. Scores of employees displayed remarkable courage and coolness while hurriedly helping 350 to 400 customers out of the store. Most were forced to flee through a winding stairs exit through the rear of the building.

Henry Nelson, a Kresge floorman, fought his way through the terrified mass and rushed to rest rooms to alert people there. Thirteen or fourteen salesgirls, lounging in a rest room in the rear of the third floor, were blocked by people in the stairway. Firemen spread a life net, and one by one the trapped victims jumped through the clouds of smoke.

Nelson had to literally push two young women who were so frightened they refused to jump. One salesperson, Helen Weeks, suffered a fractured pelvis when she missed the life net in a jump from the third floor. Harry Nelson was the last to leave via the window. He suffered severe burns about the face and a badly injured ankle when he jumped into the life net.

Several reports of the cause of the fire were made by eyewitnesses inside the store. Assistant Manager S.P. English said a wide tongue of flame seemed to sweep down the south-front wall, which ignited ceiling decorations.

A clerk, Mrs. Rae Blood reported seeing a light bulb explode, setting fire to the holiday decorations and quickly spreading to the counter of phonograph records, ribbons and art goods. A customer, Rudolph Barrick, also said he saw the fire start at this location.

As I now look back at the description of injuries in the old newspapers, those of an 18-year-old salesgirl, Miss Violet Young, sound strikingly familiar to me. The hair was burned off of her head

This is a very early photo of the S. S. Kresge Co. 5 & 10¢ Store that burned on December 21, 1932. Signs in the windows say "OPEN TO-DAY." Crowds at this store and not the others, plus the signs, indicate that this was probably the store's Grand Opening.
(Photo courtesy of Peoria Public Library)

and she was burned about the hands and face. Could she have been the one I saw running out of the building with her hair on fire?

Fire damage was confined to the three-story building occupied by Kresge's; the offices of a dentist, Dr. C. C. Landon; and Rembrandt Studios on the second floor; plus the Clarke and Co. store; the Field Millinery Store; and the Adams Music House, which adjoined the dime store. Fire Chief Charles Dickison and his crew were commended the next day for their efficient handling of one of Peoria's most spectacular retail fires.

Well, it's not exactly the way you want to remember a childhood Christmas shopping trip but, thanks to Betty, we were eyewitnesses on the outside, not the inside.

...and it seems like only yesterday!

Milton Berle took back seat to Bishop Sheen

One of Peoria's most famous radio and television personalities, in addition to Marian and Jim Jordan and Charles Correll, was one of the most unlikely, because it was not his true vocation. I'm not sure you could even call it his avocation, and sideline is another description that doesn't fit. This is all because he was one of, if not "the" most visible Catholic this side of the Pope. He was Archbishop Fulton J. Sheen.

But back in the 1950's he was not only a very prominent TV "star," his television program, "Life Is Worth Living," became the number one program on the national networks. As a matter of fact, he beat out "Uncle Miltie," Milton Berle and his Texaco Star Theater. Berle was "Mr. Television" at the time, and Bishop Sheen topped him.

Although Fulton J. Sheen was born in El Paso, Illinois, on May 8, 1895, Peoria has every right to also claim him because the family moved to Peoria shortly after he was born. His birthplace was a small apartment above his father, Newton Sheen's, hardware store at 25 West Front Street in El Paso. His Christian name was Peter John, and he was known as "P. J." but he preferred Fulton, which was his mother's maiden name.

While growing up in Peoria, Sheen attended St. Mary's Catholic grade school and graduated from Spalding Institute in 1913. While attending Spalding, he was a basketball buddy of another future radio star, Jim Jordan (Fibber McGee). Jim and his pals called him "Spike" Sheen. At this same time Marian Driscoll, Jim Jordan's future wife (Molly), was attending the Academy of Our Lady, across the street from Spalding.

After high school graduation, Sheen attended St. Viator's College in Bourbonnias, Illinois (near Kankakee) to prepare for the priesthood. He was ordained in Peoria in 1919. In later years, he was quoted as saying, "I have no earlier recollections than a desire to be a priest."

His only parish assignment was as an assistant at St. Patrick's Church in "the south end." He came back in February 1966 to attend the parish's 100th anniversary celebration.

The Most Reverend Fulton J. Sheen began his broadcasting career in March, 1930, on a radio program, "The Catholic Hour." The show was a product of the National Council of Catholic Men, and Sheen, virtually unknown nationally, was selected as its first preacher. The council later estimated that the "fringe time" radio show reached seven and a half million listeners. It received mail from all parts of the world, as far away as the Faulkland Islands, Australia, Turkey and South Africa.

But Reverend Sheen's biggest broadcasting triumph was yet to come. When he began television's "Life Is Worth Living" in 1952, he was Auxiliary Bishop of New York. He was described as "a modest, middle-level cleric who had long been heard on radio."

Sheen was the "star" and only "regular" on the weekly black-and-white, half-hour, prime-time program. His set was a simulated study and he punctuated his points with drawings scrawled on a blackboard. He came across as a charming, well-spoken Catholic bishop offering anecdotes and little lessons in morality. "Sermons" would be too stuffy a word for his messages. And he had a following that far exceeded his Catholic following.

My father is a perfect example. Dad was not Catholic, and he was also a big Milton Berle fan, but he wouldn't miss "Life Is Worth Living." And for you younger readers, let me hasten to add that this was long before VCRs were invented. So, if you missed a program, you just missed it.

It's hard to conceive today that a Catholic bishop talking alone and writing on a blackboard could not only be popular, but at his peak, become the number one TV show in America. Bishop Sheen did just that by actually beating "Mr. Television," Milton Berle, in the ratings.

Many of Bishop Sheen's messages discussed the evils of world communism. The show's most dramatic incident came in early 1953 when he gave his reading of the burial scene from "Julius Caesar." For the names of Caesar, Cassius, Marc Antony and Brutus, he substituted the then leading communist names of Stalin, Beria, Malenkov and Vishinsky. And with hypnotic forcefulness he added, "Stalin must one day meet his judgement." A few days later, the Russian dictator suffered a sudden stroke and a week later he was dead. There was never any comment from Sheen's office on this remarkable coincidence, but it was widely reported in the press.

"Life Is Worth Living" ran from February 12, 1952, until April 8, 1957. The first three years were on the old Dumont network, then it moved over to ABC. Bishop Sheen was also national director of the church's Propagation of the Faith, and before his retirement in 1969, he was credited with bringing into the Catholic faith such notables as newspaper columnist Heywood Broun, automaker

Former Peorian Archbishop Fulton J. Sheen, whose radio program, "The Catholic Hour," and television show, "Life Is Worth Living," gained him national acclaim as a broadcaster.
(Photo courtesy of Peoria Public Library)

Henry Ford II, and playwright Clare Boothe Luce. He also brought back into the church Louis F. Budenz, former editor of the Daily Worker communist newspaper, and former communist spy, Elizabeth T. Bentley.

The bishop visited Peoria on many occasions over the years. His last visit here was May 7, 1977, when he received the

Order of Lincoln, which was described as the State of Illinois' highest honor.

In 1978 my wife, Flossie, was chairwoman of the Catholic Women's League's spring luncheon. She wrote to Archbishop Sheen, inviting him to be their guest speaker. He was too ill to accept, but his answer to her on October 20, 1978, read in part..."Your invitation to address the Women's League of Peoria is one my heart would long to accept. I have my roots in Peoria, and I would love to avail myself of the opportunity of another visit. However, I have just recently been released from the hospital, and my doctors have insisted that I cancel all engagements for this year..." He signed it by his, then, title as Titular Archbishop of Newport.

Fulton Sheen died the following year, on December 9, 1979, at the age of 84. He passed away at his home on Manhattan's Upper East Side after a long battle with heart disease.

When Sheen beat out Milton Berle in the ratings, a reporter asked Milton how this could possibly happen. Berle's reply was, "Bishop Sheen had better writers."

Archbishop Fulton (Peter John) Sheen, one of our towns best.

...and it seems like only yesterday!

Marvin Hult still being the best he can be

One of the real fringe benefits of writing this column is that every so often you're privileged to write about a long-time friend. Such is the case this week regarding a former business associate, Marvin H. Hult.

Marv is still making news and continues to be actively engaged in helping our area become a better place to live. Just last week, ground was broken for the new Marvin Hult Health Education Center. No better name could be given to the facility which is planned for opening on the Proctor Hospital campus in September, 1990.

One of many health education subjects the center will cover is chemical dependency. Marv feels so strongly about this problem that awhile back he wrote a beautiful song about it called "The Best I Can Be." It was sung at the groundbreaking by the Roosevelt Magnet School Choir.

Marv began his association with Proctor Hospital in 1957, and listening to him you'd have to assume it is what he's most proud of, at least up until the naming of this new facility for him. But, at the risk of embarrassing Marv, here's just a few of his many community service accomplishments over the years.

Outstanding Young Man of the Year - 1954. J. C. Chairman of the first Heart of Illinois Fair - 1954. United Fund Co-Chairman - 1956. Red Cross Fund Drive Chairman - 1961. Advertising Man of the Year - 1980. Bradley University Board of Trustees - 1975-87. Proctor Hospital Board of Trustees - 1957-84. Chairman, Proctor Board of Trustees - 1976-79. Chairman, Proctor Health Care Foundation - 1987 to present. Governing Member, Health Education Center project - 1988 to present.

I first met Marv Hult in 1946, shortly after we both returned from service after World War II. I was managing the Madison Theater and we had arranged for a WMBD radio program to originate from the stage of the Madison. It was the Wayne West Show, sponsored by Kroger Food Stores. I walked into the auditorium just as a handsome young announcer stepped to the microphone with his hand to his ear, ala Gary Owens on television's "Laugh-In" show, doing the opening of the new program. It was the 25-year-old Marv Hult. We've been friends and business associates practically ever since.

Knowing Marv as well as I think I do, it's amazing the things I didn't know about him. He was born in Rockford, Illinois, the son of Harold and Ethel Melberg Hult. His father was one of five brothers who owned and operated the Superior Dairy there.

The family moved to Davenport, Iowa when he was very small and when he was eight, they moved to Peoria when his dad took a job with Roszell's Dairy. Marv attended Irving, Greeley and Columbia grade schools, Columbia Jr. High, and Peoria High. Then he attended Bradley in 1939 to '41 before he joined the Naval Air Force. He served on two aircraft carriers, the U.S.S. Copahee and the Bunker Hill in the South Pacific, and also flew as navigator-observer on anti-submarine patrol out of Midway.

It was here that a chance meeting led to Marv eventually achieving his then life-long ambition to become a radio announcer. A visiting USO troupe came through on a South Pacific tour. In the troupe was Lon Saxon, the music director of WGN in Chicago.

Walking along the beach, Marv told him of his ambition to be a radio announcer. Lon picked up some pebbles and told him to put them in his mouth and recite something. He also gave him other tips, such as lowering his voice

Marv Hult (right) explains a piece of business to Charley Caley, owner of WMBD-Radio. Jim Ebel is on the left. *(Photo courtesy of WMBD)*

range. When Lon got back to Chicago he sent him some material on learning to announce. Marv must have done his homework.

When he returned home he went back to Bradley, where he graduated in 1947. But in 1946, WMBD held an audition for a summer replacement announcer. Marv won the part-time job. He did everything. Regular radio commercials, inserts in the soap operas, big band remotes from the Ing and Père Marquette, and others. One local program he especially remembers is announcer for Milton Budd's Breakfast Club show each morning.

WMBD's owner and president at the time, Charley Caley, took an interest in this talented, enthusiastic young man, and Marv's rise in management was rapid. He became promotion manager and his first project was to promote the new WMBD Studios when they moved from the Alliance Life Building into the Majestic Theater. By 1948, he was a salesman, and in 1949 he became the national sales manager.

In this job, Marv traveled to all the major cities including the "big apple." One day he had been visiting CBS at their old headquarters on Madison Avenue in New York. Across the street was a "watering hole" that was frequented by many of the network's staff. Marv went in and sat down at a bar stool next to the legendary Edward R. Murrow. He introduced himself to Murrow, stating that he was from WMBD. Murrow looked it him and said, "Brook's Watson." In those days Brooks Watson was the radio newsman in Peoria. He, unfortunately, dropped dead of a heart attack a short time later.

Ed went on to tell Marv that Brooks was his right hand man during the blitz days in London during the war. He also said that of all the broadcasters, he would like to have Watson on his staff. Quite a tribute from probably the most respected newscaster in broadcast history.

By 1950 Marv was named Assistant Manager of WMBD. Then in 1951, after his good friend and WMBD program director Chuck Barnhart died an untimely death in a car accident, Marv succeeded him as P. D. Marv took over as manager of WMBD in 1952. He held this position until he left the station in 1957 to begin his own advertising business. Marv says he held every title in the station except engineer in those eleven years.

In 1957, Hult formed the Marvin Hult & Associates Advertising Agency. The company grew to become the largest ad agency in downstate Illinois. In 1982, he sold the agency to its corporation officers. It is now Hult, Fritz, Matuszak and Associates.

But Marv could never totally retire. In 1977, he and his partner, Larry Curran formed Air Vent, Inc., a national manufacturing firm with offices in Peoria. They sold Air Vent in 1986.

Marv and his lovely wife Shirley Browning Hult have two children, Randy, and Pam (Mrs. Dave Mabee.)

I won't say Marv started at the bottom of the ladder at WMBD, but let's put it this way. His first announcing job was as the area's first FM radio announcer with virtually no listeners. Hardly anyone had an FM radio back then. They had to do a promotion with Cohen Furniture Company to sell the merits of the, then, unheard of FM radio.

That's a pretty sneaky way to get an audience to listen to you, but our man Marv did it back in 1946.

..and it seems like only yesterday!

Marv Hult, Central Illinois' first FM radio announcer, doing the very first Peoria FM broadcast in 1946.

(Photo courtesy of Marv Hult)

Fall brings back memories of old-time bowling alleys

Here it is fall already, beyond a doubt my favorite time of the year. Not only because of the great weather. It also heralds the beginning of a participation sport that's nostalgic to me...bowling.

We have some very fine bowling establishments around our town today, but nostalgia sets in when I think back to when I was about six years old, and learned to bowl at the old Alps Bowling Alleys. I'll bet more than a few of you remember this combination tavern and four-lane bowling establishment at the corner of Frye, and Prospect Road. (There's a Convenient Food Store there now.)

Ours was a bowling family. Mom bowled in two or three leagues, and Dad bowled in several around town. In addition to the Alps, at one time or other, they bowled at the Saratoga, the Peoria Auto Parts, the F&J (Fulton & Jefferson), and I can faintly recall Dad bowling at the old Razz West Alleys up in Averyville.

When I began bowling, the Alps proprietors were Fred and Ede Wyss. The bowling alleys (we called them "alleys" back then, not "lanes") had hand-operated pin racks, manned by boys who were eager to earn 4¢ a line, while running the risk of being maimed for life by flying bowling pins.

The front end of the building had a corner entrance and was a tavern with pool tables, spittoons, brass rail, and was everything a "saloon" should be in those days. There was another hall-type room between the tavern and the bowling alleys, which also sported a pool table. I recall mothers putting their toddlers down for their afternoon naps on this pool table while they bowled.

At the far end of this room were a couple big open windows that overlooked the bowlers. Many an hour I sat there watching all the activity. I'd like to have all the nickels and dimes the adults gave me to buy Nehi root beer or Fridgie ice cream bars or whatever. I may hold the world record for Fridgie bar consumption.

When I first thought about writing about the Alps, I remembered that Joe Gorenz was the son of Ede Wyss. Many of you will remember Joe as a top-flight bowler. He was inducted into the Greater Peoria Bowling Association's Hall of Fame in 1970. Joe was a coal company representative for many years and is a long-standing member of the Creve Coeur Club today at age 89. But he was also a part-owner and operator of the Alps, with his mother Ede, and stepfather, Fred Wyss.

He has hundreds of stories about the old place, and his daughter Edith Gorenz (Mrs. Harold L. Anderson) provided us with photos of the Alps. Here's how Joe remembers some of the history of the place.

Joe Gorenz, Jr. as he appeared in the early days of the Alps. *(Photo courtesy of Edith Anderson)*

The Alps Beer Gardens opened in 1886 at the corner of President and Pacific. (This is now, Frye and Prospect). There were several acres of picnic grounds with picnic tables and parasols. Fresh mineral water fountains were on the grounds, mostly sulphur. A grotto was located on the side of the hill.

It was a very deep, high cave illuminated by candles and lanterns. Beer and food were served. It was delightfully cool in hot weather and warm in cold weather. Burrowed in the side of the hill, the cave was natural. The walls contained painted murals. Natural air vents kept the cave washed with fresh air. (A 1971 newspaper article mentions two bowling alleys here, but Joe doesn't recall that).

The four-lane Alps bowling establishment was opened in a building at 1300 Frye Avenue on this same corner but up from the grotto and beer garden. The property was owned by the Terre Haute Brewing Company and leased by a Mr. Fairbanks. He was part owner of the brewery and also the Hagenbeck & Wallace Circus. George Holt was the proprietor from about 1895 to 1910. Then Johnny Blanc took over the lease from 1910 to 1917. The four bowling alleys were formerly in Pete Weast's saloon downtown. They were thought to have come from St. Louis in 1895.

Johnny Blanc's lease ran out in 1917 and he closed the place, thinking the brewery would give him a better deal but they didn't. In November, 1918, Joseph and Edith (Slagle) Gorenz rented the property for $25 a month, but the bowling alleys were in bad shape and closed down. Prohibition came to Peoria on July 1, 1919, and Joseph Gorenz died five days later. He had been ill and was in St. Francis Hospital at the time.

Since the nation had gone "dry," the Terre Haute Brewery apparently wanted to rid itself of the property. Mr. Fairbanks approached Edith about buying it. She explained that she was broke and in debt, including a $200 hospital bill. So he made her an offer she couldn't refuse. He said, if she would continue to operate it, he would apply the $25 a month rent toward a payment to purchase the property. This included not only the building but also the acreage.

Ede agreed, but the bill collector was knocking on the door for the hospital bill. She agreed to pay 25¢ a week and the collector, Mr. Gorman, came out each week to collect the quarter, which he used to buy his lunch before he left.

Fred Wyss was a former Peoria motorcycle policeman. He was living with his brother Bill and his wife on Frye. Ede and her son Joe lived in a house adjoining the business, and Fred rented a room from them. He began working at the place doing all kinds of maintenance work, including putting the bowling alleys back into working operation. The alleys reopened in 1923.

Fred and Edith were married in 1925. Ede, Fred and son, Joe Gorenz, formed a

Edith (Slagle) Gorenz standing in front of her sign on the front of the Alps the year before she married Fred Wyss. It was taken on March 16, 1924.

(Photo courtesy of Edith Anderson)

partnership with each owning a third of the operation. Ede ran the business while Fred handled the general maintenance. Joe kept the books and handled the finances.

After prohibition was repealed in December 1933, beer and liquor were put in. I remember Kirby Frye was a bartender and Joe says Ed Pearce was their first bartender. Another one he recalls was Shorty Cobb.

But the big money came with the advent of gambling. At the peak of the city's wide-open gambling policy, they had nickel, dime and quarter slot machines, punch boards, and dice games. The slot machines alone took in $400 to $600 a week. But gambling was closed down two or three years later.

Eventually, Ede grew tired of working. She and Fred closed the business about 1942. The corner building was sold to the Shell Oil Company in 1945, and the rest of the property, including 14 building lots were sold to Attorney Vic Michael, where houses were built.

The Alps was part of both the quiet and not so quiet Yester Days of our town.

...and it seems like only yesterday!

Men and women bowlers at The Alps Bowling Alleys around 1930. Front row: My mother, Ann Adams, third from left (I'm just above her); Aunt Ethel Chamberlain, second from right. Cousin Betty Ann Chamberlain, is front right (with hand on ball). Top row: Uncle Ralph Chamberlain, fourth from left; Uncle Gene Adams, third from right; and my dad, Virg Adams, extreme right. The proprietors, Fred and Ede Wyss are also on right in second and third rows.
(From Bill Adams' personal file)

Jack Wedell band was popular here

About a year ago I wrote a column about two Peorians who were musical entertainers in and around our town. They later became man and wife, but they met when they were a part of a prominent musical group back in the 1930's. I'm referring to Dick and Marion (Harvey) Coffeen. Dick was a trumpet playing member of that band when Marion Harvey was its vocalist. The band I'm talking about was Jack Wedell and his Orchestra.

A few days later I received a call from David Wedell in McAllen, Texas. Ervin Knight had sent him a copy of YESTER DAYS and, since I had mentioned his brother's band, he felt compelled to call. His brother, Jack, had just passed away a couple months before that in Corpus Christi, Texas, and he wanted me to know.

I told Dave that I wanted to write about his brother's band, but lacked information. Since then Dave has communicated much, including reminiscences from Jack's widow, so let's go back to those great 1930's once again.

Our town and, for that matter, all of Central Illinois, was certainly blessed with big band music, especially during the '20's, '30's and '40's. Here's some that we've covered the past year and a half. Glen Gray, Tiny Hill, Joe Kilton, Ozzie Osborne, and Charley Cartwright, just to name a few, and there are many more to come.

But one group that took a back seat to no one was Jack Wedell and his Singing Orchestra. Jack was unique. He not only had a good big band, he was one of those rare orchestra leaders who also had a beautiful voice. When you look back at all the big name bands, there were only a handful that had this ability. Vaughn Monroe, Eddie Howard, Orrin Tucker, and maybe Tiny Hill, although Tiny's contribution was more novel. He certainly was not a ballad singer.

As a matter fact, Jack's voice was good enough to attract the attention of some of the biggest bands in the business. In the 1930's, he was offered $30 a week (a good salary then) to be a soloist for Lawrence Welk. Later on, he had an audition scheduled with Les Brown ("and his Band of Renown"), but he was ill and couldn't make it. His wife, Bonnie, says he should have called to change the date, but didn't.

A couple years after that, he had a wire from Harry James offering him an immediate job as vocalist. Bonnie says most any singer would have jumped at the offer (Frank Sinatra sure did) but Jack said he had too many signed contracts for his own band to take the offer.

The real reason, though, may have been a feeling of insecurity do to an eyesight problem. When Jack was an infant, he scratched his eyeball with his fingernail. He was taken to a doctor after the eye became infected, but instead of helping the problem, the doctor made it worse and the infection spread to the other eye. He suffered with the infliction for the rest of his life.

Dave Wedell was born on October 18, 1909, in Spokane, Washington. Brother Jack came along two years later, on December 7, 1911, in Hammond, Indiana. They were sons of John Carl and Anna (Barker) Wedell. As you might suspect, their dad was a traveling salesman. He sold women's ready-to-wear. Tiring of moving the family from town to town, he settled in Peoria and bought a house at 320 Maryland Street. This was near Glen Oak Park and dad thought it would be a good place to raise two boys.

Dave and Jack's Aunt Leita played saxophone in the Des Moines, Iowa, Ladies Band. Dave wanted to learn to play it, so Aunt Leita bought him a sax. Younger Jack would join in by keeping time beating on the dining room plates. He taught himself to play and eventually

Jack Wedell and his Singing Orchestra in a picture from the "Père Marquette Activities" brochure of March, 1934.

(Photo courtesy of Dave Wedell)

became an efficient drummer, in addition to his singing ability.

Ironically, Dave and Jack never played together. Dave played around town with other groups, while Jack eventually formed his own 10-piece orchestra. The Jack Wedell Orchestra became a mainstay in Peoria, playing at all the popular ballrooms, including the Inglaterra, the National Roof Garden, the Père Marquette, and most of the others.

Dave remembers an incident when Jack appeared at the Palace Theater. Another band was playing there and asked Jack to sing with them. It was an Armistice Day stage show and, for Jack to be a part of the group (they had their own drummer), the leader had a guitar strung with ordinary cotton string so that Jack could sit with the band and "play" the guitar, without being heard of course. Well, that's show biz!

The Jack Wedell band toured the midwest during the summers of 1934 and '35. It was during this time that Marion Harvey became the female vocalist and Dick Coffeen played first trumpet for the group.

Other members were Wilbur Frink, 2nd trumpet; Bob Terry, 1st alto sax; John Norrell, trombone; Len Bradley, 3rd alto sax; Lloyd McCain, piano; "Jocko" Lloyd Kimman, tenor sax; Carrol Hitchcock, string bass; and Hal Wasson, drums.

After his bandleader days, Jack became staff vocalist for WMBD and later for WGN, Chicago. And for a time he appeared with the Hal Kemp Orchestra.

Just the other day, Dave Wedell sent me a copy of a "Père Marquette Activities" brochure published in March 1934. It referred to itself as "Peoria's most distinguished hotel," which it certainly was. Jerry Gordon was the manager, and the hotel's musical director was Jack Wedell. Dave says that Jack's orchestra received more local press coverage than any of the big name bands when he went into the Père Marquette.

Here's the excerpt from that 1934 brochure:

"Through the soft multi-colored lights which sift down over the dancers each Saturday night in the LaSalle Room, comes the melodious voice of our own maestro, Jack Wedell, leading his sensational singing orchestra to please the patter of Peoria's dancing feet.

"Our regular Saturday night dances have become exceedingly popular for group parties. We should be happy to arrange a special table just for you and your guests. The cover charge is only fifty cents per person, and a la carte service assures you the selection of food that you desire."

1934...the Père Marquette...soft lights...and the melodious sound of Jack Wedell and his Singing Orchestra. I know to many of you out there

...this must seem like only yesterday!

Jimmie Bickel: Big star in Juvenile Theater

Having spent my 25-year career in broadcasting entirely with WEEK-TV and the companies that owned and operated it, many of my "friends" needle me for going back so often to the early days of WMBD-Radio. The reason for this is quite simple. Since the very first experimental radio stations, and up until WEEK-Radio came on the air in 1947, WMBD was the only station in town.

Now that I've explained that (at least to *my* satisfaction), I must go back once again. This time it's to remember a "big star" of WMBD's "Juvenile Theater," Little Jimmie Bickel. Jimmie and his older sister, Eleanor, were talented youngsters, the children of Henry and Mardell Bickel. The Bickel family lived at 307 Hanssler Place. Their next-door baby sitter was Mary Budd, (now Mrs. James Hayden) and, as you might suspect from the name, she was Milton Budd's sister.

Jimmie Bickel was a singer and dancer and a regular on "Juvenile Theater" from 1934 until 1941. Eleanor was "bosom buddies" with Mary Jane Doebler LeMaster, about whom I recently wrote. (Unfortunately, Mary Jane passed away shortly after the article). Eleanor became a professional dancer and was on the road

for several years with the Ernie Young Dancers. (Incidentally, Ernie Young was the producer who started Joan Crawford on her career).

But in 1939 for example, Jimmie Bickel starred in "Juvenile Theater" with another Jimmy...Jimmy Gent, and other outstandingly talented kids: Betsy Ross, Marjorie Burling, Doris and Margaret Ehrhart, Dale and Donald DeWitt, Harold Wright, Charles "Tiny" Timm, Joann Snyder, Marilyn Linden, Myrlene Wabel, Dorothy June Ristic, Nelma June Duggan, Judith Ann McDuff, Jean Power, Hazel Forde and Thelma Jean Paugh.

And by the way, these were not amateur entertainers we're talking about. They were all little professionals with very *big* talent.

Jimmie Bickel started his dance training in Peoria at the tender age of five. His first appearance was in Violet Holly's dance recital that year. Lew Goldberg managed the Palace Theater in those days, and he liked Jimmie so well he'd call his mother to bring him down to the theater so he could put him on the vaudeville bill. This was near the end of the vaudeville days, but he appeared with such big names as Pat Rooney, Sr.; Helen

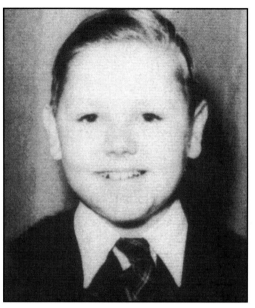

Jimmie Bickel in 1939 when he appeared on WMBD-Radio's Juvenile Theater.

(Photo courtesy of WMBD)

Kane, the original "poop-poop-a-doop girl" and composer-vocalist, Pinky Tomlin. Paul Ash had a large orchestra appearing at the Palace and wanted Jimmie to go on the road with them, but his mother was reluctant to do so.

Well, you probably haven't heard much about Jimmie or Eleanor around Peoria since the early '40's. The reason is that when Jimmie was still in his teens, the Bickel family moved to California. He hung up his tap shoes and went to college in San Francisco. After earning a degree in accounting, he had a successful career as a professional accountant in the field of public education.

A recent picture of Jim Bickel and his sister, Eleanor. *(Photo courtesy of Jim Bickel)*

Bickel had gone to Woodruff High School with Shirley O'Banion. When the family arrived in San Francisco, he heard that the O'Banion's had moved to San Jose, California. He went to visit them, and the result was that he married Shirley's sister, Betty O'Banion.

The Bickel's raised four fine sons and have recently celebrated their 40th anniversary. One of the sons is a professional musician in the San Francisco Bay area.

Jim and Betty live in San Mateo, 25 mile south of San Francisco. His father died a few years ago and his mother is now in a nursing home. His sister, Eleanor Bickle Witmer, now resides in Stockton, about 80 miles from San Mateo.

Jimmie's love for singing never left him over the years, nor his knowledge and ability to tap dance. In 1978, he did a little benefit show for his church and it went so well, he got the bug to perform again. This church show was the first time any of his sons had seen him dance.

He saw an ad in the newspaper that the Palo Alto Players were auditioning for "Guys and Dolls." He decided to audition and won a part as one of Nathan Detroit's dancing and singing gamblers. The show was highly successful and was such great fun, Bickel has been performing ever since.

To date Jim has appeared in 25 musicals with five theatrical companies on the West Coast. He's appeared with Gretchen Wyler in the San Jose Civic Light Opera's production of Stephen Sondheim's "Follies," and was also cast in a principal role in the Peninsula Civic Light Opera's "42nd Street."

Other musical performances include "Sugar," "Annie," "Evita," "Cabaret," "Carousel," "Annie Get Your Gun," "Fiddler on the Roof," "Funny Girl," "Once Upon a Mattress," "Dames at Sea," "Mame," "Anything Goes" and many more. In January of this year Jimmie appeared at the San Mateo Performing Arts Center in an All-Star Revue where he performed two old favorite numbers, "Million Dollar Baby" and "Louise." And just this August in the same theater, he sang, danced and acted in "George M." Jim says that all the scenes in this show about Mr. Cohan's vaudeville days had a very special meaning to him because of his early childhood appearances in vaudeville at Peoria's Palace Theatre.

Jim Bickel as he appeared recently in a west coast version of the musical, "Good News." *(Photo courtesy of Jim Bickel)*

All these musical productions are apparently not enough for Jim. In addition he has a cabaret-type musical act called "The Three J's," featuring Jerri, a female partner; Jim (himself); and Joan, their accompanist.

Jimmie is justifiably proud of the fact that he can still "hoof it" and keep up with younger ones less than half his age. And he wants all the folks back in Peoria who might remember him to know that James H. "Little Jimmie" Bickel is alive and well and is definitely "still kickin'" in San Mateo, California.

Time sure flies when you're having fun.

...and it seems like only yesterday!

A ride down Memory Lane on Peoria's old streetcars

One of the things I miss most about those good old Yester Days in our town is taking a streetcar ride. I can still hear the clanging bell as that orange "beauty" made its clattering way through our city streets and beyond. I can even smell the steamy heat inside on a cold wintry night, and I can hear the whir of its electric motor.

That's the great thing about nostalgia. All you have to do is think about it and you're there. Of course it's not as good as the real thing but it's not a bad second.

The reason I'm writing about it this week is because of a photographer friend of mine. His name is Lee Roten. And he told me about a publication that's coming out shortly, if it hasn't already.

You've probably noticed Lee's name under many of the pictures I've shown in the column. He has an outstanding collection of old local, historic photos and I lean on him quite a bit. When all else fails, Lee usually has just the picture I'm looking for.

But Lee has a friend by the name of Paul Stringham who is an absolute authority on the old streetcars, interurbans, and railroads. For many years, Paul's hobby has been these three modes of rail transportation, and back in 1964 he published a book titled "76 Years of Peoria Street Cars." It contained 97 old photos (more than half taken by himself) of Peoria streetcars and the most complete history of them I've ever seen.

Peoria's first streetcar made its very first run on January 15, 1870. The company was the Central City Horse Railway and they began with two cars that first day. The cars were small, and each was pulled by one horse. They seated 12 people and had five windows with venetian blinds on each side. Fares were 6¢, or 20 fares for $1.00. (The price was all the way up to 10¢ by the time I started riding them.) The line ran on Adams from South Street to the north end of the line between Hamilton and Fayette Streets.

The Central City Rail Road later bought out several companies that had been operating in Peoria, and on Sunday, September 22, 1889 at 11 p.m., they did a test run of our town's first electric streetcar. Regular service began the following morning. Their first five electric cars began operating between the north end of the line, which was by now at about 2000 North Jefferson Street, to the Union Station at Water and State Street.

These electric cars were rushed into service on that date because this was the opening day of the State Fair, which was held in Peoria in those days.

In 1979, Stringham co-authored a hardbound book titled, "Chicago and Illinois Midland Railroad." The other two authors were Richard R. Wallin of Springfield, and John Szwaikart of Brookfield, Illinois. It contains more than 355 illustrations, maps, reproductions, roster of motive power, and bibliography of the C&IM Railroad. Both this book and Stringham's Peoria streetcar book sold out, and the one on streetcars is a collector's item today.

Paul Stringham was born in Peoria in 1913, the son of Hubert and Cora Bostic Stringham. They lived at 303 Lydia Street and Paul went to Garfield Grade School and then Manual High, graduating in the Class of 1931.

He worked in the Rock Island Depot News Stand from 1933 until about 1955, when he went to work for Peoria Camera. Then from 1967, until he retired in 1978, Paul was associated with the Methodist Hospital Cafeteria.

But his lifelong interest has been rail transportation and primarily streetcars. This is because his father was foreman of the South Adams Street carbarn, between Western and Dodge. (The building still stands on the river side of the street.) But

Paul Stringham with his trusty 1936 vintage camera. *(Photo courtesy of Paul H. Stringham)*

he also credits Manual teacher, Frank Hardin, because he was the one who introduced Paul to photography. He was a charter member of Mr. Hardin's camera club, and he soon began using photography as a means to document the history of streetcars.

Stringham is 76 years old this year, so he figures it's a good time to issue a new,

updated version of the book he published 25 years ago, "76 Years of Peoria Street Cars." But there's another reason — 1989 is also the 100th Anniversary of Peoria's first electric street cars. The new book will contain some of the photos in the 1964 issue, but many of the pictures were not in the first one.

Paul began taking his own streetcar pictures in 1936 and continued until they stopped running in Peoria on October 2, 1946. He began researching the subject in 1950. Many of his photos show the personnel who operated the streetcars, and many of them show old scenes of Peoria in the background. The book is a nostalgic trip down memory lane and one I know many folks will want to take, whether they're streetcar enthusiasts or not.

Stringham's 1964 edition was published in Chicago, but this one is being published and printed right here in river city. The publisher is our old friend Lee Roten.

But this isn't the total story of Paul Stringham's rail books. He has been working for several years on another hardcover based on the interurban system that was so much a part of our early rail transportation. It's titled "Illinois Terminal — The Interurban Era." This one is being published in California by the Interurban Press and Paul is hopeful it will be released in November of this year. So it's a pretty busy time for this young 79-year-old.

And you know, it's very appropriate that Paul should come out with both a streetcar and an interurban book in the same year because, if you're old enough to remember, the streetcars and the traction both used the downtown streetcar rails at the same time many years ago.

Most oldtimers recall that the Illinois Terminal Depot was what is now the Peoria Police Station at the corner of South Adams and Walnut. But back in 1907 the IT Depot was located in the Mayer Office Building, (which later became the Pascal Hotel), at North Adams and Hamilton Streets.

Until the new depot was built in 1930, the interurban came into town up Walnut Street to Adams. It then proceeded up South Adams to Fulton, up Fulton to Jefferson, across Jefferson to Hamilton, then down Hamilton to the North Adams Street Depot. The traction would then begin its next trip south on Adams from the terminal to Walnut Street, where it would continue across the IT bridge to East Peoria and south to St Louis.

Paul Stringham's new, revised edition of "76 Years of Peoria Street Cars" is a wonderful trip back to those great Yester Days. The nearly 100 pictures alone are worth the price of the book, and the history is absolutely fascinating.

Can it possibly be 43 years since streetcars graced our city streets?

...it seems like only yesterday!

So long, matey...

This past July I wrote about a former TV associate of mine by the name of Stan Lonergan. As most Central Illinois "mateys" know, Stan portrayed the television character Captain Jinks, and held reign for nearly 20 years on WEEK-TV's legendary Captain Jinks Show. Sadly, Stan passed away this month, a victim of cancer.

It was because of his illness that I decided to not delay in writing about him last summer. Bill Houlihan had informed me that he was ill and had been receiving chemotherapy, so I called Stan and made an appointment to interview him.

He was feeling fairly well then, although he was completely bald from the therapy and obviously weak from the ordeal. But his sense of humor was just as keen as it had been back in the old days. The two of us began to reminisce and you could see Stan brighten as we talked about all the great times of early radio and TV.

We had a good time remembering, and I hope some of that joy came through in the column. Stan was truly talented and fun to work with. One of those people who could be very ordinary, yet very complex at the same time.

George Baseleon, announcer and weatherman at WEEK-TV, was Captain Jinks' first mate, Salty Sam, on the show's mythical ship, the S. S. Albatross. George passed away about four years ago at the age of 76.

So now that both Stan and George are gone, I can't help but go back and reminisce about my days working with these two and the sometimes crazy, sometimes serious experiences I remember so well.

"The Captain Jinks Show" began on WEEK-TV, (Channel 43, remember?), in the fall of 1956 and Stan assumed the role about a year later. He did the show alone until 1960, when George Baseleon put on the fake mustache and stocking cap and became Salty Sam. This, incidentally, was the same year I became the station's promotion manager.

The show enjoyed a good audience almost from its inception, but once Stan and George began bouncing their humor off one another, the show's popularity skyrocketed. I think one of the things that made these two work so well together was their difference in personality.

Stan, although he liked kids, was basically shy, and his Jinks character took on a W. C. Fields type of "arm's length" approach. This played well against Salty's warmth with the kids. If a child got too chummy with Jinks, he'd often revert to "Don't touch me, I'm a star." As Captain he could get away with it, while his first mate came laughingly to his rescue. The humor played well with kids and adults, alike.

Last July, I told some stories about Stan and the show, but here's a couple more I remember that occurred while I was promotion manager.

One of our town's big parades over the years has been, of course, the Santa Claus Parade. Back in the '60's we talked to the parade's producers and soon Jinks and Sam were a part of it. It wasn't long before they had their own float, and became a very important part of this annual event.

One year we arranged for Santa to be a guest on the show the same afternoon that the "jolly old elf" arrived in town in the annual Santa Claus Parade downtown. The parade ran long, ending just a few minutes before the program was to begin at the studios in East Peoria.

As promotion manager, it was my responsibility to get them there on time. So I was standing by as the parade ended in the 100 block of South Adams. I had my wife, Flossie's, Corvair Chevy coupe. It was small and believe me, there was just enough room in it for Jinks, Sam, a rather fat old gentleman named Santa, plus the driver. Obviously I was the only one who wasn't "incognito." By the time Santa was escorted off his float, we barely had time to make it to the studio.

I was driving over the Murray Baker Bridge and moving as fast as traffic would allow when the hood flew up on the Corvair, blinding my view. Traffic leaving town after the parade filled both lanes. It seemed like an eternity before I could slow the car down and stop on the side of the expressway.

As I got out, the passing cars were all honking at us and blowing their horns. I couldn't understand why until I looked back at the car. Here was Captain Jinks, Salty Sam and Santa, all piling out of the car to assist me with the problem. And I was the only one in the group without a fake beard.

But that wasn't the end of my dilemma. The hood of the car was sprung and now it wouldn't latch at all. There was nothing to do but take off my belt and use it to tie down the hood. Stan, in his usual good humor, offered to sit on the hood and hold it down, but I told him if I wanted a hood ornament, I'd rather it be something a little less conspicuous than a life-sized Jinks.

Well, we just made it in time for the show to begin. They ran into the studio for "the show (that) must go on" and proceeded to tell all of Central Illinois their harrowing experience at the hands of a crazy man by the name of Bill Adams.

Another experience I had with these two was even more memorable but rather than funny, it was both sad and heart-warming. It was also associated with the Christmas Season.

So long Captain! Stan Lonergan, who portrayed Captain Jinks on WEEK-TV's long-running "Captain Jinks Show", passed away in October, 1989.

(Photo from Stan Lonergan's personal collection)

Each year, Captain Jinks and Salty Sam would visit the children's wards at the local hospitals the week before Christmas. WEEK and advertisers on the program would supply gifts, which station employees would wrap so that they could give a gift to each sick child. It was my job to coordinate these visits and see that everything happened on schedule.

This particular one was at St. Francis Hospital's children's ward. Stan and George were, of course, in character, and the kids were eagerly anticipating their arrival. As we approached one room, Salty walked in first. Over in the corner in a crib, was a small child with bandages over his eyes. He apparently had just had an operation on his eyes and, obviously, couldn't see.

Salty Sam greeted the kids with "Ahoy, mateys." As soon as George spoke, this blind child shouted, "Salty Sam!" and held out his arms. George went over immediately and picked him up. The child put his arms around him, gave him a big hug and said, "I love you, Salty."

Well, I needn't tell you that both Jinks and Sam had a very hard time saying anything for the next several seconds. But, typically, George Baseleon carried this child all the way as they proceeded through the entire children's ward. I had to leave the scene. I had acquired a little eye problem of my own.

I've never forgotten the memory of that small child and how he hugged his good friend, Salty Sam.

Television is often (justifiably) criticized for what it portrays. But Captain Jinks and Salty Sam had a much more positive impact than even we realized at the time.

Thanks, Stan and George, for not only entertaining, but more importantly, for being friends to thousands of youngsters throughout Central Illinois (and to many of we adults, too).

...it truly seems like only yesterday!

The Bell keeps ringing up sales

Frankel family has been in clothing business since 1891

Bruce Frankel - As the future partner of The Bell appeared in 1954.
(Photo courtesy of Bruce Frankel)

History, nostalgia, entertainment. These three words best describe what this column is all about. All subjects are historic. Most are nostalgic to someone and as many as possible relate to entertainment. But once in a while we cover something that's not exactly in the entertainment field. This week's subject is one such, although the business has entertained the Frankel family in our town since 1891. I'm referring to a men's clothing store known far and wide as The Bell.

This fine store today is located at 4314 N. Sheridan, across the street from the Venture/Evergreen Mall complex and Peoria's first major mall, Sheridan Village. But it had its beginning "downtown" at 631-33 South Adams, where it held forth from 1891 until it closed on December 31, 1974. In addition to these two stores, the Frankels operated a third Bell store in Sunnyland Plaza from 1972 until 1983.

Flossie and I have become friends the past few years with its proprietors, Bruce and Dolores Frankel (Dee came into the store in 1982). Their son, David, worked in the store during his high school days, as his dad had done before him, and joined them in the family tradition in 1986. Talking with the Frankels about the business' history has been so enjoyable, I decided to write about it.

As best as can be determined, Bruce's grandfather, Harry, began a store on Bridge Street (later renamed Franklin Street) in 1891. That's the same year his brother Julius began his clothing store on South Adams, at the corner of Chestnut (later renamed State Street).

Possibly sometime before the turn of the century, the two brothers merged their businesses at this location. On Tuesday, September 5, 1905, The Bell ran an ad in The Peoria Star which also carried the name Julius Frankel and Co. with both Julius and Harry's names listed in the logo. This would indicate that they were possibly in the process of changing names at that time.

In any event, the store did change its name to The Bell Clothing and Shoe House, and the reason is an enterprising one, as well as fascinating.

Back in those days, around the turn of the century and later, Peoria had become a hub of rail transportation. As I've stated before, the first railroad train began operating here in 1854, and later our town had service from no less than 28 trains on Saturdays alone at the Union Station at Water and Chestnut (State) Streets. The horse drawn streetcars (and after 1889, the new electric streetcars) would bring their passengers from the Union Depot up to Adams and beyond. Those people, who planned to just shop on Adams, would walk two blocks up from the depot.

So, in order to attract potential customers to the Frankel Clothing Store, they hired a man to stand on the corner and ring an old hand-held school bell to get their attention. The brothers obviously came to the conclusion that The Bell would be an excellent name for their business, which it was.

Several years ago, Bruce talked to a man from Canton. He doesn't remember his name, but the man told him that he used to be a "sandwich man" who rang the bell for the store. He'd walk the street with a sandwich-type sign on, that advertised the store and he would also ring the bell.

Some time around 1910 Julius apparently sold his interest in the store to Harry. The reason is hazy but it may have been that there just wasn't enough business to support the growing Frankel family.

Julius then, again, went into business for himself. He would go out of town to buy soft goods at closeouts, auctions and the like, bring it back and sell it. He operated out of a store in the 400 block of S. Adams in the Gumbiner building. Julius later went into the real estate business with his sons, Harry A., Sam and M. J.

After Julius left The Bell, Harry, known by employees and customers alike as "The Boss," brought his sons Silas and Abe into the business. Harry died in 1943 and the sons continued as partners until Abe died in 1968. At this point Bruce became a partner with his father, Si, although he had been working in the store since his school days. Si passed away in 1986.

Bruce fondly remembers many stories about the old store before and during his association. One such is about the famous money conveyer that ran on a pulley attached to an overhead wire from the store clerks to the cashier and back.

This conveyance apparently operated from the stores beginning until the Adams Street location closed in 1974. At one time it was one of three such carriers which not only kept close control of cash transactions by one cashier, but also eliminated the need to buy expensive cash registers in the early days.

Twice the carrier smacked customers in the head. Si always said it was plenty high in the old days but the problem was that people were getting taller all the time. But old-time customers remember looking at the merchandise with one eye, and watching the flying copper cage with the other.

A September 8, 1934 picture of The Bell at 629-33 South Adams. The front of the building indicates the original store was 631-33. It later expanded to include 629, which had been Basil's Ice Cream Parlor.
(Photo Courtesy of R. W. Deller from Lee Roten's Historic Peoria Photo File)

Bruce also remembers that Uncle Abe had an aversion to advertising on the electronic media. He once bought a $3,000 package on Chick Hearn's WEEK-TV sports show in the mid-'50's. Bruce says it was a successful ad campaign but Abe never got over the cost of it. But when Uncle Abe died in 1968, it didn't take Bruce long to get on the radio. Abe was buried in the morning, and that afternoon Bruce signed a contract with WMBD-Radio for spots on the Milt and Bob Show.

As a child, Bruce lived in the 1100 block of N. Maplewood. After his first half year at St. Marks School, he went to Whittier, then Peoria High, Class of '49. When he was 17 he had polio, which laid him up in the hospital for eight weeks. He then graduated from Northwestern, Class of '54. He and his high school sweetheart, Dolores Stein, went together for seven years and married in 1954. They have three children, Becky (Mrs. Eric Clifton), Pamela (Mrs. Gary Schueller) and David, who recently married Ellen Kipfer.

Bruce has another fond memory of Grandpa Harry Frankel. He was a Russian immigrant, born in 1872 and naturalized in 1893. In the late '20's, his son Abe bought wheat in the futures market. Harry mistakenly thought that, since his son had bought wheat, they needed a place to store it. So he had the store's porter, Clarence, clean out the back room to make room for Abe's future wheat.

My first personal recollections of The Bell are through my Uncle Walt Heintz. The store was very popular with the skilled workers who mainly lived in the "South End." Uncle Walt was a photo engraver and he bought virtually all his clothes at The Bell. They were of good quality and, most importantly, they carried the union label. Uncle Walt was a union man through and through.

Surprisingly, to me at least, Bruce tells me this is still true today. He says about 90% of their suits are still union made. That has a nice "ring to it," if you'll pardon the pun.

Well, it's true. The Bell has "rung up" a lot of sales and friends since 1891.

...and it seems like only yesterday!

TV marked beginning of Hollywood's decline

...and those good old tearjerkers!

For my money, the golden era of Hollywood motion pictures was the 1940's and early 1950's. Maybe that's because it coincided with most of the exciting years I spent at the Madison Theater. I left the theater in early 1959 and during those last few years I saw the beginning of Hollywood's decline. The star system was on the way out and the studios were struggling with an upstart industry that we were actually forbidden to mention in management meetings ...television.

I wanted out, too. The handwriting was on the wall. Popcorn and candy sales were becoming more important than the boxoffice and the glamour of the movie business was gone. Theater managing was becoming about as exciting as running a drug store concessions counter. So, I devised a plan to force myself to leave a business I had really enjoyed, but was now beginning to dislike.

I took a job offered me by John McGinnis, to be production manager of TV TimeTab. From the beginning, I considered this to be merely a stepping stone to going to work for WEEK-TV.

Having lived next door to Bob Burton ("The Bounder"), a radio and television personality there, I met many of the people at that station. I felt, since TV had ruined the movie business, "If you can't lick 'em, join 'em!" So I did.

But from my ushering days in 1941, until I was drafted into the Navy after high school in 1944, Hollywood was in high gear. Of course the war gave the industry much great additional story material. The only negative was that many of the male stars went into the service, too. But they came back if you'll remember.

One of MGM's biggest promotional gimmicks was, "Gable's Back and Garson's Got Him!" What a line for Clark Gable's first post war movie, "Adventure," opposite Greer Garson. It played the Madison for a week starting Friday, April 26, 1946.

Although it was held over for a second week at the Rialto, the promotional line turned out to be better than the movie. But fans were hungry to see "The King" once again.

Promotion was a way of life on the local scene, too. In addition to action-packed war pictures, there were great "weepers" for the ladies as well. As a matter of fact we used to refer to them as "One (two, three or four) hankie" pictures, the way Jerry Klein and Bill Knight keep track with stars today.

By the way, one of these just appeared on cable TV recently. It was "Sentimental Journey," starring John Payne and Maureen O'Hara. The story line was about a dying actress (O'Hara) who adopted a little girl to give her husband (Payne) a companion when she was gone. This was a really maudlin weeper that was almost too uncomfortable to watch on TV.

But I suspect it had a similar reputation when it played the Madison beginning Saturday, June 13, 1946. Because it played only five days and our Class "A" movies almost always played for at least a full week back then. The other giveaway was that Hollywood gave it a title that was an obvious effort to fool the public into believing that it had something to do with a very popular song of the time.

Les Brown's orchestra, with vocalist Doris Day, hit the top of the charts in 1944 with their recording of "Sentimental Journey." Would Hollywood stoop to such an underhanded trick...especially back in those wonderful halcyon days? Are you kidding? By the way, the critics only rated it as a "two hankie" (I mean star) picture.

But the biggest "hankie" picture I recall was one that was perfectly titled and its star was one of Hollywood's biggest

Madison Theater newspaper ad that appeared on Sunday, Nov. 22, 1942.

Bill and Flossie Adams standing in front of the Madison Theater in June, 1946. "Sentimental Journey" was the movie playing and Bill had just returned from service that April. *(From the Adams' personal collection)*

and most beautiful females. The 1955 movie was "I'll Cry Tomorrow" and starred Susan Hayward.

Miss Hayward portrayed an earlier Hollywood star, Lillian Roth, who was a victim of alcoholism. She had many broken marriages because of it but overcame her problem in the end. This was at least a "four-hankie" picture that Leonard Maltin still rates at 3½ stars.

As an aside, there is an interesting story about Lillian Roth that concerns Peoria. For years a rumor floated around town that the real Lillian Roth had retired quietly and was living in a small home on Prospect Road in Peoria Heights. The rumor turned out to be untrue but it persisted here for a number of years.

"I'll Cry Tomorrow" was a theater manager's promotional dream. We had various tie-ins around town with book stores, department stores and the like. The promotion I recall most vividly was a tie-in with the linen department of Block and Kuhl's. We had several hundred folded linen handkerchiefs printed with the picture title and theater name, which were given out around downtown and in the store.

We used washable ink so the hankies could be reused. Flossie still has one of them. How did she get it? Well, she was one of our best criers. Although we never made any money off of her, she was a good barometer as to how many hankies we could predict on a given picture.

Great States Theaters (Madison, Palace, Rialto and Apollo in Peoria) were

very promotional minded in the '40's. They were always looking for different ways to plug a movie. We would have days, weeks and months (and sometimes years) using a certain promotional theme.

One such month was November, 1942 and the theme was, "Let's Get Acquainted!" In addition to the movie, newspaper ads ran artwork caricatures of some of the service staff. The Madison's ad on Sunday, November 22, 1942, showed line drawings of L.C. Worley, Manager. Len was actually city manager but the Madison's manager, Bill Harding, had just left for service. Worley was filling in until a new manager was named. (It turned out to be me in 1943).

Other employees in the ad were my, later, close friend, Bob Hagen, assistant manager; Louise ('Muz') Heath, cashier; Ethel Claudin (Muz's daughter), cashier; Wm. Adams (whoever he is), chief of service; Lenora Selburg, cashier; Jackie Huff, candy sales (nighttime candygirl); and Dorothy Graham, candy sales (daytime candygirl).

Oh, incidentally, the movie that week was "The Major and the Minor," starring Ginger Rogers and Ray Milland. And, not so incidentally, the prices at the Madison were: Adults — matinee 30¢, evening 40¢. Kids were 10¢ and 15¢. And this included a 10% Federal Defense Tax, too.

These were (mostly) days of great movies, great stars, great promotions and really great prices!

...and it seems like only yesterday!

End of baseball pool marked end of The Empire

Peoria got a "bum rap" back in the good old Yester Days. It acquired a bad reputation as being a wide-open "frontier" town, among other things. Well, I suppose it was wide open. But the interesting thing to me is that everything seemed to be run above board. There may have been deals made, but there was practically no gangster influence.

Virtually every drug store, newsstand or tavern operated punch boards and slot machines, and I suppose this was unlawful but it was obviously "winked at" by the city fathers, and as far as I know it all operated as a legitimate (at least in Peoria) business.

Although gambling was prevalent, there was only one major lottery-type operation and that was the baseball pool, and it held forth in the Empire Recreation Parlor and Restaurant at 139 S. Jefferson Street. Bill Urban was its proprietor and the business thrived until the baseball pool was closed down on May 29, 1953. Shortly after that the former cigar store closed its doors for good.

My dad was good friends with Bill Urban back then along with another Empire employee, Les (Babe) Scott. For several summers when I was a teenager, my family was invited up to the Urban's cottages on Upper Gull Lake, just north of Brainerd, Minnesota. These vacations are among my fondest memories.

I recently met Mr. and Mrs. William Hall. Bill's wife, Isabelle is a daughter of Ray Scott who also worked at the Empire, and we talked about those days. Babe Scott was her uncle, and he later bought the building that housed Jack Adams' Clover Club on Fulton Street.

I've also talked to Willard Urban who operates a tax accounting business on Western Avenue and also in Farmington, Illinois. Willard is the son of Bill Urban and remembers many of those days at the Empire, having worked there.

But Bill Urban was born in St. Joseph, Missouri in 1886. The family came to Peoria when he was about six years old. He married Emma B. Schultz of Peoria here on April 2, 1919. (He refused to be married on April Fool's Day.)

Bill and Emma had three children: Elaine, whose married name is Schneider, has for many years lived in Nashville, Tennessee, Willard R. and Mary Katherine, now Petruzzi, both of Peoria.

Bill Urban began working in the Empire as a young man for the, then, owner and operator, Billy Black. He began by cleaning cuspidors and racking up balls for the pool tables. Even then the Empire "Cigar Store" had gambling in the form of card games, punch boards, slot machines and the like.

After Black died, Urban bought the lease and continued to operate it as The Empire. According to Willard, his dad conceived the baseball pool idea and put it in operation sometime around 1918. The lottery was unique, and in no way was involved with fixing baseball games (Remember the Chicago Black Sox scandal of 1919?).

Baseball pool tickets cost 25¢ and you played it by shaking up "peas" with numbers on them from 1 to 16. Numbers 1 through 8 represented teams of the National League and 9 through 16, the American League teams. Each team was assigned a number. You drew eight peas, which represented your teams. The lottery winner was the one with the biggest cumulative total of the actual scores of the teams playing that day. There could be one or more daily winners.

20¢ of each 25¢ purchase went into the payout, the house kept 5¢. The daily total cash awards were big for those days, usually anywhere from $5,000 to $10,000.

The game was played seven days a week, and Saturdays were traditionally the biggest pots.

Now the Empire was strictly stag, no ladies allowed. So, in order to make it possible for women to play the baseball pool, Urban opened The Alcazar, just around the corner at 414 Fulton Street, which did cater to the ladies. The same game was played at both operations. In addition to that, this lottery was so popular, other taverns around town would buy tickets to take back and sell at their own establishments. The other taverns would mark them up another nickel, to 30¢.

And a Springfield business came in and bought several hundred tickets every week. That was Bench's News Stand there. These tickets were made up ahead of time, using old score cards. But Willard Urban was part of a big news story with his dad back in 1930. The two were kidnapped, and it made national headlines.

As he explains it, he was seven years old at the time. His dad had bought farmland out on Route 91, near 150, and they were in the process of building a barn. His dad took him along that day, and they drove over to Radnor to check on some lumber. On the way back to the farm, two cars blocked an intersection and four men took them captive. They had obviously been "cased."

They dropped young Willard off about two miles from home, and then took Bill to Chicago Heights where they held him for ransom for about a week. The ransom was ultimately paid and Urban was

An H. G. Crawshaw photo of The Empire building with its wrought-iron balcony across the front and cupola above the roof. As it appeared shortly before it closed in 1953.

(Photo courtesy of R. W. Deller from Lee Roten's Historic Peoria Photo File)

Some of the employees and customers in the Empire on May 29, 1953, its last day of the baseball pool. The sixth man from the right (peeking around the man in the straw hat) is Bob Petruzzi, who married Mary K. Urban.

(Photo courtesy of Bob and Mary K. Petruzzi)

released unharmed. The ransom was in the neighborhood of $100,000, a huge amount of money in those days.

The gang of four was headed by a Chicago hood named "Handsome" Jack Clutis. Willard says he was a brilliant young man who graduated with honors from Illinois University. The gang all wound up either killed or with long jail terms.

Kidnappings were becoming commonplace back in the depression days. This may have been the same gang that also kidnapped Frank Dougherty who owned the Inglaterra ballroom, and

attempted to kidnap Clyde Garrison and his wife as they were returning home one night. Clyde pulled a gun, however, and began shooting. His wife was killed in the crossfire.

But the Empire was more than a cigar store, poolhall, saloon or gambling hall. It also was an excellent restaurant. Mrs. Urban's brother, John Schultz, was the cook. They served excellent prime rib for 15¢. Pork sandwiches and hamburgers were 10¢, and they were noted for their excellent chili.

Well, today's off-track betting parlors, the state lottery and the future riverboat gambling has nothing on Peoria's biggest lottery of yesterday, the baseball pool at Bill Urban's Empire. The only difference is, now they've made it legal.

...and it seems like only yesterday!

Band's one-night stand lasted 25 years

I've talked about many musical groups who've played in our town over the years, including Tiny Hill more than once. But there's another Hill who's been a big part of the scene since the late '30's, and he's still doing his thing today. I'm referring to a great guy and fine musician, Billy Hill.

Willis Howard Hill was born on Idaho Street in Peoria, the son of Howard and Clara Hill. His parents divorced when he was three and Bill lived with his grandparents for four years on a farm at Cramer, Illinois. His mother, then, married Allen Rice and Bill, his mother and step-father lived in Hanna City, Peoria, Washington, and then again in Hanna City. He graduated from Farmington High, Class of '40.

He remembers that his family was poor when he was a child, and while living on Armstrong in Peoria, he liked music but couldn't afford an instrument. So he filled old beer bottles with varying amounts of water and made his first music by hitting them with a stick. Seeing his interest in music, his step-father bought him an old guitar.

After they moved to Washington, the McKinney School of Music would come there and give lessons at the Community Center. He later took guitar lessons from Floyd Mathews in Peoria. When the family moved back to Hanna City, Walt Williams and Johnny Nack took him under their wings, and he played with them.

Bill has the distinction of leading the orchestra for the first, ever, dance at the Hub Ballroom in Edelstein. He says it was more of a farm implement show than a dance. He played guitar in a 9-piece orchestra from Farmington called Eleanor McKinney and her Music Makers. They were hired to play the Hub, but, since Eleanor played piano, she had Bill wave the baton. He was devastated because he had to lead the band instead of play guitar.

Hill served in the Coast Guard during World War II from 1942 to '45. About 1947 he played in an orchestra on the Idlewild riverboat that plied the waters of the Illinois and Mississippi Rivers that summer. Others in that band included "Bugs" Burnham, Eb Campbell, Jack Edie, Bill Trone, Bud Weaver and Dick Mills (who later went with the Charlie Spivak orchestra.)

The Idlewild season ended in the fall, and in October 1947, Billy formed his first "Billy Hill Trio," and went to work at a place called Earl's. It had formerly been Tony's Subway. It was here in February, 1948 that Bill met his future wife, Marilyn Hinds. She and her identical twin sister, Marcia, came in one night with Chuck Etter who played with the Charlie Barnet band. That December they were married.

When Bill and Marilyn were dating, she couldn't play, although she was a big band fan. One night he took her to the Clover Club and they saw the "Stan Nelson Trio." Stan's wife played bass fiddle and Marilyn thought she'd like to try it. So Bill taught her. They later formed a trio, which included Marilyn's twin sister, called the "Twin Tone Trio." It consisted of Marilyn on bass, Marcia on combo drum, and Billy on accordion. (He says he began playing accordion because all the pianos were out of tune.)

About 1949 Billy met Vernon Combe. He and Marilyn decided to go on the road, so they joined Vernon in Detroit where he lived. Verle Bogue, who had a band here for several years, was an agent for MCA at the time, and he booked them around the Michigan area. They were known as the "Vernon Hill Trio." Bill on piano, Marilyn on bass and Vern on guitar.

One of their favorite rooms was in the Rowe Hotel in Grand Rapids, Michigan.

All the big names would stay there and they met many of them, including Guy Lombardo and his brother, Carmen; the four Ames Brothers and their wives (Ed was a blonde then); and the man who started Perry Como on his career, Ted Weems. One of Billy's best stories is about Ted.

Back in the prohibition days Ted Weems' orchestra played in the speak-easys in Chicago. He told Billy that the gangsters would come in and request songs for the orchestra to play. When the "hoods" would stump the orchestra with a song they didn't know, one of them would pull out a gun and shoot a hole in the bass drum.

This gave Weems an idea. He created a radio program in 1940, featuring his 14-piece band and singers, Perry Como and Marvel Maxwell (Marvel became Hollywood star, Marilyn Maxwell), "Country" Washburn, and blind whistler, Elmo Tanner. The show's name was "Beat the Band," and its MC was Gary Moore.

Weems invited Billy to join his orchestra but Hill didn't enjoy the life on the road, so he and Marilyn came home in 1952. He went to work for Byerly Music and she took a secretary job with the Junior Chamber of Commerce. They had two children, Mark and Becky, and Billy later opened his own Hill Music Co., first on War Memorial Drive near Prospect, and later on California Street.

But upon returning to Peoria, they also organized the "Billy Hill Trio," with Bill, Marilyn and Bob Dubois on trumpet. Then Frank Clary joined them on drums

Early photo of Billy Hill's five-piece orchestra. Left to right: Ben Curtis, vibraharp; Frank Clary, drums; Lance Willock, trumpet; Billy Hill, accordion; and Marilyn Hill, bass.
(Photo courtesy of Bill Hill)

to do a club date in Canton, and they became the "Billy Hill Four."

Their longest reigning job, however, began in 1954. Dick Raymond's orchestra was the house band in the Hotel Père Marquette. Dick had booked his band out of the hotel one Saturday night, and asked Billy if he could fill in for that date. Billy did and, not only played that night, they remained in the Peoria Room for the next 25 years, until 1979. (Not a bad one-night stand).

Over these years the band varied from five to ten pieces, depending on the hotel's needs. Then about 1976, they went back to four pieces. And over these years many local musicians were a part of the Billy Hill orchestra in the Peoria Room.

Gene Farris was one of the early ones, and Gene still entertains around the area

with his singing and great piano. But back in the '50's with Billy he played tenor sax. (Hill says he didn't even know Gene could play piano then.) And today Gene is hard to stump on a song he doesn't know but back then Billy says the only song he'd sing was "Pink Elephants."

Others who have contributed their talent over the years are; Lance Willock, Ross Summerville, Gene Foster, Wally Marsh, Dave Moore, Chuck Cunningham, Ron Swenson and many more. The, later, four-piece group with Billy and Marilyn included Mike Grimm and Chris Curtis.

When Marilyn died in June, 1984, Billy laid out for awhile, but music is so much a part of him, he had to get "back to work." He began again with Mike Grimm and Ron Swenson. Billy has since written a song dedicated to his wife, titled "Marilyn," but he doesn't do it publicly. He can't get through it.

But the great music rolls on. Today Billy sometimes plays single for private parties and other dates, but the trio appears around the area as well. Two favorite places are Uncle Al's in Sunnyland and The Chateau in Pekin. Today's trio features Joe Frakes who sings and plays drums, and Ron Swenson on sax, with Billy at the keyboard.

Twenty-five years in the Père Marquette's Peoria Room. What a one-night stand.

...and it seems like only yesterday!

George Manias settles down

Shoeshine parlor & hatters in its fifth location

Some earthshaking news happened recently in downtown Peoria. The "World Headquarters" moved to a new location. Not only that, this was the fifth move downtown in its long and prosperous past. You doubt this rather dubious statement? Well, don't take my word for it, talk to Ray Becker. Or, better yet, go directly to the source himself, George Manias.

Okay, so I'm not talking about Caterpillar. I'm referring to maybe its most famous neighbor, George's Shoeshine and Hatters, which has also been dubbed World Headquarters. Its latest move brings these two world powers "CATercorner" across the street from one another. Is there a merger in the offing? If so, George isn't talking.

As I understand it, several years ago Ken Gerber, with an assist from some of the top Cat executives, gave George's the World Headquarters moniker. Its chief executive, George Manias, is a friendly, gentle man. And many know he was, without doubt, the best friend of another man we wrote about recently, one Robert Merle "Chief" Coy.

For years Chief made George's his own personal headquarters. But what you may not know is that, even though George speaks with a thick Greek accent, he is actually a *native* Peorian, born at Proctor Hospital, (when it was still on Second Street). How could this be? Well, George's father, Emanuel, came to America from the town of Rethimnon on the Isle of Crete, Greece, in 1906. He settled in Canton and worked in a factory for $1.00 a day. And, believe it or not, he saved enough money to open his own combination grocery and restaurant there. Around 1909 he moved to Peoria and opened another restaurant in the 500 block of South Adams.

Emanuel became a U.S. citizen and was drafted in World War I. He served from 1916 to '18. After the war he bought back the same restaurant, which he ran until 1928 when he returned to the old country to get married. He brought his bride, Katena Atklidakis, back to Peoria in 1929. He tried to buy back the restaurant, but the owner wouldn't sell, so he opened another one further south in the same block of South Adams.

George's sister, Angela, (who now runs Angela's Candy Nuts & Stuff in the Twin Towers) was born at St. Francis Hospital in 1930 and George was born at Proctor in 1931. But in 1936, George's grandparents were ailing in Greece, so his father sold once again and moved the family back there to take care of them. George's younger brother, Emanuel, Jr. was born there in 1937.

His grandparents both died, and Emanuel, Sr. was having the paperwork prepared to move back here, when World War II broke out. Crete became occupied by Italian and German troops in the spring of 1941. This became a dangerous and scary time. The enemy discovered that Emanuel was a U. S. citizen, took his money and possessions, and threw him in prison.

George was made to peel potatoes, dig trenches, and worse. He recalls seeing a man steal a loaf of bread to feed his starving family. The soldiers caught him, made him dig a hole and they buried him alive in it. There was a curfew at sundown. If anyone was found on the streets after dark, they were shot.

After Crete was freed by the Allies, George's father was released from prison. Having no money, he applied for a loan, and the family returned to America in 1945. Angela was 15, George was 14, and Emanuel, Jr. was 8. None of the kids could speak English.

George's sister and brother went to school, but George got a job shining shoes at the Paris Shoe Shine Parlor, and he went to night school at Woodruff to learn English. After about six months he went to work for the Rialto Cleaners &

Hatters. Phil Storey taught him how to clean and block hats. Then he bought one shoe shine chair, put a sign on the sidewalk, and "George's Shoe Shine Parlor" went into business in Ed and Roy's Barber Shop, next to the Rialto Theater. At night he and brother, Emanuel, moonlighted by cleaning Hickey's Restaurant and the Rialto theater.

He remained at Ed and Roy's until late 1950, when he opened George's Cleaners, Hatters, & Shoe Shine Parlor in the old Niagara Hotel Building at 106 S. Jefferson. He was 19 years old. George might still be at that location if it weren't for progress (something he's had to learn to contend with ever since).

After 18 years there, the Niagara Hotel was torn down in 1968, so George moved to 402 Fulton, next to the Fulton News Stand. Later, Ray Becker bought the building for the location of his new Twin Towers development. Ray had become a good friend and customer of George's. He told him he'd have to move, but not to worry about it. He'd help him find another choice downtown location, which he did.

In March of 1980, with Becker's help, George again moved his business. This time to the 100 block of South Jefferson in the Lehmann Building. Ironically, this was just across the street from his old Niagara Hotel operation. There was nothing in writing between Ray and George. It was done with a handshake.

But progress once again crossed George Manias' path. Now it's time to tear down the Lehmann Building so, once

Every chair is filled with men and women at the Fulton Street location, getting their shoes shined by George and Charles. Standing at left is Ken Gerber of Caterpillar.
(Photo courtesy of George Manias)

again, his friend Ray Becker came to his aid. Ray bought, and is completely refurbishing, the old Central Bank Building for the new home of his Community Bank. And who has the choice location just inside the main entrance? None other than George's Shoeshine and Hatters.

So, man and boy, George Manias has had no less than seven downtown locations over the years, and the last five have been his own business. Today's new plush operation is one you can see in his prideful eyes. George is president of this world headquarters and his partners are vice president, Charles Holk (with him over the past 35 years), and Jimmy Tillman, assistant to the vice president (12 years).

And over the years many world dignitaries visiting Peoria have come to George's for a shoe shine. Caterpillar executives bring people there from all over the world, as does his good friend, Bob Michel and others.

Back in 1982 Congressman Bob brought one of his best friends in for a

The Manias family posing in the Lehmann Building location (this was after Emanuel, Sr. had passed away). Left to right: Emanuel, Jr; Angela; mother, Katena; and George Manias.
(Photo courtesy of George Manias)

shoe shine, President Ronald Reagan. The president sent George a nice letter from the White House thanking him for his fine service. In December, 1986, USA Today ran a front page story and color photo of George and Charles Holk posing with the letter, and it was seen by their friends all over the free world.

But for many years George's was also headquarters for his good friend Chief Coy, who became a fixture there for many years. When Chief became ill and began to suffer from Alzheimer's, George saw to it that he had his meals, visited him at the Hotel Jefferson, and finally had him moved into the nursing home. At the end, the only one Chief could remember was his best friend, George.

So George, now that you have made (hopefully) your last move, I can think of nothing more fitting to do than repeat the words of your old friend, Chief Coy. Have a "Lovely Day!"

...and it seems like only yesterday!

C.C. Castle's sing-song radio ads still remembered

Several years ago Bill Little's daily column included an inquiry from a reader, Sherman O. Miller, about a man by the name of Charles C. Castle. Mr. Miller had run across an old song attributed to him titled "Peoria-We Do."

I contacted Bill about it at the time, as I knew a little bit about Mr. Castle. Another one who wrote him was a daughter of C. C. Castle, Mrs. Mary Leaver of Pekin. Mr. Castle was an accomplished musician and Peoria businessman who was prominent in the South Side Businessmen's Association, and died relatively young. After digging deeper into his background, I've found other facts about him that you might find interesting as well.

Like so many people with artistic talent, Charley Castle had many jobs and businesses as a young man. At one time or other, he was a barber, a music teacher, a music store proprietor, a candy salesman, an insurance salesman, a real estate broker, a merchandising counselor, and a newspaper advertising salesman. But his great love was music, and with his obvious sales ability, he was making local "music" with it until his untimely death.

Charles Cameron Castle was born on April 24, 1886, in Washington, Indiana. He was the son of Thomas Edgar and Mollie Lawrence Castle, and he probably got his newspaper interest from his father.

His mother wouldn't move with his dad who went out West in 1889 to pursue his craft as a newspaper printer. In 1915 he became editor of "The Madisonian" newspaper in Virginia City, Montana, and later became owner and publisher. It was the successor to the "Montana Post," the first newspaper in the Montana Territory. But Mollie and three-year-old Charles stayed in Pekin, and after a divorce, she married Frank Knoll. Young Charles used the name of Knoll, until he achieved adulthood and married Minnie Sunken.

He and Minnie had three children. Mabel was born in 1906 (She later married Mark Sommer of the Keystone Steel and Wire family). A son, Charles Cameron, Jr. or "Bud" as he was known, was born in 1907, and another daughter, Helen J., was born in 1914. Helen died in December, 1916 of spinal meningitis at age two. His wife Minnie had also died in 1915 in the TB Sanitarium at age 27.

Helena Wierschem lived with her parents, John and Mary Albers Wierschem, on Sumner Avenue in the "south end." In 1917 Charley was a barber, with his C.C. Castle Tonsorial Parlor at 825 Lincoln Avenue near Sumner. He also had a music store next door where he sold Gibson guitars and other string instruments, and gave music lessons.

Helena was a very pretty girl, and she would walk up to Herzog's Tavern (next to Charley's barber shop) to get a pail of beer for her German parents. When Charley saw her coming with her empty pail, he'd run out the back door of his barber shop to the tavern next door. He'd arranged it to wait on her. They married in August of 1917 and had four children; Vernon Julius, Mary Lou (who wrote to Bill Little), Florence Evelyn and Thomas Edgar.

As mentioned, Charley tried many means of endeavor in his short life, but the two major ones, music and advertising, stayed with him. He was an excellent salesman, and had a knack of incorporating his music into some very unique promotional ideas. He taught music, especially in the string instruments, and at one time had his own all-string orchestra. He also published instructions on how to play. A specific one I've seen is on how to play the mandolin. He also composed both words and music.

Back in the early radio days he got the idea of writing songs and jingles as a means of advertising various businesses and products. I'll bet there are more than one reading this that recall a slogan for a

Charles C. Castle (center) and his all-string orchestra, circa 1920. Others members unknown. Can you identify any of them?
(Photo courtesy of Mary Castle Leaver)

Charles C. Castle and the front cover of his song, "Peoria-We Do!," as it appeared in the Peoria Journal Transcript on June 2, 1929.
(Photo courtesy of Mary Castle Leaver)

local jewelry store. Do you remember "It's Okay to Owe Kay"? Well, that identification line came from a song Charlie wrote especially for Kay's Jewelry Store and it was heard hundreds of times on WMBD-Radio. Another musical jingle was written for a famous local beverage. It was titled "Rostock Peoria Beer."

By 1927 C. C. Castle was working for the Daily Journal Company. Its publisher was Henry M. Pindell and its papers consisted of The Peoria Transcript (morning), The Peoria Journal (evening) and the Sunday Journal-Transcript. Charlie worked for Mr. Earl H. Maloney, its advertising manager. He handled the advertising of Peoria's South Side, and also wrote a column called "South Side Smiles." He had found his vocational niche.

But he also continued to write music and brain-storm other advertising ideas to promote his songs. In 1930 he printed a business card listing his home address and

"C.C. CASTLE, Composer-Publisher of Castle's Catchy Songs". It showed a price list for a front cover ad on his sheet music. This particular one was a song titled "When You Go To Church On Sunday," and he sold it to the Zion Lutheran Church on Easton Avenue.

Mr. Castle must have been an above-average salesman because he, not only sold advertisers, he obviously sold his employers at the newspaper, too. From 1929 until 1931, his songs appeared in the Journal-Transcript Sunday edition, in the form of sheet music. A full-page was used with two quarter-page ads side by side at the top. The sheet music was printed upside-down on the bottom half of the page. When you folded it in half, then folded over the quarter-page, you had a front and back ad for two advertisers, plus two pages of his words and music inside.

I'm aware of 12 of his songs that were published in the Sunday paper. Some of the titles are: "Let's Be Sweethearts Again" (a song he wrote when he and Helena temporarily separated), "Why Did You Play With My Heart?," "When You

Go To Church On Sunday," "Remember The Golden Rule," "Love Or Gold," "Girl And Boy Scouts" (Grand March), "Oh! But You're It," "I Will Tell My Daddy Bye And Bye," and, of course, "Peoria-We Do." (Although it wasn't listed in the Peoria paper, he also wrote a song for our neighbor city titled, "Pekin Has It.") And some of the advertisers who appeared with the songs were Schwab's Dairy, Peoria Baking Co., Adam J. Kohl Insurance, P.&P.U. Railway, Peoria Water Works, Illinois Light & Power, and the Père Marquette Hotel.

Charley also copyrighted ideas other than his songs. He wrote many books, one of which explained legal words and phrases to the public, aimed at getting lawyers to advertise. (He was obviously ahead of his time.) Another book was titled "Our City," and contained a 52 week newspaper ad campaign based on "Patronize the merchants in Peoria (Our City). They are reliable and fair."

Mr. Castle was successful with his many endeavors and was still with the newspaper when he died of a sudden heart attack in 1934 at the age of 48.

I never met Charles C. Castle but he was, obviously, an interesting and creative man. I wish he would have lived at least a few years longer because, you see, he would have been my father-in-law. But he passed away when my wife, Flossie, was just eight years old. She was a much more mature 15 when I first met her while I was ushering at the Madison.

...and it seems like only yesterday!

Journal Star Christmas Sing part of Peoria's tradition

Many holiday traditions have evolved over the years in Peoria's history. Some live only in our memories, while others have continued over the years to be a part of our lives even today. A perfect example is the Santa Claus Parade.

But such is also the case tonight with an annual event in the Courthouse Plaza when Mayor Jim Maloof once again leads thousands of Peoria-area folks in songs of the Christmas Season. It's the Journal Star's Annual Christmas Sing. Courthouse Square has been its home since it began on December 22, 1948. That very first Christmas Sing was created and sponsored by the then Peoria Journal. When the papers merged in 1954, it became the Journal Star Sing.

Maybe some of you were part of that crowd of 8,000 on the east side of the "old" courthouse that cold night in 1948. If so you remember that its MC was WMBD's Milton Budd. And the female soloist was the young lady who remained a part of it for many years, Miss Ann Dooley, (now Mrs. Stan Steinau). Another musicmaker from WMBD was its organist that very first night, Herman Hampy.

But in addition to that fine group, the first crowd was entertained by the combined choruses of Caterpillar Tractor and R. G. LeTourneau. They were alternately led by Caterpillar's chorus leader, Tom Godspeed, and LeTourneau's leader, Henry Esser.

Three local radio stations carried the event. WWXL did a direct broadcast at 9 p.m., while WEEK delayed its broadcast until 10:15 p.m., following the news, and WMBD carried it the next morning between 7 and 8 a.m. on Milton Budd's "Musical Clock" program.

On that first sing the words to the Christmas Carols were printed in the Peoria Journal the day before and readers were asked to tear them out and bring them with them. The next year a large sheet was put up and the words were projected on it for all to see.

The second annual sing on December 22, 1949, was a bitter cold one. The 12° temperature held the crowd down to around 3,500, but those that attended once again warmed the air with their exuberance. Its MC was another WMBD favorite, who was as round and jolly as Santa himself, Wayne West. Ann Dooley and Herman Hampy, once again, lent their talents. This time the Keystone Choristers, directed by John Diemer, provided additional caroling. The first projectionist in 1949 was motion picture operator Nick Frasco. Nick stayed on as a fixture in that capacity until 1970. He retired in 1971, and he and his wife left town to join the Peace Corps.

In 1950 a crowd estimated at 7,000 braved the 6° temperature. That year's song leader was Howard D. Kellogg, Jr. who joined MC Charles Barnhart of WMBD, and soloist Ann Dooley. This one also featured the Junior Red Cross Choraleers, made up of high school students, led by Joann Jordan with Mrs. Shirley Mannion, advisor.

In 1951 Howard Kellogg became MC as well as male soloist, and he and Ann Dooley remained a part of the Christmas Sing until it took a hiatus from 1961 through 1966 while the new courthouse was being built and the old one was torn down. Old friend Ozzie Osborne replaced Herman Hampy as organist in 1952.

That last Sing for Howard Kellogg and Ann Dooley in 1960 was a memorable one for them for another reason. The temperature dipped to 1° below zero and frost bite became a real concern for the 300 brave souls who came out that night. To make matters worse, Howard came with a bad case of laryngitis, and baritone James Bowers conducted the second half of the program. It also took two electric heaters and a charcoal grill to keep Ozzie Osborne and his fingers from freezing to the organ.

By 1967, the courthouse work was completed and the Christmas Sing resumed once again, to the delight of young and old alike. Dirk McGinnis took over as song leader-vocalist and he also directed the "Young Folk" who came to lend their young voices to the festivities. The organ music was once again in the capable hands of Ozzie Osborne, but this time the weatherman cooperated with a comparatively balmy 37°.

In 1968 a young man with a strong tenor voice took over as MC and song leader. Jimmy Maloof had already been entertaining Peorians for more than 25 years. Jim became song leader and master of ceremonies, a role he has handled ever since. He received a 20-year plaque last year as he began his third decade with the Christmas Sing. 1968 also saw a return of the Young Folk, this time under the direction of Gene Holmes.

Ozzie Osborne continued as organist through 1979, and the following year Tom Neal provided the organ music. In 1981 Ozzie's former partner Rox Bucklin assumed the sometimes bone-chilling job, and he's been doing it ever since.

Only once has a scheduled Christmas Sing been cancelled and it was due to impossible weather conditions. Dave Schlink, Journal Star Public Affairs Director, has been supervising the event since the early '70's. In 1983, the County Health Department advised him to cancel

Getting ready for the 1957 Christmas Sing. Seated, Ann Dooley. Standing, (left to right); Howard Kellogg, Howard "Lefty" Tyler (Peoria Journal Star); and Ozzie Osborne.

(Photo courtesy of the Peoria Journal Star)

the event. He did so, reluctantly, but it was a wise decision. That night the temperature dipped to 10° below zero. That and an accompanying high wind caused a windchill factor that would have been dangerous to all who might show up.

When Nick Frasco left in 1971, projectionist and stagehand Harold Johnson, took over the projection work until 1983. By now Harold was in his '70's and his eyesight was failing, but he still came and climbed up to that cold booth every year to contribute to this community event. Harold died the following May at age 74. Harold's son, Loren Johnson, helped his father his last three years, then took over the duty in 1984 and will continue to do so tonight.

There is an amazing statistic concerning the Christmas Sing. In its 42-year existence, just seven people have served as master of ceremonies and singers: Milton Budd, Ann Dooley, Wayne West, Charles Barnhart, Howard Kellogg, Dirk McGinnis and Jim Maloof. And Jimmy has presided over 22 of the 42 years. And in all that time there have been just four organists; Herman Hampy, Ozzie Osborne, Tom Neal and Rox Bucklin; and three projectionists; Nick Frasco, Harold Johnson and Loren Johnson. This has to be a labor of love.

The invocations have been given by so many of the clergy of various denominations. This tradition began with Dr. Leonard Odiorne in 1948, and continued with Catholic Bishop John Meyers last year. Tonight, Reverend Ben Baier of Faith Missionary Church in Bartonville will do the honors.

The past two years Andi Bedel has been song leader for the hearing impaired. Tonight this will be handled by Lois Reese. Also tonight Santa (Neil Skow) and the Shrine Funmakers will also entertain as they have done in past years.

So, "O Come All Ye Faithful." Bundle up, bring your family and friends. Feel the inner warmth and pleasure of singing with joyful hearts as area families once again get into the true Christmas spirit of togetherness and sharing.

1948...the First Annual Christmas Sing.

...and it seems like only yesterday!

Christmas at the Madison

Back in the 1940's and '50's, our family Christmas was tied in closely with the Madison Theater. Not by choice, but by necessity. The reason was that, as a theater manager, I spent long hours working (over 80 hours a week), including every holiday. Our children were growing up in front of my eyes, and I wasn't able to give them my quality time. Frankly, I was developing a deep feeling of guilt, and it's the main reason I decided to make a vocational change in 1959.

But the Christmas season was always a special occasion at the Madison, which had its fringe benefits. Len Worley and I spent many hours decorating its interior. We started when Santa hit town, and by the time New Year's rolled around, we had overdone the trimming by more than a little bit.

Len and his wife, Lottie, had no children, so their Christmas was the theater. Len and I had our differences but, over the years, we developed a father-son relationship. We would string streamers across the outer lobby, along with appropriate lights and evergreen boughs. The huge Christmas tree went into the center of the main inner lobby, between aisles two and three. Len bought too big a tree each year. This huge beauty would always have to be cut shorter to fit in the oval circle of the inner lobby, extending up into the mezzanine foyer. It really was the perfect location for a Christmas tree.

But the concession stand was probably the most sinfully over-decorated area in the entire theater. Our candy sales should have taken a noticeable drop because, by the time Christmas Day arrived, it was all a customer could do to see the candy in the case. It was bad enough before, but when they came out with flocking in aerosol spray cans, Len used it so generously on the glass and mirrors, it was dangerous to get your clothing near the area.

Back in the days after World War II, the employees all chipped in and bought Worley a Sealyham Terrier. His pedigree name was Mr. Frost, which soon became Frosty. This dog became as loved (and spoiled) as any child ever could. He was the child the Worley's never had.

But when decorating the theater, there was one quiet spot that lent itself most to a homey Christmas atmosphere. It was the beautiful white marble fireplace at the very end of the inner lobby. We would decorate it every year, including a simulated fire in its grate, but it lacked something. Then Flossie decided what was wrong. Christmas and fireplaces (we had none at home), brought to mind the setting in the poem, "The Night Before Christmas," and there were no stockings hanging on it. This was 1954 and we had two daughters at the time, Kim, going on eight, and Kerry, four-and-a-half so, why not hang their stockings on the Madison Theater fireplace?

We wrote their names in sparkle dust (like they now sell in the malls), one for "Kimmy" and one for "Kerry." A great idea we thought, but I noticed a bit of a sour expression on Len's face when I told him of our creative plan. Then it hit me. He was obviously jealous...Kim and Kerry would have stockings but Frosty wouldn't. We decided to surprise him, and quickly made a third stocking for "Frosty." When we put up the three of them, you never saw a happier old man. Needless to say, I made points with the boss that year.

By the way, Kim and Kerry both went on to Knox College in Galesburg. Kim finished at American University, and married John Post, whom she met at Knox. They now live in Rochester, N. Y., and have two boys. John is a vice-president of Ryan Homes and Kim is a career counselor.

The Adams daughters at the Madison Theatre fireplace in 1954. (Left to right), Kim and Kerry. That's Len Worley's dog, Frosty, with them.

(From the Adams' personal collection)

"The Hoboken Four" with Major Bowes between appearances on radio's Original Amateur Hour. That's Frank Sinatra on the right.

(Photo by Richie Shirak.)

Kerry went on to get her law degree at Washington U. in St. Louis, and is an attorney. She married Doug White, also an attorney. They have one son and reside in Washington D.C.

And speaking of 1954, the movie at the Madison that Christmas was one of the better ones to come out of Warner Brothers' studios that year. It was "Young At Heart," and co-starred a couple of singers who both began with earlier big bands. Doris Day (real name Doris Kappelhoff), and a fairly good crooner by the name of Frank Sinatra.

Doris Kappelhoff was born April 3, 1922, in Cincinnati, Ohio. She sang briefly with Bob Crosby's orchestra in 1940. Then she went with Les Brown and his Band of Renown from mid-1940 to early 1941, when she quit to give birth to a son. She rejoined Les Brown in 1943 and gained fame with the hit recording "Sentimental Journey." Ironically, she had earlier worked with Sinatra for a brief time in 1947, on radio's "Your Hit Parade."

Doris had some small roles in minor films from 1939-42. But she later landed a good part in the 1948 movie, "Romance on the High Seas," in which she sang the hit tune "It's Magic." She became box office magic through the '60's and in the late '60's and early '70's had her own TV sit-com.

Francis Albert Sinatra was born on December 12, 1915, in Hoboken, New Jersey. As a member of the "Hoboken Four," he toured for months on Major Bowes Amateur Hour, where he also was heard on network radio for the first time. (I have a tape of his first radio appearance.)

Frank was singing at the Rustic Cabin in Englewood, N.J., in mid-1939 when he was hired by Harry James. He joined the Tommy Dorsey Band in early 1940 and his popularity began to rise. He left Dorsey in late 1942. Sinatra became a sensation in January, 1943, when he appeared at the Paramount Theatre in New York. He was greeted by screaming

hordes of bobby-soxers and began rivaling the popularity of Bing Crosby.

Frank had his own radio show in 1943, then sang on "Your Hit Parade" in 1944, and became a regular on it from 1947 to '49. His movie career began in 1941 while still singing with the bands. Then in 1943 he began in movies on his own, mostly in uneventful roles. His career was all but over when he landed a supporting role in 1953. He won the Academy Award as "Best Supporting Actor" in "From Here To Eternity." It revived his career and led to better roles. Two pictures later he starred with Doris in "Young At Heart," and his version of the title song in the picture became one of his big recording hits.

A 1954 Adams family Christmas memory at the Madison, and the movie that was playing.

...and it seems like only yesterday!

Dec. 31, 1946 —
Joe Kilton at "The Ing"

Hap-p-p-p-y NEW YEAR! And *my* New Year's resolution? To write a column about a memorable New Year's Eve. So, let's take a look at December 31, 1946. That was about the first one when all of our men and women in the armed forces had enough points to be back home with their loved ones.

That night both the Madison and Palace Theaters were advertising New Year's Eve "Frolics," with a special midnight show. The Madison's special price was an exorbitant 85¢, a full 20¢ above the normal 65¢. But the movie was well worth it. It was Irving Berlin's "Blue Skies," starring Bing Crosby, Fred Astaire, Joan Caulfield, and Billy DeWolfe. The Palace was a big bargain. For 55¢ you could see a double-feature. Dennis Morgan, Jack Carson and Joan Leslie in "Two Guys from Milwaukee," plus "Boston Blackie & the Law," starring Chester Morris.

The nightclubs and dance halls were featuring interesting music. Tony's Subway was promoting The Subliner's dance band. And at Eddie's Tavern at 3219 N. Adams, it was Bob Walton's new band "in the garden." The private service clubs were celebrating, too. The Amvets was featuring Marie Weber's orchestra,

and at the Moose Lodge it was Ray Dixon's Band.

A short drive away, the Hanna City Tavern featured Baxter's Five Kings, while Mackinaw Dells had Rae Scott & her 14-piece all-girl orchestra. And at The Hub in Edelstein, it was The Freddy Stevens orchestra and a gala floor show, plus a Jitter Bug Contest with cash prizes.

But in our town the biggest reveling spot was "The Ing," and the music was provided by Joe Kilton and his orchestra. Hats, favors, noisemakers, and more, were included in the $1.50-per-person admission price.

Joseph M. Kilton is a Peoria boy, born here on April 19, 1910, the son of Miles V. and Olga Huber Kilton. His father was from Monticello, Illinois, and he came to Brown's Business College, where he met Olga. His parents decided to go into business and opened a variety and hardware store, "M.V. Kilton's 5 & 10" at 739 Lincoln. They later moved the store down Lincoln, across from Manual High.

Joe went to Lee School and graduated from Manual in the class of 1927. He says he might have gone on to college, but his parents bought him a trumpet for grade school graduation. From then on music

was his life. Young Joe was just 15 when he was offered a spot playing trumpet in Lou Weber's six-piece Orchestra in 1925, and he joined the union. They played mostly small town theaters in Illinois, Indiana and Iowa.

Kilton stayed with Weber a couple years until he joined an eight-piece orchestra in 1927 called Paul Mehlenbeck and his Arcadians. (Paul named it Arcadians because he lived on Arcadia Avenue and liked the sound of it). They played mostly ballrooms and dance pavilions, one of which was the Peoria Automobile Club near Chillicothe. It later became Shore Acres.

But in 1927, Mehlenbeck landed a weekly radio program on WOC in Davenport, Iowa, a half-hour every Thursday from 5 to 5:30 p.m. For this, the band was called Paul Mehlenbeck and his Farrow Chanticleers, because it was sponsored by "Farrow Chicks." (A Chanticleer is a rooster).

Kilton played with Paul for three years. Then the drummer, Carl Hayne took over the band, keeping the name Arcadians, and expanded it to ten pieces. They went into the Inglaterra for the first time in the early '30's, at the very depth of the depression. At this time marathon dancing was the rage. The Ing ballroom was divided by a partition. The marathons were held in the front half, and regular dancing continued in the rear. The Arcadians played four nights a week for the regular dancing. After the Arcadians broke up in 1932, Joe went with Harry

Newell and his orchestra. This was a Toledo, Ohio group who were staying at Mackinaw Dells. They moved to rooms in Peoria's Seneca Hotel.

Joe married Ella Dixon in 1932. She was Ray Dixon's sister, and her sister, Ruth, also married an orchestra leader, Bob Black. Ella studied music and played piano but didn't play professionally. The Kilton's had one son, Tom, who now lives in Urbana. He taught language at U of I, and is now with its modern language library. Ella died in June, 1985.

The Newell band played the summer of 1933 in Manitou Beach, Michigan. When they returned to Peoria, Kilton joined Red Deames' orchestra of ten, including vocalist Rosie Short (Kramm). He played in Deames' group for two years and was also working at the Jefferson Bank.

After Deames, Joe jobbed around with several local bands. He left the bank in early 1936 and that fall Bob Black needed a trumpet player for his band in the Père Marquette. The Père manager, Jerry Gordon, had an aversion to loud music in his hotel. But in order to play the popular music of the day, Black talked him into allowing *one* trumpet, and Joe got the job. Kilton remembers that he had to keep one eye on the entrance to the Peoria Room. When he'd see Gordon coming, he'd immediately grab the mute and put it in his trumpet. It wasn't easy to satisfy the dance crowd and Mr. Gordon at the same time.

On August 21, 1937, Joe Kilton and Huber Sammis opened the Peoria

Joe Kilton as he appeared at The Inglaterra in the late 1940's. *(Photo courtesy of Joe Kilton)*

Joe Kilton and his original 1943 orchestra. Joe and his trumpet, surrounded by (clockwise): Ed Breuer, Stacy Gebhards, Paul Zimmerman, Herb Gehrke, Gene Larson, and Harley Goodman. *(Photo courtesy of Joe Kilton)*

Camera Shop, "37 steps from Main on South Monroe." Then in 1950 the store moved to the corner of Main and Monroe. In 1967 they sold out to Bob Wilkinson and his partner, Reverend Knappe. The Wilkinson's still operate the store, which is still at that corner location.

Kilton remained with Bob Black until 1938, and then free-lanced until 1943 when he formed his own orchestra. He was encouraged by a former cashier at the bank, Harold Newsam, who was then managing the Inglaterra. The Joe Kilton orchestra continued to play for 27 years, until 1970.

In December, 1951, Senator and Mrs. Everett Dirksen's daughter, Joy, married a young man by the name of Howard Baker. Howard, of course, went on to big things in Washington politics. The reception was held at the Peoria Country Club, and Joe's band provided the music. But

the original 1943 group consisted of Ed Breuer, piano; Stacy Gebhards, tenor sax & clarinet; Paul Zimmerman, bass; Herb Gehrke, drums; Gene Larson, baritone sax & clarinet; Harley Goodman, guitar; and Joe on trumpet and leader.

When Paul Zimmerman went into service, Bob Wilkinson replaced him on bass. Ed Breuer was later replaced on piano by Frank "Duddy" DeNufrio. Wiltz Chenoweth took over on drums after Herb Gehrke's illness. DeNufrio later had a heart attack and was replaced by Budd Kramm.

So, that's the story of Joe Kilton and his orchestra. And they were playing at The Ing that post war New Year's Eve of December 31, 1946.

...and it seems like only yesterday!

Singin' in real "Rain"

A few weeks ago four couples got together and decided it might be fun to go see a local stage musical re-creation of "Singin' in the Rain." We joined Stu and Peg Sheehan, Norma and Bob Toniny, and Bob and Dorothy McNamee, and drove to Farmington's Main Street Dinner Theatre. Now this is not your average table of eight, in more ways than one. In addition to being musical fans, this group (at least collectively), can critique a show on a par with either Jerry Klein or Bill Knight, especially in the vintage area.

If you regularly read this column, you'll remember that the McNamees were our partners in a European adventure on the Orient-Express this past summer.

Longtime friends, Stu and Peg Sheehan, have not only joined us on other entertainment jaunts, but they have also assisted by bringing me into the twentieth century in the humbling experience of writing a column by computer. Stu has been especially beneficial with his knowledge and help. And even now, when I'm completely stumped, I call him and he advises me on what to do, with three little words, "Read the book!" (Sometimes he uses four words.)

As for the Toninys, we've been friends for years, but we don't go back as far as the mid-'30's when Bob taught dancing at the National Roof Garden. Maybe you do, but that's another column.

So, on a recent Friday night this group settled back to be entertained by Don Grant Zellmer, Di-Anne Harper-Zellmer and company, and/or to critique the performances of same. I'm happy to report all we had to do was settle back. The rest was sheer delight.

Don took the part Gene Kelly portrayed in the movie, that of silent movie idol "Don Lockwood." Di-Anne re-created Debbie Reynold's character, "Kathy Seldon," a beautiful young starlet. And a young man by the name of Ron Kimbrell, came close to stealing the show in Donald O'Connor's "Cosmo Brown" role. These three can sing and dance up a storm, in this instance a rain storm.

Ron, by the way, (along with Jeannie Welch) also filmed and edited all the movie footage seen in the production, and was part of the technical crew that actually made it rain on stage. (The rain sequence designer was Jim Kumer.) The other starring parts were portrayed by Wendy Keith in the comedic, non-singing role of "Lina LaMonte," which was so ably done in the movie by Jean Hagen. Daniel Wieland was "Roscoe Dexter," the effeminate silent movie director, and David Nidiffer was "R. F. Simpson," head of the Hollywood movie studio.

Marianne Campbell played two parts, Dora Bailey, the Hollywood gossip columnist and the diction coach. In real life she is Di-anne's mother. And David Newton, the musical director and pianist is outstanding. His musical support keeps the entire performance moving, and his piano accompaniment for the the silent movie bits is especially entertaining.

In addition to an excellent evening of entertainment, the food was very good as well. And to add to our delight, our waitress was also Wendy Keith. Her performance at our table was almost as good as her portrayal of Jean Hagen, and Wendy's voice could also nearly "shatter glass."

But I'm delighted to say that these young professionals in Farmington not only succeed as performers, they really do make it actually rain on stage, not once but twice, at every performance. And if you sit too close, they'll prove it to you, as they did us.

This isn't the Adams' first nostalgic trip with the Zellmer's. We also experienced their talents a few weeks ago when we brought our daughters, sons and their spouses to see "Mack & Mabel." It was the story of Mack Sennet and Mabel Normand, and also went back to Hollywood's silent movie days.

Now, the main reason I probably wax so nostalgic over "Singin' in the Rain," is the fact that it was a great technicolor musical movie that played the Madison

Theatre in 1952, when I was still managing that grand old theater. As mentioned, it starred Gene Kelly, Debbie Reynolds, Donald O'Connor and Jean Hagen, and it has since been suggested that it may have been the greatest movie musical of all time.

And like all great musical movies, it was originally a stage show, right? *Wrong!* The story was originally fashioned for this motion picture by Betty Comden and Adolph Green from a catalog of Arthur Freed-Nacio Herb Brown songs. The setting was Hollywood during the transition from silent to "talkie" movies. Gene Kelly's dancing and singing (in the rain) rendition of "Singin' in the Rain" and Donald O'Connor's acrobatic presentation of "Make 'Em Laugh" were two classic routines in the same picture. And Jean Hagen's comedic performance as Kelly's silent screen costar, with a voice that could shatter glass, was probably her greatest effort.

It was co-directed by Gene Kelly and Stanley Donen and the supporting cast consisted of Cyd Charisse (another fair hoofer), Millard Mitchell, as the studio head, Douglas Fowley, Madge Blake and Rita Moreno. Gene Kelly's rain sequence was, of course, memorable, but Donald O'Connor's timing in "Make 'Em Laugh," was something to behold, especially his run up the wall and flip.

This routine obviously took hours to rehearse, and according to O'Connor, he only did it once without support, and that was the "take" for the rolling cameras, the one you saw in the movie. It was perfect, and he says he never did it again.

Gene Kelly in his famous "Singin' in the Rain" number in the picture of the same name. *(An M-G-M photo)*

Debbie Reynolds was outstanding as Kelly's love interest. She was the unknown starlet just coming up in Hollywood. Since "Lina LaMonte" (Hagen) didn't have a voice that would make the transition to "talkies" (a problem that actually did cause many silent stars to disappear over night), "Kathy Seldon" (Debbie) became the behind-the-scenes voice of the mimicking movie idol, Lina.

A scene from the 1952 MGM musical, "Singin' in the Rain." Left to right; Donald O'Connor, Debbie Reynolds and Gene Kelly. *(An M-G-M photo)*

The first showing of "Singin' in the Rain" at the Madison was a sneak preview at 8:30 p.m. on Wednesday, April 9, 1952. It then began a one-week run the following day. Sneak Previews, by the way, were only done with exceptionally good movies. The idea was that word-of-mouth would get around faster if an audience coming to see another picture happened to like it. Which nearly everyone did on this one.

It sold a lot of tickets and probably umbrellas, too, because it made you want to pick one up (raining or not), and hum a few bars as you left the Madison back in April, 1952.

....and it seems like only yesterday!

Jane Pauley: A "class act" leaves "Today"

Having been associated with NBC for 25 years, I've watched the occurrences on the "Today Show" the past several months with, possibly, a little more critical eye than most. Another reason is because I've been a Jane Pauley fan, and this partially stems from the fact that Flossie and I met her very early in her network career. For my money she has not only been outstanding on the show the last thirteen years, of late she has been the bond that has kept the show together while others, such as Willard Scott and Bryant Gumbel grumbled.

Jane began on the "Today Show" in October, 1976, and that following May we attended an NBC convention in Hollywood. We were at Victoria Station, adjoining the Universal studios. This particular evening of wining, dining and dancing was just one of several hosted by the network. The music that night was being provided by none other than Bob Crosby and his Bobcats.

During the evening we were privileged to visit with many network and Hollywood celebrities. High on Flossie's list was Mr. and Mrs. Jimmy Stewart, and an "accidental" meeting with the new kid on the "Today Show" block, Jane Pauley. They met, as many ladies do, in the ladies' room.

Jane was "paying her dues" that night, visiting with various guests of NBC. And she seemed to be enjoying herself, dancing with some of the guests and the network brass. But with Bob Crosby's music, it couldn't be too hard an assignment. Jane was just 25 years old at the time. In addition to being a beautiful young lady, her honest, straight-forward midwestern personality was most pleasing and we enjoyed visiting with her.

But Jane Pauley was just a little over one year old when the "Today Show" first aired on NBC on January 14, 1952. It was the brain-child of then NBC vice-president Sylvester (Pat) Weaver. If you'll recall, the first host was the easy-going Dave Garroway. His announcer and "second banana" was Jack Lescoulie, and "Today's" first newscaster was Jim Fleming. Dave was later joined by Betsy Palmer, Frank Blair and a chimp named J. Fred Muggs.

Many hosts and co-hosts have come and gone including John Chancellor, Hugh Downes, Frank McGee, Barbara Walters, and Tom Brokaw. Jane Pauley replaced Barbara. You may already be aware that Margaret Jane Pauley was born in Indianapolis, Indiana. That was on October 31, 1950. She is the younger of two daughters of Richard and Mary Pauley. Her dad was a food products distributor. Her older sister, Ann, is a nuclear engineer. Jane says she grew up in a "middle-middle-class neighborhood."

She was a shy child but overcame the handicap by becoming a top-notch debater and public speaker in high school. Bradley forensic students might be interested to know that she was active in the National Forensic League where she wrote and delivered speeches for the schools speech team, capturing several awards and prizes.

Following graduation from high school, Jane enrolled at Indiana University where she was an A-minus student in political science and a member of Kappa Kappa Gamma sorority. She left college at the end of 1971 with a B.A. degree, intending to eventually return to law school. She went to work in the 1972 Presidential campaign of New York City Mayor John Lindsay. She was hired as an aid and was assigned to the Arizona primary. When Lindsay's campaign fizzled, she returned to Indianapolis and took a job with the Indiana Democratic Central Committee.

That fall she heard that WISH-TV, the Indianapolis CBS affiliate, was looking for a female news reporter. She interviewed and, to her surprise, was hired, although she had no TV or news experience. She started as a cub reporter but within fifteen months had worked her way up to co-anchoring the midday news and anchoring on weekend evenings.

At this time WMAQ-TV, the NBC affiliate in Chicago, was floundering in third place. A network official saw her perform one day and urged her to try out for the Chicago position. She was hired in September, 1975 to co-anchor the 5 p.m. and 10 p.m. weeknight programs with Floyd Kalber. (You may remember Kalber many years ago on Peoria's WIRL-Radio). Jane became the first female co-anchor in Chicago.

While Jane Pauley was establishing herself as a Chicago broadcast journalist, Barbara Walters was at the height of her popularity as co-host of NBC's "Today Show." In April of 1976, Barbara resigned from NBC to join ABC News as co-anchor of its evening newscasts at a reported annual salary of one million dollars.

In a nationwide search to find a replacement for Walters on "Today," NBC screened videotapes of more than 250 applicants, which was eventually narrowed to 60. Six of these were selected for on-the-air tryouts on "Today" in the summer of 1976. Among them were the experienced Catherine Mackin, NBC's Congressional correspondent; Betty Furness, WNBC's consumer affairs reporter; Kelly Lange, weather forecaster for NBC's Los Angeles affiliate; and Jane Pauley. After the on-air tryouts, the network polled some 2,000 viewers in ten

Celebrating twenty-five years of "Today", on the set in 1977. (Left to right) Barbara Hunter, Tom Brokaw, Floyd Kalber (who was once with WIRL-Radio), Gene Shalit, Jane Pauley, and Lew Wood. A Raimondo Borea photo. *(Photo courtesy of NBC)*

major markets. They overwhelmingly favored Jane and she was chosen on the strength of her audience appeal.

Jane's first broadcast as a "Today" show regular was on October 11, 1976. On her first show she joined "Today" host Tom Brokaw in interviewing Walter F. Mondale, then the Democratic vice-presidential candidate, and James T. Farrell, the proletarian novelist. She held her own with the more experienced Brokaw and earned good notices from the media critics.

The show had been losing ground, even before Barbara Walters' departure, but by the end of Jane's second week it had stabilized and Nielsen gave the program 31% of the early morning audience, compared to 18% for ABC's "Good Morning America," and 15% for the CBS "Morning News."

Jane weathered thirteen years on a somewhat volatile "Today" show. Five with Tom Brokaw, and the last eight with Bryant Gumbel. Those inside the network will tell you the past few haven't been easy. But Jane Pauley has been the level, quiet, unassuming, yet strong personality, who has come through it all, until another "upstart" female newsperson, Deborah Norville, came along and NBC began grooming her to replace Jane.

But on her last "Today" show on Friday, December 29, 1989, Willard Scott summed it up in two words (which isn't easy for Willard). He simply said Jane is a "Class Act." I couldn't agree more. She is a class act, and has been for all of her thirteen years. I'll also predict she'll continue to be because that's her style.

Jane married "Doonesbury" cartoonist Garry Trudeau in June, 1980. They have three children, including twins, and live in New York City. She has always maintained a low social profile, which is partly because of her turned-around work schedule. For this reason alone, it seems time for a program change and to try a new lifestyle.

So, now that Jane has moved on, it might be appropriate for those remaining on "Today" to remember how Dave Garroway signed off each show back in the beginning..."PEACE."

...and it seems like only yesterday!

Riding the Traction

Last October, I talked about two modes of rail transportation in our area's Yester Days, the streetcar and the "traction." And thanks to a local historian and author named Paul Stringham, it's now possible to take a nostalgic trip back to those glorious days, via two books he's recently published. Peoria is fortunate to have a man who has dedicated his life to remembering them, and his over forty years of effort is now well documented in two new publications.

He had published a most comprehensive book about Peoria streetcars in 1964 titled "76 Years of Peoria Street Cars," and last November he came out with a new 25th Anniversary Revised Edition of the book. (1989 was the 100th anniversary of Peoria's electric streetcars). But Paul has also authored a brand new book on the Illinois Traction System. The title of this beautiful hard-bound coffee table type book is "Illinois Terminal — The Electric Years," published by the Interurban Press of Glendale, California. So, with Paul Stringham's permission, let's take a peak at this major interurban electric railroad of the past.

What later became the Illinois Traction System (ITS), originated in 1900 in the unlikely city of Danville, Illinois, with a population of 16,354. The original incorporation was the Danville Paxton & Northern Railroad, intended to be a steam train road, but was changed to an electric line. It was unable to post a $25,000 performance bond and the project was halted.

William B. McKinley and his syndicate from Champaign were already heavily involved in public utilities. He bought the Danville Street Railway & Light Co. in July, 1900, and then the defunct DP&N Railroad. In 1902 he incorporated a new railway and work began to join Danville, Urbana and Champaign. It was completed in 1903.

The Peoria Bloomington & Champaign traction incorporated in 1905, and was an extension of a Decatur-Bloomington project to Peoria. Then the McKinley Syndicate bought the Central City Railway Co. of Peoria in January 1906, which was their first practical means of getting to the heart of our city. Grading began in March 1906 and construction of the Illinois River bridge began that April. By May four crews were working between Peoria and Morton. In April 1907, the first electric car ran from Bloomington to within 400 feet of Farm Creek Bridge in East Peoria. Regular service to the east end of the bridge began the next day. The first passenger car crossed the Illinois River bridge at 2:10 p.m. on April 20, 1907, and regular service began the next day.

Before the Peoria Bloomington and Champaign project was complete, the McKinley Syndicate announced plans to build a line from near Mackinaw to Lincoln, closing the gap separating Peoria from Springfield. This would give Peoria a direct route to St. Louis and on July 4, 1908, an excursion train made the first Peoria-Springfield through run.

The streetcars and traction shared Peoria's downtown rails from 1907 until the new, modern traction terminal was built at S. Adams and Walnut in 1930. From April through December of 1907 they shared the Peoria & Pekin Terminal, located in a small three-story addition of the Mayer Building, which was across Adams street from the Mayer Hotel. This depot was up Hamilton street from the corner, next to the County Jail. Then, on January 1, 1908, ITS moved its depot into the main floor of the the Mayer Building, and it remained there until October, 1923. This Mayer Building later became the Pascal Hotel, which burned. (Today the location is the site of the DeKroyft-Metz Co.

In May, 1912, ITS bought the site of the National Hotel at Hamilton and Jefferson. Plans were to build a seven-story station and office building, with an off-street train shed for boarding passengers. Construction was actually begun but only the foundations were in when World War I broke out. The work was halted and never completed. At the Mayer Building, there was no provision for trains in the building, so they remained in the middle of Hamilton Street while at the depot. But in 1923

Peoria streetcars were generally rerouted. This new plan brought Heights streetcars around the courthouse and the interurban cars standing in Hamilton Street now interfered. So, on September 1st, ITS moved its station one half block down to 211 Hamilton, on the other side of the street at the alley between Adams and Washington.

This was an unattractive store front, but it had to serve until 1930 when the new station was built at Adams and Walnut. This new, modern station served as the Peoria Terminal until service into Peoria was discontinued in June of 1950. (This is now the Peoria Police Station).

The Illinois Traction System eventually ran from St. Louis to Peoria via Edwardsville, Staunton, Carlinville, Springfield, Lincoln, and Mackinaw. Mackinaw Junction also provided the service from Peoria to Decatur via Bloomington and Clinton. Another connection at Springfield allowed east-west service between the state capitol and Danville via Decatur, and Champaign-Urbana.

But did you know there was also ITS traction service in northern Illinois? It connected with the Chicago-Joliet Electric Railway at Joliet, and provided service between Joliet, Ottawa, Streator, LaSalle, and Princeton. And did you also know there was a Chicago Ottawa and Peoria Railway Company at one time? It never did connect Chicago and Peoria, of course, but the plans were in place around 1910 to run a line from Peoria to Eureka, and another from Mackinaw Junction to

From 1907 until 1923, the ITS used most of the main floor of the Mayer Building at Adams and Hamilton Streets. The first few months it used the Peoria & Pekin Terminal, which was the main floor of the three-story addition to that building at left (where the men are standing).

(Photo courtesy of R. W. Deller from Lee Roten's Historic Peoria Photo File)

The Traction Terminal that might have been — In 1912 this was proposed as the new ITS station and office building at the corner of Hamilton and Jefferson. It was the former site of the National Hotel.

(Photo courtesy of R. W. Deller from Lee Roten's Historic Peoria Photo File)

Eureka, which would then proceed on up to Streator, thus connecting the two electric services.

The reason it never happened was due to the mounting popularity of the automobile. This and the outbreak of World War I put the project on hold, and by the war's end in 1918, it had already become impractical. But the traction provided clean, comfortable, fast (70 mph) transportation to St. Louis and other cities in-between. It provided luxury parlor and sleeper car service and friendly personnel. Although the overnight runs arrived in the early hours, sleeping passengers could stay

aboard and debark at their leisure. It was a popular way to travel.

Paul Stringham's newest book "Illinois Terminal — The Electric Years" is a hard-bound 263-page coffee table book jammed with over 40 years of his research. It also contains myriads of historic black and white pictures and beautiful color photos, too.

Both the streetcar and the traction books are now available. Contact your local bookstore. If local history is important to you, these books are a "must."

...and it seems like only yesterday!

"Soaps" began on radio

Watching "soap operas" on today's television, you'd never know they had their beginning on old radio. I know my age is showing but, while I thoroughly enjoyed many of those old radio programs, I can't bear to watch one on TV.

And did you know that Peoria's own Jim and Marian Jordan were in at the very beginning of the radio soap opera? Before they introduced "Smackout" on WENR and WMAQ in Chicago, they were regular members of the cast of another WENR program called "The Smith Family," which began around 1925. It is credited as being the very first soap opera. "Fibber McGee and Molly" didn't come along until 1935, a good ten years later.

By the mid-'30's the soap opera was fast becoming a national institution. I was just a kid when I first listened with my mother during school summer vacations, and I got hooked on some of them myself. Some of my favorites were "Ma Perkins," " Vic and Sade," " David Harem," "Lorenzo Jones" and "Aunt Jenny's Real Life Stories."

So, let's go back to those "puritanical" days and take a look at what America's housewife was listening to the week of November 15 to 19, 1937. (I'll also note the sponsors of some of them.)

"Bachelor's Children" (Old Dutch Cleanser); "The Goldbergs"; "Hope Alden's Romance"; "Linda's First Love"; "The Story of Mary Marlin" (Ivory Snow); "Stella Dallas"; "Young Widder Jones" (before Widder Brown); "Pretty Kitty Kelly" (Wonder Bread); "Mrs. Wiggs of the Cabbage Patch" (Old English Wax); "Oxydol's Own Ma Perkins" (The product was part of its name).

"Myrt and Marge" (Super Suds); "John's Other Wife" (Louis Philippe); "Just Plain Bill" (Anacin); "Pepper Young's Family" (Camay); "Betty and Bob" (Gold Medal Flour); "Happiness House"; "Today's Children" (Pillsbury); "David Harum" (Bab-o); "The O'Neills" (Ivory Flakes); "Road of Life" (Chipso); "Mary Noble, Backstage Wife" (Dr. Lyons Tooth Powder); "Vic and Sade" (Crisco).

"Big Sister" (Rinso); "Aunt Jenny's Real Life Stories" (Spry); "Girl Alone" (Kellogg's); "Romance of Helen Trent"; "Our Gal Sunday" (Anacin); "Arnold Grimm's Daughter" (Gold Medal Flour); "Dan Harding's Wife"; "Kitty Keene, Inc."; "Lorenzo Jones" (Phillips); "The Guiding Light" (White Naptha Soap); "Life of Mary Sothern" (Hinds) and "Hilltop House" (Palmolive Soap).

There's also a local connection with one of the more humorous of these early soaps, "Vic and Sade." It was created and written by Paul Rhymer of nearby Bloomington. Paul went to work for NBC's continuity department as a kid fresh out of college in 1929. One day in 1932 a network production manager came into the office looking for a writer. He needed a family-type script to audition a prospective actor.

Rhymer worked over the weekend, and on Monday presented him with a 10-minute script about the homespun Vic and Sade Gook, who lived on Virginia Avenue in the town of Crooper, Illinois (it very much resembled Bloomington.) Vic worked as a bookkeeper for Plant Number 14 of the Consolidated Kitchenware Company. Sade was his homebody wife. The Gook's later adopted a son, Rush. He was the son of Sade's sister, who couldn't afford to keep him. (It *was* the depression, you know.)

During its heyday, "Vic and Sade" was heard on NBC's Red and Blue Networks, and then on NBC and CBS simultaneously. It ran as a 15-minute show, five days a week until September 29, 1944. Art Van Harvey, a former grain dealer and advertising man played Vic, and Bernadine Flynn, a veteran stage actress played Sade. Billy Idelson was originally cast as Rush.

But an obscure couple with journalistic backgrounds rose up in the soap opera business until they practically controlled the market. They were Frank and Anne Hummert. Frank worked for the St. Louis Post-Dispatch before joining the Chicago advertising agency of Blackett and Sample in 1927. (Chicago was the hub of national radio programming in those days.)

Hummert was involved in radio copy and in 1930 the agency hired Anne Ashenhurst as his assistant. She had written an advice to the lovelorn column for the old Baltimore News, and later worked for the Baltimore Sun and the Paris Herald.

Frank and Anne's first two serials were "Just Plain Bill" and "Betty and Bob." Their success grew and by 1935 they were both high-ranking company officers. Hummert's first wife had died, and he and Anne married. Their fortunes continued to rise and in 1944 they left the agency to form their own Hummer Radio Productions, Inc. It became the largest operation of its kind, an assembly line for producing soap operas and other programs.

But a very strange incident occurred in our house in 1951, and it was associated in a startling way with a soap opera the Hummerts didn't write. It was a CBS offering called "The Second Mrs. Burton." This soap was the story of Terry Burton, the second wife of Stan Burton, and her search for happiness. They lived in a small town and were under the constant control of Stan's domineering mother.

At the time we were renting a small house owned by my grandmother, Beulah Bowman, in the 600 block of Butler Street. Our first two daughters were quite small. Kim was four and Kerry was about 10 months old. It was a hot summer day and Flossie had put them down for their afternoon nap. She turned on the radio as background for the girls to sleep and was listening to "The Second Mrs. Burton."

A favorite old radio soap opera was "Ma Perkins." Left to right: Virginia Payne, made up to look like an older "Ma" for publicity purposes. (She was 23 when the show began.) Murray Forbes played "Willie" and Charles Egelston was "Shuffle."
(An NBC photo)

In the plot of the program, Stan's mother had recently married a very sinister man. He had obviously married Mother Burton for her money. He then took out a big insurance policy on her life and began plotting to get rid of her.

He had gone up into the attic and loosened the rafters so that the ceiling would crash down on Mrs. Burton while she slept. Suddenly, at the climax to this particular day's episode, Mrs. Burton's ceiling (on the radio) came crashing down. At this very instant the same thing occurred in our daughters' bedroom! *Really!* Their ceiling actually collapsed and big chunks of plaster fell into their bed.

Flossie was in shocked disbelief. She grabbed the kids and went running to Grandma Bowman's and called me at the

"Vic and Sade" was created and written by Paul Rhymer from Bloomington, Illinois. Left to right: Billy Idelson as "Rush," Bernadine Flynn as "Sade," and Art Van Harvey as "Vic."   *(An NBC photo)*

theater to hurry home. It was a hot summer day and Kim had moved to the end of the bed to get closer to the open window. Ironically, the majority of the plaster hit at the very spot her pillow had been before she moved. The baby was unhurt but the bed was full of plaster, dirt and dust.

Flossie was so unnerved by this simultaneous event that, to this day she doesn't recall what happened to Stan Burton's mother. So, if any of you know what happened on that program 39 years ago, please call and let her know. The suspense is beginning to get to her.

Yes, the soap operas could be very realistic on old time radio, but I doubt that they could become any more real than "The Second Mrs. Burton" did that day in our house.

...and it seems like only yesterday!

Remember old radio's kid shows?

Last week when we went back to November, 1937 and remembered all the old radio soap operas, I couldn't help but recall all the wonderful kid shows, too. After all, I was only twelve years old at the time.

So, at the risk of "over nostalgia," here's what we kids were listening to right after the soap operas, when school was out. Most of them ran weekdays from 4:15 through 6:45 (Peoria time), while others ran on Saturday mornings or early evening: "Terry and the Pirates"; "Don Winslow of the Navy"; "Kellogg's Singing Lady"; "Jack Armstrong, the All-American Boy"; "The Air Adventures of Jimmy Allen"; "Charlie Chan"; "The Tom Mix Ralston Straightshooters"; "Little Orphan Annie"; "Junior Nurse Corps"; "Adventures of Speed Gibson"and "The Lone Ranger."

And here's a few more you may remember that were heard before or since that date: "The Adventures of Superman"; "Archie Andrews"; "Bobby Benson and the B-Bar-B Riders"; "Buck Rogers in the 25th Century"; "Smilin' Ed's Buster Brown Gang"; "Captain Midnight"; "Chandu, the Magician."

"Coast-To-Coast on a Bus" (White Rabbit Line); "Dick Tracy"; "Gene Autry's Melody Ranch"; "The Green Hornet"; "Henry Aldrich"; "Hoofbeats" with Buck Jones; "Hop Harrigan, America's Ace of the Airways"; "Hopalong Cassidy"; "Let's Pretend"; "Maggie and Jiggs"; "Mark Trail"; "Red Ryder"; "Renfrew of the Mounted"; "The Roy Rogers Show"and "Sergeant Preston of the Yukon."

If you were a kid anytime between the late 1920's and early '50's, and don't remember some of them, well, you just didn't have a radio. And they came along at a time when money was scarce for many families but these adventures didn't cost a dime, unless you had to have one of the many premiums offered. Then it might require "Ten cents in coin and a boxtop...."

I know I couldn't have made it without the decoder or shake-up mug Little Orphan Annie kept talking about. And if you didn't have a compass ring that glowed in the dark, how could you ever find your way through the jungles of South America with Jack Armstrong? And his pedometer that told him how far he had walked through those jungles was also a must.

And of all those great programs, the ones I followed every day were "Little Orphan Annie"; "Jack Armstrong"; "Tom Mix"; "Terry and the Pirates"; "Dick Tracy" and "The Lone Ranger." So, let's take a closer look at three of the best known of the group.

"Little Orphan Annie" was the first juvenile adventure serial radio program, first heard on April 6, 1931, on the Blue Network. It was 15-minutes, six days a week, an adaptation of Harold Gray's comic strip. It's theme song, "Orphan Annie," was played on the organ and began, "Who's that little chatter box? The one with pret-ty auburn locks? Who-oo can it be? It's Little Orphan Annie!"

And do you remember its announcer, Pierre André? Annie lived with Mr. and Mrs. Silo in the make-believe Tomkins Corners. Shirley Bell played the part of Annie. It was later played by Janice Gilbert. Annie went on her adventurous escapades with her pal, Joe Corntassel, who's part was played by Allan Baruck, and another young kid you heard a lot from later, the multi-talented Mel Tormé. The other characters on the show were also taken from the comic strip, such as Daddy Warbucks, Punjab the Giant, and Captain Sparks. Ovaltine sponsored Annie until 1940. "Little Orphan Annie" left the air in 1943.

And another show that became synonymous with its sponsor was "Jack Armstrong, the All-American Boy," brought to you by "Wheaties, the Breakfast of Champions." You may also

A 1975 photo of Jim Ameche, holding an art portrait of Jack Armstrong, the All-American Boy. He played the role from the show's beginning in 1933 until 1939.

(A World Wide Photo)

remember that Jack and his cousins, Billy and Betty Fairfield went to Hudson High School. These three, and their uncle Jim Fairfield, travelled the world seeking adventure. Do you remember the words to their school fight song that opened the show? "Wave the flag for Hudson High, boys. Show them how we stand; Ever shall our team be champions. Known through-out the land!"

It was first heard on CBS originating from WBBM, Chicago on July 31, 1933, and ran until August, 1947, as a 15-minute program. It was later carried on NBC, Mutual and then the Blue Network (ABC). It finally became a twice-a-week, half-hour program until 1950. That fall another, more adult version, "Armstrong of the SBI," aired but shortly vanished on June 28, 1951.

And do you remember the actor who first created the role? He was Jim Ameche, the brother of Don Ameche. (Don also appeared on the early Jack Armstrong programs as Captain Hughes). The part of Jack was briefly played by John Terrell and Stanley Harris from 1938 to 1939, until Charles Flynn took the role. Then he played Jack until 1950, when he was nearly 30.

Billy was played by several actors, including John Gannon, who later became a Cook County Circuit Court judge in Chicago, and Dick York, the later star of TV's "Bewitched." Scheindel Kalish and Sarajane Wells played Betty and of several announcers, the first was David Owen and later, Franklyn MacCormack, among others.

"A fiery horse with the speed of light, a cloud of dust and a hearty Hi-Yo Silver! The Lone Ranger rides again!" That and the William Tell Overture theme music told you it was time for another action-packed adventure of the Lone Ranger, and his faithful Indian companion, Tonto. It was first heard January 30, 1933, on WXYZ, Detroit.

The western hero was the creation of George W. Trendle who, along with John H. King, had bought the Detroit station, WXYZ. After it severed its connection with CBS, the station was loosing money. But Trendle had an idea. He planned to develop a new program, a wholesome Western with a bigger-than-life hero. This character became The Lone Ranger. Trendle hired Fran Striker, a young writer from Buffalo, who fleshed out the Tonto character, came up with the silver bullet idea, added the "Hi-Yo Silver" cry, and further developed the program. Its fame spread beyond WXYZ in Detroit, going to WGN in Chicago, then WOR, New York. These stations became the the the nucleus of the Mutual Network in 1934.

Jack Deeds was the first brief voice of the Lone Ranger. Within a month George Seaton took the part. (He later became a famous Hollywood film director). In May 1933 a WXYZ staff announcer, Earle Graser took over until his untimely death in an auto accident on April 8, 1941.

The Lone Ranger was written out of the show for awhile, leaving Tonto to carry on alone. Tonto was played by John Todd virtually all the way. When the Lone Ranger came back, the part was played by Brace Beemer. He played it from 1941 through 1955. And the best known of several announcers on the show was Fred Foy.

"The Lone Ranger" went on to big things in the movies and on TV, but the radio version finished as a three-a-week program on May 27, 1955.

When I think back to all those fond radio memories, I feel a little sorry for our children and grandchildren, even with all of today's entertainment at their disposal. I wish I could convey the joy it was to "see" those wonderful adventures through our "mind's eye." We could imagine them to be anything we wanted. A truly memorable experience.

...and it seems like only yesterday!

End of an Era

You really don't realize just how fast time flies until you see something like the closing of the Varsity Theater. What hit me most was the fact that the Varsity is 51 years old. How can that possibly be?

The Varsity was the second Peoria theater project of a very young George Kerasotes who represented the Springfield, Illinois firm of two Kerasotes brothers, Gus, George's dad, and his uncle, Louis. Their first Peoria theater was the Beverly, which is actually two years older, having opened in 1937. So, let's go back and revisit these two theaters from the beginning.

Plans for theater construction at (then) 1805 N. Knoxville was first announced on February 23, 1936. The new building cost was estimated at $75,000 and planned seating capacity was 800. Total cost, including the land, building and furnishings was an estimated $100,000. C. W. Kent was to be the owner and builder and the original name was to be "The Astaire Theater."

That plan apparently fell through because in October 1936, a construction permit was issued to Kerasotes Brothers to build the Beverly Theater and J. Fletcher Lankton was named architect. The young 26-year-old George Kerasotes was named managing director.

The Beverly Theater opened its doors for the first time at 6:30 p.m. on St. Patrick's Day, March 17, 1937. The opening film was "My Man Godfrey" starring William Powell, Carole Lombard, Gail Patrick, Alice Brady, Eugene Pallette, Alan Mowbray and Mischa Auer. WMBD-Radio broadcast a special program from in front of the theatre opening night.

Two old friends (and my former theater competitors), Howard Young and Frank Larkin began their theater careers at the Beverly. Howey was an usher there from opening night. Frank began as parking lot attendant across the street in 1938, and says he had to "work up to usher." Howey recalls some of the theater's opening staff: Willis "Bill" Ford, manager; Arnold Lawrence, chief of service; Howard Young; Herbert Bush; and Bob Eberle, ushers. Margaret Smith and Cecile Strum were the cashiers. A few days later Bill Massey was hired as outdoor doorman, handling crowd control. (Frank says the Beverly had capacity evening crowds for its first full year of operation).

In addition to Frank Larkin, some other ushers to later join the staff were Bob Epstein (a future competitor of mine from WMBD and also a next-door neighbor), Bill Keys, Tim Norman, and

George Yeager, and Betty Bergquist also became a cashier. A young lady was later hired to sell encyclopedias as a way to increase matinee attendance. Her name was DeMova Merchant. Dee later became a candygirl at the Beverly and then the Varsity. She also became Mrs. Howard Young. Bill Ford was named city manager of both theaters after the Varsity was built, and Lloyd Shannon replaced him as Beverly manager. Howey Young then replaced Shannon as manager until he joined the Marines in 1941, and Wade Fehr was his chief of service.

Just two years after the Beverly opened, the Varsity Theater opened its doors at (then) 2107 Main Street. This new luxury type theater was the, now, 28-year-old George Kerasotes' entry into show business "on his own." He had graduated from the University of Illinois and later completed courses at the Lincoln College of Law at Springfield. But George came from a theatrical family and show business was more interesting to him than law.

Bill Ford was only 30 years old when he became city manager, but he had spent 14 years in theater work. He started at the Princess Theater in 1925 while attending Peoria High School. Four years before the Varsity, he had been named manager of a theater in Macomb.

The firm of J. Fletcher Lankton was also selected to be the architect for the $155,000 Varsity Theater. Another young 26-year-old of that firm was assigned as its designer, Cletis Foley. Like Mr.

The original staff for the Beverly Theater opening on March 17, 1937. Standing, left to right: Willis J. Ford, manager; Howard Young, usher; Margaret Smith and Cecil Strum, cashiers; Bill Massey, outside doorman (hired a few days later); Jack Phillips, chief-of-service. Kneeling l to r: Dick Bush and Alan Walshauer, ushers.

(Photo by Ruth Robertson - courtesy of Howard Young)

Kerasotes, Mr. Foley also graduated from the University of Illinois.

The Kerasotes company stated that the new, modern Varsity was dedicated to the entertainment needs of the West Bluff and especially to Bradley Tech (then Bradley Polytechnic Institute), which was the inspiration for its name.

The outer lobby entered into a foyer and lounge done in imported walnut and natural woods. Directly forward in the center was a semi-circular lounge seat recessed into the wall and decorated with a mural depicting college life at Bradley. It was by Miss Lee Mock, who was awarded the honor of painting the scenes in a contest held in the Bradley College of Art.

Crowd lined up the street for the Grand Opening of the Varsity Theater on April 14, 1939. Standing in front is WMBD's live radio remote truck.

(Photo by Ruth Robertson - courtesy of Frank Larkin)

Frank Larkin recalls working at getting the Varsity ready for opening night while still on the Beverly staff. He had the honor of putting up the first letters on the marquee for the grand opening. Howard Young also came over from the Beverly and worked the opening night. Frank went into the Navy in 1943. When he returned in 1947, he took on-the-job training at the Varsity. He later became city manager of the Beverly and Varsity and added the Starlite Drive-In before opening the Rialto for Kerasotes in 1951. Howey Young immediately followed as Rialto Manager.

But the new Varsity Theater opened its doors for the first time at 6:30 p.m. on Monday, April 14, 1939. The feature motion picture was "Out West with the Hardys." It was the third of the very

popular Hardy Family series from MGM, and starred Lewis Stone, Mickey Rooney, Cecilia Parker, Fay Holden, Ann Rutherford, and Sara Haden.

The theater policy was to show only the better pictures, shortly after their downtown runs, at the "popular" adult prices of 15¢ (matinee) and 20¢ (evening). Children were 10¢ at all times. (Those would sure be popular prices today, even for the popcorn).

But Frank Larkin recalls that the picture policy changed over the years in order for the Varsity to survive. In November, 1953 it became an "Art Theater." This was the creation of Sue Maxwell, head of Bradley's theater department, and Bradley students were given free admission in the balcony on Monday nights.

In the 1970's the Varsity even became a soft-porn picture house. Russ Meyer's "Vixen" was one that ran to large crowds for eight months. Then in the 1980's the Varsity became a "split-screen" theater to compete with the "shoe box" multi-screen complexes that were now doing the bulk of the business.

Well, the once "new, modern" Varsity Theater is no longer. It closed its doors for the final time on Thursday, February 1st with the split-screen showings of "Tango & Cash" with Sylvester Stallone, plus "The Wizard" and "Mask of the Red Death."

It's hard to believe that the Beverly and Varsity opened over 50 years ago.

...it seems like only yesterday!

Looking ahead

Riding the rails to Chicago again

Every week we take a trip back in time to talk about some memorable experiences in our past. But with this week's subject, the best way to go back might be to take a trip into the not too distant future.

So...The year is 1995. We are in Chicago's beautiful recently remodeled Union Station on Canal Street. We're walking to the boarding area for the new, sleek, modern Amtrak train, leaving shortly for Peoria. That's right, *Peoria!* It's named the "Riverboat Gambler" and is scheduled to leave at 6:30 p.m. The 2½ hour trip will get us home by 9 p.m.

There are a couple hundred people boarding this evening, and I'm told this is about average for a weeknight. Many are coming from Chicago and other midwestern cities to visit Peoria and take advantage of the new activity on the Illinois River — riverboat gambling.

We are boarding today to return home after an extended weekend in Chicago. We recognize some other Peorians aboard who are also retired. We know from experience that retired people would much rather travel by train than drive to and from Chicago, and it sure beats the hassle, not to mention the cost, of flying.

But many people are coming to Peoria for more than the lure of wagering a few dollars while plying the waters of Lake Peoria. They are coming to shop the new Bielfeldt Mall also located on Peoria's river front. While in Peoria, many people will take the time to tour other points of interest, such as Wildlife Prairie Park and Grand View Drive. Others will take advantage of sports and theater events at the Civic Center, or a baseball game at the new, recently completed downtown stadium. And many business people are now visiting Caterpillar's World Headquarters by train (It's conveniently located near the depot).

Our train is now underway, slowly picking up speed as it threads its way out of the congested area of Chicago's inner city. As I look out at the snarled traffic on the expressway, I can't help but appreciate the luxury of train travel even more. Our route will take us southwest through Joliet to Chillicothe on the Sante Fe line, then we'll connect with the newly improved rails south to Peoria.

As our train nears the Peoria suburbs, it reduces speed before its final destination at the downtown depot. This building is now called the River Station Restaurant, but back in the heyday of railroads, it was the Rock Island Depot. A portion of this historic old building once again serves as a train depot and ticket office.

As we step from the train, I can't help but look around me with pride. What a difference with all the new activity here on our riverfront. It all began with Jumer's Boat Works, the Spirit of Peoria riverboat and the adjoining restaurant. With the addition of the new riverboat casino, this area has become a hub of activity both day and night. And on the other side of the railroad tracks is the new super mall, bringing shoppers back downtown. Eckwood and Liberty parks also combine to make our once unattractive riverfront a thing of beauty.

Well, that's some trip into our future. But it's just fantasy, right? A figment of our over-active imagination? Maybe. But as you know, much planning has gone into the mall project and, hopefully, this year the developers will have good news for us about its future. And thanks to the newly signed Illinois law, (aboard the Spirit of Peoria), riverboat gambling is going to happen and, like it or not, Peoria is positioning itself to be the recipient of this newly formed activity. And a study is again underway to investigate a downtown baseball stadium.

But what about the train to Chicago? We attempted this idea back in 1980, and it proved unsuccessful. That's true, but many things were admittedly wrong with that experiment. The East Peoria depot

An Amtrak engine, similar to one that might one day operate once again between Peoria & Chicago.
(Photo from Passenger Train Journal magazine.)

The old Rock Island Railroad depot at Water and Liberty Streets shortly before the clock tower was removed in 1939. This is now the location of the River Station restaurant.

(Photo courtesy of Paul Stringham, from Lee Roten's Historic Peoria Photo File)

was an inconvenient location for many living on the other side of the river. The depot's poor quality and inadequate parking, plus several other problems, added to the dilemma. But it didn't fail because of a lack of public need.

Now there's a local group called "Peoria Rail" who are working on a new plan. They are Peoria-area people, chaired by Dan Phillips, interested in train transportation and concerned about Peoria's lack of service. They feel times have changed, that we have learned from past mistakes, and that rail service is not only feasible, it answers immediate transportation needs between Peoria and Chicago.

An advocate to restore rail service is Charles Ginoli, a local CPA, who has been involved in transportation since he studied the problem at the U of I in the 1930's. In 1950, he formed Ginoli and Company, an accounting firm which he managed until his recent retirement.

Ginoli has served for many years on the City Traffic Commission and was chairman of the Greater Peoria Transit District where he increased his interest in rail travel. He recalls the many problems facing the Rock Island Railroad back in the '60's. Its road bed was deteriorating, its downtown depot was too costly, and the road was going bankrupt. This forced them to move the depot from downtown to a smaller, less expensive one at the foot of Morton street. But passenger service finally ground to a halt in 1979.

In 1987 the state legislature created the Illinois Rail Task Force Commission. They hired a consulting firm to determine which corridors in Illinois had potential for rail service. They found two were feasible: Peoria & Chicago, and Quad-Cities & Chicago. The study also recommended the Peoria-Chicago line should use the Sante Fe rails from Chicago to Chillicothe, then connect with the old Rock Island rails to downtown Peoria. This is now in the hands of the Illinois Department of Transportation.

The Peoria Rail group is now working toward a public hearing before members of IDOT. That hearing is planned for the very near future. They encourage everyone interested in, or curious about, the resumption of passenger rail service to attend this meeting.

Now, I'm one of those people who feel that passenger service would not only be important to Peoria again, but popular as well. But there's also another big reason for this service to be in place as soon as possible. High-speed rail service is now in the early planning stages in the U.S. When it happens, the trains that are in operation nationally have an opportunity to become a part of that future network. Those cities without it (as Peoria is today), will have no opportunity. Peoria would once again "miss the boat" or in this case "the train." We can't afford to let that happen to us again.

You know, 1995 may be none too soon.

...it seems like only tomorrow!

Peoria Stadium

Athletic field was once a racetrack

When you drive past Peoria Stadium today, you see a football-shaped sign that identifies it as "Peoria Public Schools Stadium." Its primary use is for high school football, track and field events, and other occasional uses. But the football field and quarter-mile track only uses a small portion of the entire acreage with ball diamonds and soccer fields taking up another portion of the space. So, why all the extra space? Because it began as a horse race track, *one full mile* in length.

That mile oval track ran from the grandstand, circling around to what is now War Memorial Drive, all the way across to New York Avenue, up that street to nearly Lake Street, and back around to the grandstand.

Now, if you're as old as I am you might relate to one of the greatest of all football events held here, "The Turkey Day Game." This was the traditional game played for so many years between Manual and Central. (Later, Woodruff and Spalding also played in the afternoon). Bradley also played football here.

I also vaguely remember when this was a fairgrounds, and years ago it was an amusement park, too. But from before the turn of the century until the early 1930's, it was a racetrack. Not only for horse racing but, later, dog racing as well.

And thanks to research done by Paul Stringham for his streetcar history, and Lee Roten's documentation of it, with accompanying photos, much of the data on this and other major events have been preserved.

It all began in 1895. A race track committee composed of four gentlemen, Messrs. Voorhees, Schnellbacher, Bunn and Irwin, met at City Hall on the evening of Wednesday, February 27th and it was unanimously agreed to proceed with plans for a horse race track. They were also trying to interest the Central City Rail Road Company (which had begun electric streetcar service in 1889) to extend its service to the proposed site. They also agreed to form a stock company with $50,000 capitol for the purpose of purchasing the Allaire farm with 20 additional acres of the Hines farm on the north. With the purchase of the land, they saw no trouble in providing money for the erection of necessary buildings.

By the second week of May surveyors were laying out the "mile track," and John Jobst was awarded the contract for grading. By mid-June the contract was let to Charles Sutter for buildings at the "fairgrounds" and the mile track work was rapidly progressing. Work on the buildings began on June 25th and work on the track's amphitheater started in July.

Tuesday, July 30th was a tragic day, however, when the amphitheater collapsed while under construction. Several men were injured, two were badly hurt. William Rosenberger and Michael Schearer were working on top of the structure and fell nearly 40 feet.

A windstorm had blown down the partially completed structure the previous Friday night, and it had no sooner been erected again, when it collapsed. But the work continued. The track was finished by August 31st, and the amphitheater was completed on September 6th. Two days later, the streetcar extension to the fairground entrance was done and on September 10, 1895, the first races were held by the Peoria Trotting and Agriculture Society. The first week's races ran from Tuesday through Saturday. (There was no racing on Sunday in those days.)

Up to this time, the Knoxville streetcar line ended at Corrington. The extension to the racetrack entrance came across Corrington to California, then up along side that street to a turn around at the main gate on Reservoir Boulevard (now War Memorial Drive.)

On the day of the first evening's races, track officials were still busy with last minute details. Underneath the grand-stand, tables in the dining hall were put in place and all was ready to serve full meals or lunches. Next to the dining room, but separated by a partition, was a large bar.

The day was very warm with no clouds in the sky. It dried out the track which was wet from a previous rain. Everything was painted white from the fence to the grandstand, even the roof. Plank walks lead from the various gates to the grandstand.

Over the years the area was to become used for various events other than racing. In May, 1912, buildings were added for the "Implement Show." In 1913 plans for additional buildings began; three ornamental horse barns and an exposition building. 1915 saw two more buildings added, one for liberal arts, the other for swine. In 1916 a new, larger grandstand was planned. It was eventually contracted for by Val Jobst in 1923. In 1920, an aviation field was put in, and one airplane eventually used the facility for exhibition flights for a time.

In August, 1926, work got underway for an amusement park at the fairgrounds. It was designed by John A. Miller of Homewood. It opened the night of August 28, 1926. The fairgrounds was also the location for the Peoria County Fair for several years, and sulky horse racing became a part of this annual event.

A Knoxville streetcar on the turn-around at the main gate of the fairgrounds and dog race track, on Reservoir Blvd. at California Avenue. Photo taken by Bill Janssen on March 1, 1931. The dirt street on right is now War Memorial Drive.

(A Bill Janssen photo courtesy of Paul H. Stringham)

Paul Stringham remembers the amuse-ment park as a teen-ager. He recalls that the rides were all undercover, except the big, wooden roller-coaster. He recalls a merry-go-round, dodge 'em cars, the whip, and a house of mirrors, among others.

But at 8:15 pm. on Thursday, June 30, 1927, a new racing sport began on the mile track. It was Greyhound dog-racing, and was named the "sport of queens" because of its popularity with women. That night a crowd of more than 5,000 swarmed the Exposition Park oval to view the first eight races of a thirty-night season. The dogs, chasing the mechanical rabbit, had the huge throng on its feet in almost every race. The event was sponsored by the Peoria Kennel Club.

The first race's winning dog was named "Lindy." A $2 ticket on him paid $14.30 to win, $4 to place and $4 to show. U.S. Congressman William E. Hull presented the winner of the fifth race with a trophy.

Dog racing held forth at the fair-grounds track until September 21, 1931. This was at the depth of the depression, and financial difficulties between the promoters and the lack of patronage caused it to close.

So in July, 1935, the Peoria School Board voted to purchase the old fairgrounds from Clyde Garrison. The WPA began clearing many of the old wooden structures, including the administration building, for a new Central Athletic Field to be used for sports events by the city schools.

It was an energetic project that was only partially executed. The mile track was eliminated and the grandstand would become a part of a new football field, quarter mile track, added bleachers across from the grandstand, practice fields, baseball diamonds, tennis courts, children's playground, picnic area, field events and archery range. A site for a new school on Lake Street was also proposed but never completed.

Well, many of the pieces of the original plan, sans the new school, did occur and the new Central Athletic Stadium was dedicated on Thanksgiving Day (naturally) with the 26th annual football game between Manual and Peoria Central. An estimated crowd of 6,500 fans watched Central beat Manual 19 to 0 in their first, ever, game in the new facility.

Horse racing, dog racing, exposition park, fairgrounds, amusement park, and, finally, an athletic field. To some old-timers still around

...it seems like only yesterday!

An aerial view of the mile race track where Peoria Stadium is now located on War Memorial Drive. Photo was taken by Ray Barclay, sometime before the razing of the horse barns. The current quarter-mile track and football field area can be seen in front of the grandstand.

(Photo courtesy of R. W. Deller from Lee Roten's Historic Peoria Photo File)

Showboats entertained old Peoria

Since "Big Jim" came to our town (and a couple others) the other day to sign the new Illinois law legalizing riverboat gambling, I thought it might be timely to go back to that romantic era of our past when riverboats were common around here. I recall some of the last ones such as the Avolon (formerly the Idlewild), but riverboats have been coming to Peoria since the l830's, and showboats came to entertain our ancestors since the 1850's.

A while back I read an old Peoria Star newspaper clipping. It was an interview of an unknown old Peorian who entertained on those showboats, and it gave a great insight to life here in early Peoria.

In April 1938 a couple writers from that paper were visiting in Eckwood Park on a Sunday Afternoon. One of them saw an old man about 75 years old sitting alone on a park bench. He had lifeless gray hair, his clothing was shabby and he wore scuffed shoes. But he was clean shaven, and his clear blue eyes had a wistful look as he gazed out over the water.

One of the reporters sat down at the other end of his bench, and not a word was said for about half an hour. The old man never so much as lifted his head. Suddenly, above the din of people's voices and children playing in the park, the air was filled with three sharp blasts from a boat whistle. The old man stirred, came alert, and looked downstream. The bridge opened and slowly the blunt noses of coal scows shoved through, coming upstream and being pushed by a grimy tow boat.

The barges and boat slowly passed in front of them and disappeared behind the riverfront's warehouses and wharf boats. Finally the old man crossed his legs and relaxed, with one arm resting on the back of the bench. A half-pathetic sigh escaped his lips as he said, "Nothing about the river's as it used to be."

The reporter answered, "Yes, modern transportation has greatly changed the aspect of the river. The old steam packet, picturesque and romantic in its time, has had its day. You're not by any chance an old steamboat man?"

He shook his head, "No, not a steamboat man. A showboater, the same as my father and mother before me. It's said, 'Once a trouper, always a trouper.' Once the virus gets into your system, it stays there for life. And the saying applied equally to showboat people. It was right here in Peoria, way back in 1853, that my father became a showboater."

"What, here?" the reporter asked.

"Yes, right here." the old man countered. "He'd come from the East and worked his way down from the lakes on a canal boat. Times were hard, and for a couple of years he eked out a living playing an accordion and singing comic songs to people that gathered in the saloons.

"It was the Fourth of July (1853). After playing the up-river towns of Peru, Hennepin, Henry, Lacon and Chillicothe, the show boat owners Spaulding and Rodgers had steamed their floating palace, a great aquatic amphitheater surpassing all American theatres in sumptuousness and comfort, as they styled it, up to the levee during the night and made it fast.

"I've been told of it so often by my father that I can picture the Peoria of those early days. There wasn't much to it: a handful of people living back under the hills, and a few warehouses, general stores, livery stables, and saloons strung out along two main streets, paralleling the river, that with no pavements were either a morass of mud or ankle deep in dust, according to the season."

The Belle of Pike was a popular steamboat on the Illinois River in 1859. Its captain was Henry Detweiller, for whom Detweiller Park was named.

(Photo from the Thomas H. Detweiller collection - Peoria Public Library)

"Spaulding and Rodgers" was the first showboat ever to ascend the Illinois. They were to give three performances, one at 9:00 in the forenoon, another at 2:30 in the afternoon, and a final one at 7:30 that evening. Their coming was well advertised. People came from the nearby towns by stage, and farmers drove their families in from their prairie homes. At 50¢ for box and main floor seats and 25¢ for those in the regular and colored balconies, the huge barge was jammed to capacity.

"The first and second performances, according to my father, went fine. But there were many steamboats tied up at the levee that day. When the actors weren't on the stage they visited with the captains and officers they had met along the river.

Many visits were made to the saloons a few steps away across Water street, and before it came time for the final show most of the players were drunk.

"Old Man Spaulding was frantic. With at least a thousand people packed on the barge, most of the actors was laid out. My father said, 'In a rage he (Spaulding) started up-town, dropped into a saloon where I was playing, saw several of his actors laid out, and said to me, 'Get on that boat and help us put on a show!' Well, I didn't know much about the show business, but I could play and sing a little. So, with the few who were able to appear, I helped Spaulding and Rodgers put on a show that at least amused the crowd.'

"He must have made an impression, for when they pulled out, Spaulding and Rodgers took him along."

The old man spoke of showboats old and new. Of those on which he passed his childhood, and others in his later years. He called them "floating theatres," French's Sensation; Showboat(s) Number One, Two and Three; Emerson's Cotton Blossom; Price's Columbia; The Floating Palace Theatre; River Maid; Bryant's Showboat; French's New Sensation; and The Goldenrod.

In the 1870's, '80's, and even later, the showboat was his family's only home. Married couples were provided rooms on the main barge. Unmarried members were on the steamboat that served as pusher.

When the final curtain rang down, the band played while men, women and children trudged down the gang-plank, back to the humdrum monotony of every-day life.

"No," the old man said, "the river's not as it used to be. My father married a showboat woman. I was born on board, grew up to the feel of grease paint and later continued in the footsteps of my parents. There isn't much more to say. That's the sort of life I lived and it suited me to a Tee. I married, but we never had a settled abode. My father, though, always called Peoria home because it was here he joined the troupe. So, when there no longer was a place for us on the rivers, it was here we came to pass our declining days."

The old man's name was never mentioned, but he painted a personal life portrait of birth, youth, love and marriage, of a simple family life aboard the old showboats of the past.

I couldn't help but think that, as he reminisced, he was obviously saying to himself...

"It seems like only yesterday!"

"The Cabin" of the Grand Republic river steamer was 300 feet long, 30 feet wide, and 18 feet high. Furnishings were equal to the finest hotels. It burned Sept. 17, 1877 at St. Louis wharf.
(Photo from the Thomas H. Detweiller collection - Peoria Public Library)

When the barge was made fast in front of some rising prairie village, the actors and actresses in gala attire, and the bandsmen in bright uniforms would climb onto the river bank to stir the main-streeters with rousing music of the day.

Huddled close together in the narrow seats, the crowd somberly watched actors and listened to jokes that long ago had sprouted whiskers, and plays that had been Broadway hits half a dozen years before.

Brickhouse made it big in baseball

Many Peoria area people have made it big in the entertainment arena over the years. And this one did it via radio and television, but he entertained us in the world of sports, and he did it so well for so long, it took him all the way to the Baseball Hall of Fame...Jack Brickhouse.

John Beasley (Jack) Brickhouse came into the world at Methodist Hospital in Peoria on January 24, 1916. He was named after his father, John William (Will) and his grandfather, Beasley Brickhouse.

His mother, Daisy, was an immigrant from Cardiff, Wales, and her father followed the coal mines to America. He was killed in the Cherry Mines disaster at Cherry, Illinois. Jack's father and family resided in Clarksville, Tennessee. Young Will ran away from home at the age of 14, with an itch for show business. He became a sideshow barker, he was buried alive, and he ran concessions at White City, a great amusement park in the heyday of early Chicago, among other things. Jack says he also originated "split-week vaudeville."

When Daisy was 15 she got a job behind a cigar counter at a Peoria hotel. She was 5 foot one, and weighed 90 pounds. Will was 39 then and stood 6 foot 5 and weighed 225. He was a travelling man and stayed at the hotel. They met once and he left town. Then he returned three weeks later and married her.

But the marriage had no chance of lasting. Their philosophies of life were as different as their ages and dimensions. Will was outgoing, a super salesman who won and lost shows and acts in card and crap games. Jack's parents separated, and his father died of pneumonia in Chicago at the age of 42. Jack was just two years old at the time.

Jack says he regrets that his dad died before he knew him. John Balaban of the Balaban & Katz theater chain (my old boss) told him years later that Will Brickhouse taught him the rudiments of selling film. John said, "I learned more from your dad than anyone else. He took me under his wing. I never was treated better."

But Daisy Brickhouse was brave and proud, and a teen-age widow with a small son. She earned $14 a week as a food checker, cashier, and hostess at the hotel. Jack's grandma lived with them and she served as a cook at Proctor Hospital. Jack spent many days after school delivering food trays to the patients. He says it was a good way to keep from getting hungry.

Daisy remarried but destiny frowned on her again, and that marriage was also eventually dissolved. But she placed high emphasis on Jack's education and he knew better than to bring home poor grades. He says that even with all the economic ups and downs, he had a pleasant childhood.

When Jack was 11, he first sold Peoria Journal extra papers when Lindbergh first flew the Atlantic in 1927. They sold like hot cakes. He bought them for 2¢ and sold them for 3¢ plus tips. It seemed a good way to make "big bucks," so he got a paper route. He soon found that the action was downtown, and the Jefferson Building became his territory. He sold both the Peoria Journal and Peoria Star and was enterprising enough for the Hartman brothers (who were Peoria's major newspapers distributors) to offer him a job. But he turned it down. He finally quit to become a caddy at the urging of his chum, Stanley Cox.

Jack lived in the 500 block of Second Street, and later on Fisher, between Second and Third. He went to Lincoln Grade School, and then Manual Training High School, where he was captivated by speech and dramatics. His speech teacher was Hazel Conrad (later, she was my principal at Irving), Lily Dean was his dramatics teacher, and Gertrude Applegate, his English teacher. He says he owes them a debt of gratitude for changing his life.

He also captained the swimming team at Manual, but says, "we were just good enough to avoid drowning." Jack graduated from Manual in 1933 in tough times. He entered Bradley Tech (now University) and Daisy signed a note at a loan company for his fee and books, and Milo Reeve co-signed.

Jack finally got a job as dishwasher at the Père Marquette Hotel, where Daisy worked. From 5 a.m. to midnight he washed dishes, attended classes, worked out with the freshman basketball team, then studied until midnight. Then got up at 4:30 a.m. to do it all over again. He lost 20 pounds on an already skinny frame. He left Bradley after one semester.

WMBD Radio staged a "So You Want To Be An Announcer" contest, and Jack entered. He came in fifth but someone at the station heard something in his delivery they liked, and invited him to work on a one week trial basis without pay. After a third payless week he balked. He needed money, so they decided to pay him $17 a week as part-time announcer and switchboard operator.

By 1938, he was well established in Peoria broadcasting as the only sports announcer at the only radio station in town, but Jack says you haven't lived until you've frozen your posterior off conducting the Lowenstein Furniture's "Man on the Street" program on icy winter days in Peoria. Gomer Bath had originated the show and Jack took over from him.

But Jack likes to tell a story on himself about the phony poll he did in order to

A 1939 photo of Jack Brickhouse with his typewriter between his legs, typing his sports script for a WMBD radio broadcast.
(Photo courtesy of WMBD)

broadcast Bradley's "Famous Five" basketball games. He was anxious to broadcast the games and Bradley wanted him to but WMBD frowned on it. They were committed to a CBS prime time schedule. So Jack and program director Harold Bean attempted to sell the brass on recording the games and playing them back late at night.

The station was doubtful that anyone would listen to a game after they knew the outcome. So Jack suggested taking a poll. WMBD agreed but they made a big mistake. They let *him* take the poll. He went down to the corner of Main and Jefferson and asked 10 people if they would listen to delayed broadcasts of the games late at night, even though they probably already knew the score. Eight answered "no" and two were undecided.

So Jack threw the cards down the sewer and went down to the back room of the Saratoga Pool Hall and did his own poll. He marked 62 ballots "yes" and 14 "no." The rest were undecided. He took the phony poll to the station, and they agreed to do one broadcast, the Bradley-Louisville game from the Peoria Armory. It was a huge success. Soon fans were going to the games, then running home to hear it again on the radio. It resulted in a full schedule of delayed broadcasts. In time it became fashionable in Peoria to hold basketball-listening parties.

Well, Jack Brickhouse left Peoria on April 15, 1940 for WGN, to understudy Bob Elson on Cubs and White Sox broadcasts. His career soared over the years in many sports, as well as many other major news events, and in July, 1983 he was admitted into the Baseball Hall of Fame.

In his acceptance speech he had one paragraph that especially caught my fancy. This was, of course, before lights were put in Wrigley field, but Jack said: "In the fantasy of my dreams, I have imagined myself as the announcer for a Cubs-White Sox World Series. A series that would last 7 games, with the final game going extra innings, before being suspended because of darkness at Wrigley Field."

Jack Brickhouse says he loves Peoria like a mother and Chicago like a wife. Quite a guy, and Peoria's own.

...and it seems like only yesterday!

(Much of the data for this column came from the book, "Thanks for Listening" by Jack Brickhouse with Jack Rosenberg and Ned Colletti.)

South End theaters revisited

Over the past couple years we've covered many Peoria theaters. But when I was a kid growing up in the "South End," I wore out a few seat cushions in some neighborhood theaters down there that you may recall.

My first remembrance of movies where when my parents took me to the Madison and Palace downtown. But when I was a little older, I'd go with my cousins or friends to see those great action-packed adventures (I now know they were "B" movies) at the Garden and, later, the Avon Theater in the former Szold's Department Store area of South Adams and Garden Streets. Later on I found my way up to the Grand Theater, which, even later, became the Warner Theater. And at one time there was a Gem Theater on South Adams, just past Western Avenue, but I honestly can't recall going there. So, let's take a look at these neighborhood houses, and some history that may have been nearly forgotten along the way.

The Garden Theater was at the beginning of Garden Street at Adams, just in front of Szold's main entrance. My first recollections of seeing movies there were with my cousin, Larry Williams, and some of his friends. He's a little older than

me, so I'm sure I was considered a tag-along he was shackled with from time-to-time. But Larry and his wife, Shirley, both have fond memories of movies at the Garden.

I've heard of vaudeville at the Garden in addition to movies, but this may have been before my time. However, I sure remember the old Hoot Gibson, Tom Mix, and Tex Ritter films of that era. This may be why I was such a Tom Mix fan later, when the Ralston Straightshooters were daily fare on old radio. But the real Tom Mix was never on the radio program. Curley Bradley is the actor I remember as radio's Tom Mix.

The Imperial Theater was first listed at 2204 South Adams in the Peoria City Directory in 1914. I don't remember it, but I certainly do recall the next theater that was listed at this same address. It was the Avon, and it was across Adams Street from the Garden. Adolph Szold owned and operated both theaters, but closed the Garden when he opened the new Avon.

The Avon opened its doors for the first time on May 6, 1937. Its first feature picture was a good action-adventure, Jack London's "Call of the Wild" starring Clark Gable, Loretta Young, Jack Oakie,

Reginald Owen and Frank Conroy. This 1935 film was directed by William Wellman.

Jim Murphy of Bergner's Madison Park store, recalls those days of the Avon. He remembers going to the movie and then visiting Roxy's Sweet Shop next door. Ten cents would get Jim a five-cent ticket to a movie that included a double feature, a cartoon and that week's chapter of a serial. Flash Gordan and Buck Rogers were big serial heroes in those days.

And Jim recalls, if he was one of the first 500 kids attending the Saturday matinee, he also received a free ice cream bar. But if he wasn't, he'd save the other nickel for a big ice cream cone at Roxy's after the show. Another of his memories is the Roxy banana split. A real treat for a kid of that era.

And I just found out something that Jim Murphy might like to know. My good friend and photographer, Lee Roten (who supplies many of the photos for this column), was one of the ushers who may have handed him his free ice cream bar at the Avon's Saturday matinee. Roten was an usher there for Adolph Szold in 1941 and '42. The Avon was remodeled by Lankton-Ziegele architects, and Lee thinks it was an expansion of the old Imperial, which originally took up only half of the building.

Lee remembers a lady named Pauline, who sort of ran the place for Szold, including the office and was also cashier. Conrad "Cooney" Ockenga was the ticket-taker, and John Schlabick was chief of service. As he recalls, some of the ushers were Bob Piper, Bob Matulis, Lyle Sparks, and Jack Giebelhausen. And Jim Raynet was a projectionist.

Now, closer to town, in the 1200 block South Adams Street, was a theater that had four names over the years. If you'll remember, it was right across the street from Wilton's Mortuary. I remember it best as The Grand. But it began as the Palace Theater and probably dates back to the teens. It was a small neighborhood silent motion picture house then, and this was before Ascher's Palace Theater on Main Street, which opened in January, 1921. After that the name became a problem for the smaller Palace, so it was changed to the "Little Palace."

Larry Williams also remembers the Little Palace as a small child, living on Johnson Street. But a few years later it became the Grand, and as I recall it in the '30's, it was a burlesque house which also ran sound motion pictures.

I remember as a youngster, it was kind of adventurous to walk down around that theater, and you'd better be careful which side of the street you were on. You never knew when you'd be seen by a friend or, Lord help you, a relative that might suspect you were sneaking in to see a live burlesque show.

Well, after burlesque the Grand became strictly a movie house. In its heyday it was owned and operated by Billy "Bozo" Stone but two gentlemen by the name of Chambers and Harrington are

A 1934 photo of the Garden Theater, taken by Bob Mehlenbeck. They were still reminding folks they were showing talking pictures.
(Photo courtesy of George Krambles)

credited with being its founders. Then in 1941, the old theater was remodeled and reopened as the Warner Theater, and it operated under that name until it closed in 1957.

By the way, although the inside is gutted, the building is still standing. It's now being used as a warehouse. If you drive by, you can still see the white ceramic brick that was once the theater front. My good friend Harry Schindler of Bartonville, recently gave me a prized possession. An old, hand-tinted glass slide that was used at the Grand.

Another South Adams Street neighborhood movie house was the Gem Theater at 3119 South Adams, just below Western. It was opened in 1916 by William McClintock and Joe Hendricks. Former projectionist, Nick Frasco, remembers that Mr. McClintock lived on Western Avenue, just below Hayes Street.

He also recalls that it was later operated by a Mr. Harris (but not Ed Harris, who later operated the Princess and

A 1942 photo of the Avon Theater, taken by Ray Barclay. You can see a part of Roxy's Sweet Shop on the left. Note War Bonds advertising on the front of the marquee.
(Photo Courtesy of R. W. Deller from Lee Roten's Historic Peoria Photo File)

Columbia), and Charles Lynch. Harris funded the operation and Lynch was projectionist and booked the movies. Nick recalls seeing his first movie there in 1918. It closed in1927, when sound came in.

Then in 1933, Nick Frasco and Dan Wytcherly added sound, and reopened the Gem, which had about 300 seats at the time. They thought the area could support a theater with reasonable prices. But it was at the height of the depression, and they closed after several months.

Well, that's a quick look at the Imperial, Avon, Garden, Palace, Little Palace, Grand, Warner, and two versions of the Gem, but they were actually in just four South End locations.

...and it seems like only yesterday!

Gene Autry dominated westerns

Last week's column about the South End's neighborhood theaters reminded me of one of those Hollywood stars who made our early movies so memorable. Westerns were a big part of those action-packed days, and from 1935 to 1942 (when he went into the service), Gene Autry was the biggest cowboy hero of them all.

Now, I'm sure I must have seen him for the first time at The Garden Theater, since he began his movie career in 1934. But I associate my teenage passion for his adventures with the Rialto Theater during the late '30's and early '40's.

Gene Autry says it all began when he was 22 years old. He was a relief telegraph operator in Chelsea, Oklahoma. It was a quiet, rainy night, and he was killing time by strumming a guitar and singing to himself. An older man came by to send a wire. After staying to listen to Gene sing and play some more, he said; "You belong in Hollywood, boy, playing the guitar instead of that telegraph instrument. Your heart ain't in it. Why don't you get yourself a job singing on the radio?" Autry took the compliment casually, until he looked at the stranger's signature on the telegram. It was Will Rogers.

Well, Autry heeded the older man's advice, and within a few years, Gene would become as well known as Will Rogers himself. And he did first become a radio entertainer, and then a singing cowboy in the movies. He built a vast financial empire that included oil wells, radio and TV stations, and a major league baseball team, among many other things. In 1950 his holdings were estimated between $4 and $7 million. By 1970, the figure was somewhere over $100 million and climbing.

Unlike most Hollywood cowboy stars, he was a true westerner. Orvon Gene Autry was born in Tioga, Texas, in 1907. His parents were of French-Irish descent, and his father was a cattle buyer, tenant farmer and circuit-riding preacher.

After the family moved to Oklahoma, Gene got a job as a railroad baggage handler when he was 16. Then he graduated to the job of relief telegrapher for the Frisco line. He bought a guitar for $1.00 down and 50¢ a month, and learned to play it, sing and yodel. After his meeting with Will Rogers, he quit the railroad job and headed for New York.

Recording executives there told him to go back home and get some experience, which he did. He became "Oklahoma's Yodeling Cowboy" on Tulsa radio station KVOO. A year later he returned to New York and recorded "That Silver-Haired Daddy of Mine." He and his friend, Jimmy Long, a train dispatcher, had written the song during his railroad days. It became an immediate hit, and has sold over 5 million records. This lead to weekly appearances on "The National Barn Dance" over WLS radio in Chicago. The NBC network coverage of the show gave him national exposure, and four years later he was Hollywood bound.

During the early '30's Gene would travel with the WLS Barn Dance troupe, and they played here at the Palace Theater and the Inglaterra Ballroom. In February, 1935, he appeared, not once but twice, at the Inglaterra. On February 15th the show was billed as "WLS Stars in Person with Gene Autry and his Round-Up." Five days later he returned to the Ing, and the billing this time read "WMBD Barn Dance & Gene Autry and his WLS Round-Up."

The man who appeared as Gene's sidekick in most of his movies was Lester Alvin (Smiley) Burnette. He appeared with Autry on the WLS National Barn Dance. Gene had heard Burnette on a Tuscola, Illinois radio station, and offered him a job for $35 a week, which was twice as much as he made at the station.

Smiley could play 52 musical instruments and he also composed over 350 songs, including "It's My Lazy Day," "Hominy Grits," and "Riding Down the Canyon." But in most of Gene's movies he was known as Frog Millhouse. And interestingly, Gene Autry and Smiley Burnette both began their film careers in the same movie. It was "In Old Sante Fe," starring Ken Maynard, and produced by Mascot Films.

While at Mascot, Gene also appeared in two 12-chapter serials; "Mystery Mountain" (1934), also starring Ken Maynard, and again with Smiley, but by 1935 his first starring role was in the serial, "The Phantom Empire." Smiley was his sidekick and Gene's horse, Champion, had third billing.

In 1935 Gene signed on with Republic Pictures, and his popularity began to soar. His first big hit was "Tumbling Tumbleweeds" for Republic that year, and his last was (appropriately) "Last of the Pony Riders" in 1953, produced by his own company. Gene made 56 movies until he went into the service in 1942, with star billing in all but the first two.

Autry came back to Republic Studios after the war in 1946, and did five more pictures for them. But while he was away, Republic had groomed a new cowboy star by the name of Roy Rogers. So Gene formed his own company called Flying A Productions. He made 32 of his own movies and released them through Columbia Pictures. If you're counting, that's 93 motion pictures (including two serials). Smiley Burnette was in 61 of them, and Pat Buttram played comedy relief in 17. George "Gabby" Hayes was in four, and Sterling Holloway in five. From 1937 until he enlisted in the Army Air Force in 1942, Gene Autry was named the top box-office star of western pictures. He was also voted among the first ten box office stars in the entire industry, the first western actor to do so.

Smiley Burnette (left) and the Sons of the Pioneers, join Gene Autry in a song from Republic's "The Big Show" (1936). The man standing on the right with the guitar was Dick Weston at the time. He changed his name to Roy Rogers and became Autry's movie rival after World War II.

(A Republic Pictures photo - courtesy of Peoria Public Library)

At one time his records outsold Bing Crosby three to one, and his biggest was the unlikely "Rudolph the Red-Nosed Reindeer." It alone sold over 10-million records. He had his own radio program, "Melody Ranch," and he toured the country with his Gene Autry Rodeo. His fan mail climbed to 40,000 letters a month, 60 percent from females, and it exceeded Greta Garbo's, Clark Gable's and Shirley Temple's.

Now, years ago I heard a story about Gene Autry that supposedly happened here in Peoria. I think I may have heard it from Len Worley, but it was so long ago, I can't remember. Anyway, here's the story.

Back in the early '30's Gene Autry was in Peoria on a tour and heading for Hollywood to take a shot at the movies. While here, he went to a local film studio and had a short motion picture made of himself. He took this "pilot" film with him to Hollywood to show to the producers. According to the legend, this helped him break into the movies.

So, awhile back I decided I'd try to corroborate the story. I wrote to Gene Autry and asked him if this ever occurred. Well, it took some time to get a reply, but a few months later I received this response from his Administrative Assistant, which said in part:

"The story you heard is quite true. Although the time frame cannot be pinned down exactly, Mr. Autry did stop off in Peoria very early on in his career, possibly before coming to Hollywood and (filmed) a short piece where he sang a song. In fact, he was most interested to find out if anyone in the area might have access to the piece and if you have any information on this it would be most appreciated. (Signed) Maxine Hansen, Administrative Assistant to Mr. Gene Autry."

Well, obviously, I don't have any more information, but if anyone out there does, please contact me. Mr. Autry would appreciate it and so would I.

..and it seems like only yesterday!

Harry Cool and the Big Bands

It's no secret by now that I'm a big-band fanatic. I have been since I've been old enough to reach up and turn on a radio. Now, one of my all-time favorites was a band that operated out of Chicago's Aragon Ballroom back in the '30's and '40's. And it always began with the announcer saying, "Here's That Band Again!" That's right, it was Dick Jurgens and his Orchestra. But my friend Bill Ryan is as big a Jurgens fan as I am, if that's possible. He lists Jurgens at the very top of his list (with the possible exception of Jan Garber.)

Dick Jurgens is still living in California at last notice, but his band continues to travel, and every time they come to The Hub, I get a call from Bill Ryan asking if Flossie and I would care to join him and his wife, Margene, to hear them. We've done this a couple times in recent years, and the band still draws big crowds, too.

There were three great male vocalists with Jurgens over the years; Eddy Howard, Harry Cool and Buddy Moreno. And Ronnie Kemper also did novelty vocals. But did you know that Harry Cool came to Peoria and lived and worked here after his big years with the orchestra?

He, along with Phyllis Fabry and John Phillips, formed the "Harry Cool Trio" here, which consisted of Phyllis at the keyboard, John on bass, and Harry as vocalist. He could still sing but all the years of nightclubs and dance halls had taken its toll, and his voice wasn't what it used to be.

Dick and Bev Vance had an afternoon show on WEEK-TV (Channel 43, then). Bev was about to have a baby and the trio was invited to fill in temporarily on their "Coffee Time" afternoon show. As it turned out, they stayed on for three or four years.

The trio also appeared at two prominent places in Galesburg for a couple years; Harbor Lights Supper Club, and Frank's Place. And in Peoria they did a stint at Louis D'Amico's Supper Club (the old Clover Club.)

I've talked to a couple of Harry's friends back then. Phyllis Fabry, of course, and Bill Houlihan. Houli knew Harry and his family well. They were neighbors, living on Ellis Street in those days. Both Phyl and Houli recall Harry as a wonderful person. He was a big, tall, handsome man and a real nice guy, but fate dealt him a low blow.

I was still managing the Madison Theatre back in the 1950's, and Harry was selling radio time for one of the local stations. He would call on me to buy time, and during one of those visits he told me a sad personal story. I'll try to relate it as close as I can. (But keep in mind this was around 35 years ago.)

If you'll recall, Harry Cool had a strong baritone voice, and was an excellent pop singer. He was on a par with Dick Haymes, Perry Como, Eddy Howard and far above many other big name, big band vocalists. He had been in show business and on radio for several years before joining Dick Jurgens. He joined about the time Eddy Howard left to form his own band around 1939. Harry stayed with the band until about 1943 or '44, when he, too, formed his own orchestra.

It was at this time that Harry was about to receive his big break. His popularity was at its peak, and he was approached by an advertising agency that was planning a new daily 15-minute radio show. The sponsor for the show was to be a name-brand cigarette.

The setting for the show was to be a fictitious night club, and the host would be the popular Harry Cool. He would also be the vocalist and feature his own orchestra. It would closely resemble the remote big band broadcasts that had been so popular on radio for years.

Harry was on "cloud nine." It was his big chance and stardom was in the offing. He knew it. He could feel it.

He had several meetings with the agency while negotiations were going on, and he noticed that at every meeting there was a little man, whom he never met, sitting in the back of the room. The man never said anything, he just seemed to observe the proceedings.

Finally the big day came to sign the contract for the new program which would assure Harry Cool stardom and big bucks. The lawyers representing both sides were there. The agency people were assembled and Harry was ready to put ink to paper, when this little man in the back stood up and cleared his throat.

He said, "Gentlemen, I've been watching the proceedings on this program for quite some time now. Through it all something has been nagging at me, but I haven't been able to put my finger on it until now. The thing that has suddenly occurred to me is this. Are we making a mistake to hire a man by the name of Cool to host a new show to promote Chesterfield cigarettes?"

Harry told me he was dumbfounded, as were all the others in the room. Apparently no one had associated his name with the competitive cigarette named "Kool." They discussed changing his name, but if he did the agency couldn't capitalize on his previous popularity. So the whole deal fell through, along with Harry's chance of a lifetime. And he never got over it.

In 1944 he did replaced Dick Haymes on the "Here's to Romance" radio show, and in mid-1945 he took over the Carl

Harry Cool as he appeared with the Dick Jurgens Orchestra after they reformed and played The Hub Ballroom back in the 1970's.
(Photo courtesy of The Hub Ballroom)

Ravazza orchestra, a smooth hotel type band. And he continued to play and record through the '40's and into the early '50's.

But the program that nearly belonged to Harry Cool did go on the air, and it was a huge success. It was called "The Chesterfield Supper Club" and became the musical springboard for two top big band vocalists, Perry Como and Jo Stafford. It first aired on NBC on December 11, 1944. Como was on the show three nights a week and Stafford, two nights. The announcer was Martin Block.

The years on the road and in the dance halls took its toll and Harry Cool virtually lost his voice. He just couldn't project anymore. It was at this time he came to Peoria. A few years later he went

Dick Jurgens in a publicity photo promoting his record album, "Here's That Band Again Today."
(Photo courtesy of The Hub Ballroom)

back to Chicago and was a night club manager at a popular supper club. And when the Jurgens band reorganized, he rejoined it and learned to sing with the band again by lowering his volume and singing up close to the mike.

The last time I saw and heard him perform was when the band came back to The Hub in the 1970's. This new orchestra came out with an album in 1971 titled "Here's That Band Again Today." I bought a copy at The Hub, and Harry's renditions, using his new singing technique, were excellent. His vocal numbers on this album are: "Raindrops Keep Falling On My Head," "Why Don't You Fall In Love With Me?," "Do You Ever Think of Me?," "What A Wonderful World," and "Sweet Georgia Brown."

Well, "the fickle finger of fate" sure played a nasty trick on one of the real nice guys in the business, and one of the top vocalists, too, Harry Cool.

...and it seems like only yesterday!

Top-flight lady golfer

Phyllis Sprenger Evans won her last city title at age 59

Years ago, one of the early public golf course pros in our town was one Frederick C. Sprenger. Now, Fred was a pretty good golfer in his own right, but probably his greatest contribution to the game came in the form of his pretty daughter, Phyllis Sprenger (now Evans).

Phyllis not only became a prominent golfer, she still holds the record (later tied by Judy Coker) of nine Peoria Women's City Tournament Championships. She was also runner-up five times, medalist six times, and shares the record (with Betty Mackemer) of most consecutive wins at three. 42 years separate her first and last wins, and under three names; Sprenger, Anderson, and Evans. But, to me, her greatest statistic is winning her last City Tournament at age 59.

Her wins of the Mt. Hawley Country Club Women's Tourney numbers somewhere in the double digits, but the records were not kept, so the exact count is unavailable.

Her father was advised by his doctor to play golf for his health, and a few years later, he became a member of Mt. Hawley. Her mother, Anne Ossenbeck

Sprenger played golf with him and she became a fair player, too.

When Phyllis was eight years old she remembers driving way out Knoxville Avenue from their home on Bigelow with her dad and Walter Murray, then president of the Peoria Park Board. They walked around a big corn field and Mr. Murray described where all the holes for a new golf course would be. It became North Moor Golf Course (now Leo Donovan), and little did she know she'd be winning golf tournaments there some day.

When Phyllis was thirteen, her dad was playing in a foursome with Colonel Cox, Bill Boyd and Walter Davis. He would bring her along, put a club in her hands and she learned by watching and trying to keep up with the men. She later played with Howard Kellogg, Sr., director of the Orpheus Club, Milton Budd of WMBD, and Bob Black, the Père Marquette orchestra leader, among others. It was playing with men where she learned to hit a long ball.

Phyllis says she wasn't a student of the game. In fact she didn't like golf at first. But by the time she was fifteen the

Western Open was being held at Peoria Country Club, and she planned to enter. She needed a little polish and Johnny Lang became her first true instructor.

North Moor became Peoria's second public course, with Kenny McCracken as pro, and Phyllis entered her first Peoria City Tournament there in 1931. The tourney began in 1930, with Mrs. Marie Topping winning the first one, and Mrs. Omega Mackemer winning the second one.

In 1932, Mackemer was defending her title when young Phyllis Sprenger beat her in the quarter-finals. It was her first taste of victory. Phyl went on to play Betty Lord in the finals but lost to Betty's stymie on the eighteenth green. And, believe it or not, two years later (1934) Betty stymied her again on the eighteenth green in the finals to beat her.

(Golfers are now allowed to place markers for balls on putting greens, and stymies, where one ball lies between another player's ball and the hole, no longer exist.) But in between, 1933 became Phyllis' year to win her first Peoria Women's City Tournament. It was the fourth year of the tourney and Phyllis' third effort. She beat Dorothy Lehmann Field in the finals. And she recalls there were between 1,500 and 2,000 in the gallery that day. The win was celebrated the following evening with a party at Lekas' Sugar Bowl on Main Street where she and her friends had dinner, and dates later.

Phyllis remembers that the clubs she used to win that 1933 tournament were a pretty sorry lot. Her father had won the driver years before in a K of C Tourney. There was a split in the head and a screw held it together. The brassie was one that Johnny Lang had given her, and the irons consisted of a mid-iron, a mashie, a niblick and a putter.

Father Fitzgerald had promised her a matched set of clubs and a bag if she won the '33 tournament. And he kept his word by giving her a set of Hagen irons and woods, and bag to put them in.

Phyllis has fond memories of Gus Moreland, too. She was a senior at the Academy of Our Lady in 1934. Peoria had a Three-I League baseball team that played at Woodruff Field. On opening day that year, she, Gus Moreland and Johnny Lang hit golf balls off home plate into the river there. And she recalls the Jackson-Keenan Driving Range across the railroad tracks on the other side of Knoxville from North Moor. Lang and Bill Kurek gave lessons there and it was a great hangout for golfers.

When Phyl was nineteen, it was suggested to her father that she become a pro. She wasn't old enough and her dad was opposed to it. But she had no desire to do it anyway, so nothing came of it. And she says she has never once regretted it. But Phyl has played in a lot of out-of-town tournaments, and won her share of them. She won the State Senior Tournament in 1971, and was runnerup in 1972. She entered the National Senior Women's Tourney at Point Clear, Alabama, in 1974 and came in 15th in a field of 150.

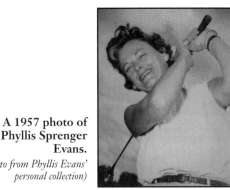

A 1957 photo of Phyllis Sprenger Evans.
(Photo from Phyllis Evans' personal collection)

She has also played several years in the Fort Madison, Iowa tournament, that hosts champions and excellent players from Missouri, Iowa, Illinois and Wisconsin. She won it in 1953, the first year she entered it, and repeated in 1967. But Phyllis lost the desire to travel to other tournaments after her good friend and travelling companion, Joyce Metzger, died in October of 1979. But along the way she has played with Babe Didrickson in the St. Petersburg, Florida Women's Open and has had exhibition matches with Patty Berg, Mickey Wright, Louise Suggs, Betsy Rawls, Betty McKinnon and Marlene (Bauer) Hagge.

But with all this golf, it took her 47 years to make a hole-in-one. In 1976, while playing with Maria and Chris Thompson and her husband, Wick Evans, she holed number 17 at Mt. Hawley Country Club. But she claims her biggest thrill came a few weeks later when she eagled the five-par 15th at that same club. Finally, in 1983, the area recognized her by admitting her into the Greater-Peoria Sports Hall of Fame, with a plaque at the

Civic Center. She was the second woman sports figure to be so honored.

Now, I've known of Phyllis and her golf prowess for many years, but Flossie and I became friends with Phyl and Wick Evans when we first joined Mt. Hawley many years ago. And I'm not ashamed to say it, I've been in awe of her ability since one particular day about 20 years ago.

Phil Mergener and I were entertaining a couple clients at the club one afternoon, and we were about to tee off on the five par number 15 (that same hole she later eagled), when Phyl and Wick played up behind us. We invited the twosome to play through. Wick hit his drive, and then Phyllis addressed her ball as we stood back watching. She uncoiled and hit one nearly out of sight and right down the middle. It was as long and straight as nearly any man's drive I've witnessed.

She smiled nicely, they thanked us, and the two walked on up the fairway. Our foursome just sort of looked at one another for a minute. And finally, I broke the silence. "Fellas," I said, "I can't follow that act. I'll meet you back at the bar, and I headed toward the club house. Well, I did come back and finish the round, but I've never felt so humbled in my life.

A few years later I told Phyllis this story about the day she nearly caused me to give up golf. She just laughed and said; "I have to admit it. I love being able to hit the ball, especially when someone's watching.

A great lady golfer, and a great lady, too. Phyllis Sprenger Evans

...and it seems like only yesterday!

Bob & Ray Show rarely used a script

Half of the last of those great old radio comedy teams left the scene last month. Ray Goulding passed away at the age of 68. He was, of course, the "Ray" half of "The Bob and Ray Show."

Both men had been in radio since before their Army days during World War II, and they perpetuated radio comedy from 1946 until recently, having last appeared on Public Radio in the 1980's. And one of the things that made the Bob and Ray show unique was that they rarely used a script. Even the major comedians in early radio wouldn't think of going on the air without a script, but Bob and Ray were almost totally unscripted.

As a matter of fact, they rarely rehearsed, but each had a sixth sense of where the other was going with the "bit" they were doing, and they could time themselves from very short programs of less than five minutes for "Monitor", to the nearly impossible task of filling an entire afternoon, when a ballgame was rained out.

Raymond Walter Goulding was born in Lowell, Massachusetts on March 20, 1922, and Robert Brackett Elliott about a year later in Boston, March 26, 1923. Ray graduated from Lowell High School, and in 1939 he auditioned for a radio announcer job at the local radio station. He won the $15 a week job. Incidentally, the one who came in second was another Lowell High graduate, Ed McMahon, who went on to become Johnny Carson's sidekick.

Ray's older brother Phil was also a radio announcer and he coached Ray on announcing techniques. After a little over a year, Ray went to work at WEEI in Boston, and McMahon was then hired to replace him. Ed still does pretty well in the second-banana department.

In November, 1942, Ray entered the Army and was stationed at Fort Knox, Kentucky where he was an instructor in officer's candidate school. He was discharged with the rank of captain in April, 1946. While at Fort Knox he met Lieutenant Mary Elizabeth Leader, an Army dietitian who later became his wife.

He returned to Boston and went to work at WHDH, where he was assigned to read the newscasts on Bob Elliott's morning disc jockey show. Bob Elliott grew up in Winchester, a Boston suburb. At Winchester High he put on "radio" shows over the school's public-address system. Following high school graduation in 1940, he enrolled in the Feagin School of Drama and Radio in New York City. He earned his tuition by working as an usher at Radio City Music Hall and as an NBC page.

His first professional radio assignment was in 1941 when he did a weekly show billed as "a page boy's impressions of radio" over WINS. A year later he got a job at Boston's WHDH. He was an announcer for a women's program presented by Jane Underwood, who later became his wife.

In 1943 Bob joined the U.S. Army, serving in Europe with the 26th Infantry and participating in the Battle of the Bulge. He was discharged in 1946 and returned to his job in Boston where Ray soon came to work.

The team of Bob and Ray was formed by accident. While Bob did his disc jockey show, Ray delivered the news on the program, and began staying on after the news to exchange "on-the-air" conversations with Bob between records. The listeners demanded more, and in May 1946 WHDH gave them a daily half-hour show of their own called "Matinee with Bob and Ray." But Boston fans wanted still more, so they were given a morning hour show called "Break Fast with Bob and Ray." For over five years they built a tremendous Boston audience.

In 1951, John Moses, a talent and booking agent, happened to be in Boston watching a tryout for "The King and I." He heard their show and thought they were potential network entertainers. He went to Bud Barry, an NBC executive in New York, who immediately brought them in and launched them on an NBC 15-minute, five-day-a-week show which premiered on July 2, 1951. Soon they were also doing a one-hour program on Saturday nights with full orchestra and guest stars.

They began a morning show and then got their own TV program. An unknown actress named Audrey Meadows aided them on television. She, of course, went on to be a star opposite Jackie Gleason on "The Honeymooners."

In 1952 the prime-time show was revived as a half-hour program, while the pair also did a two-hour and forty-five-minute morning show in New York. In 1953, the pair moved from NBC to ABC-TV, and in 1954, they returned to local radio. Then in 1955, they began their five-minute live routines on NBC's "Monitor."

In 1956, they signed as disc jockeys with Mutual, and in June 1959, they began another 15-minute, five-day-a-week show for CBS, after which they left radio to do commercials. Then in 1962, they went to WHN for a four-hour late afternoon program for three years.

Their Broadway show, "The Two and Only," opened in 1970, and three years later they were back on WOR, the home station of the Mutual Network. They departed from commercial radio in 1976, but in the 1980's, they were again doing their thing on the Public Radio Network with "From Approximately Coast-to-Coast, The Bob and Ray Show."

A rare photo of Bob Elliott (left) and Ray Goulding appearing to enjoy their work on the Mutual Radio Network. They rarely laughed at their own stuff. This is a Maxwell Coplan photo from Cosmopolitan Magazine, dated August 1, 1956.

The fun of Bob and Ray was zany but simple. It developed out of ad-lib interviews of one another. They developed characters such as Ray's Mary McGoon and Charles the Poet, while Bob did Wally Ballou. Ray did Mary McGoon, Natalie Attired, and other female voices in a falsetto voice. Mary usually did a recipe and menu show, while Natalie was a song sayer. She didn't sing songs, she said them...to the accompaniment of drums. Charles the Poet read drippy poetry, accompanied by sentimental music and chirping birds.

Bob's Wally Ballou character was a bumbling nasal-voiced radio reporter who's mike was usually dead when he began his report, so it began "...y Ballou here..." And he would end being cut off in the middle of a word.

But, to me, their funniest material was the parodies they did of other radio programs in the early days. Program titles like: "Mary Backstayge, Noble Wife"; "One Feller's Family"; "Mr. Trace, Keener Than Most Persons"; and "Jack Headstrong, the All-American American."

Other parodies included: "Hartford Harry, Private Eye"; "Helen Harkness, Sob Sister"; "The Life and Loves of Linda Lovely"; "Wayside Doctor, Hawaiian Ear, Eye, Nose and Throat Man"; "Kindly Mother McGee"; and "The Gathering Dusk," which was introduced as "the heartwarming story of a girl who's found unhappiness by leaving no stone unturned in her efforts to locate it."

And they offered their own commercial premiums. The Little Jim Dandy Burglar Kit; The Bob and Ray Home Surgery Kit, and others. Well, Ray Goulding is gone now, but not his humor. And I'm sure he would enjoy our ending the way they ended all their shows. It best describes their wonderful feel for funny dialogue.

"This is Ray Goulding, reminding you to write if you get work..."

"And this is Bob Elliott, reminding you to hang by your thumbs."

It was funny stuff back in those great old radio days.

...and it seems like only yesterday!

Two actors had plenty in common

Back in 1921, two Peorians were born who went on to become Hollywood motion picture stars. Not only that, they were both male stars, born on the same day, July 6th, and believe it or not, they looked just alike. All this is phenomenally true. But the reason? They are identical twins. And their names are Billy and Bobby Mauch.

The Mauch twins were very talented kids from the very beginning. While still quite small they sang and danced at various Peoria functions. And before they moved to New York City, they performed on several WMBD-Radio programs, but they were a little ahead of "Juvenile Theater."

Their father, Felix Mauch, came to Peoria from Chicago as chief clerk for the Toledo, Peoria & Western Railroad. He married a Peoria girl by the name of Margaret Burley. The Mauch twins were born here and spent their first seven years in Peoria and received early voice training here.

A radio scout heard about them, and their mother decided that they should be where the action was, so she took them to New York. A short time later their father negotiated a move with the TP&W. He was assigned to a position of New York agent for that railroad, and he joined his family there.

While living in New York City, Billy and Bobby appeared on network radio on such programs as "The Lucky Strike Program"; "Beauty Box Revue;" "The March of Time"; "Court of Human Relations"; "Showboat"; the kid show, "Let's Pretend"; and others.

But their big Hollywood break came in 1936 when a search was made for a juvenile that would resemble Fredric March enough to be believable in the part as March as a child. It was for a part in the Mervin LeRoy production "Anthony Adverse" starring Mr. March, along with Olivia de Havilland, Donald Woods, Anita Louise, Edmund Gwenn, Claude Rains, Louis Hayward, and Gale Sondergaard. Billy Mauch won the part. (Incidentally, the film garnered three Oscars that year. Miss Sondergaard as best supporting actress, along with awards for best musical score and best cinematography).

So the Mauch family once again made the big move to further the boys' careers. Although Billy was hired for the Anthony Adverse role, Bobby was also hired as his stand-in. Mother and boys moved to Hollywood, and once again their father negotiated a transfer to the TP&W's Los Angeles office.

Identical twins were something new to the Hollywood studios. They knew the boys had talent, but they were at a loss as to just how to use them. It took Warner Brothers some time to figure out what to do with them.

In the meantime Billy made another 1936 movie, "White Angel," without brother Bobby. Directed by William Dieterle, this one starred Kay Francis, Ian Hunter, Donald Woods, Nigel Bruce, and Donald Crisp. It was a biography of Florence Nightingale with Miss Francis as the 19th century British nursing pioneer.

Then, in 1937, the studio produced "Penrod and Sam," a picture based on a couple Booth Tarkington characters. This time Billy Mauch received star billing, followed by Frank Craven, Spring Byington, Craig Reynolds, and Bernice Pilot. The story line had to do with Billy Mauch getting involved with bank robbers.

The Mauch twins were fun-loving boys who were always up to some prank, and during the filming of the movies Billy was in, they would often swap roles. Bobby would act for Billy while Billy did the stand-in job. The reason they could get away with it was because they really were identical.

No one could tell them apart. As a matter of fact, their mother was the only one who could, except when they were asleep. Then, even she couldn't do it.

It took Warner Brothers until the fourth picture to know what to do with identical twin actors. They purchased the rights to Mark Twain's, "The Prince and the Pauper," and this time both twins would not only appear in a motion picture together for the first time, they would both star in it.

"The Prince and the Pauper" had originally been purchased by MGM for Freddie Bartholmew to play the dual role until the studio was persuaded to sell their rights so the Mauch Twins could play the starring parts.

This epic was directed by William Keighley. (You might remember him as the director who filled in as host of radio's "Lux Radio Theater" when Cecil B. DeMille refused to pay $1.00 for a union card.) The picture also starred Errol Flynn and Claude Rains, with Alan Hale, Montague Love, Henry Stephenson, and Barton MacLane. It was a story about two young look-alikes, one a mistreated urchin and the other a prince, who decided to exchange places with one another. But director Keighley became the victim of their old tricks of switching roles, and a 1937 Life magazine article said that "only the twins themselves can say for sure which was which in any particular scene."

"The Prince and the Pauper" was not only a well-done movie of an excellent story, its release date was very timely since it included scenes of an English coronation, and an actual one was taking place that year.

A scene of Billy and Bobby Mauch starring in the Warner Brothers 1938 movie, "Penrod and His Twin Brother." A Warner Bros. photo.

(Photo courtesy of the Peoria Public Library

King Edward VIII of England had abdicated his throne in December of 1936 to marry an American divorcée, Mrs. Wallis Warfield Simpson, after he "found it impossible...to discharge my duties as King as I would wish to do without the help and support of the woman I love." His brother, George VI and his wife were crowned king and queen on May 12, 1937.

After "The Prince and the Pauper" was finished, Warner's thought they

would save money and hire only one of the twins until it found another story for them. But Mrs. Mauch nipped that idea in the bud by threatening to sign the other boy to a rival studio.

Warner's had a sudden change of heart and signed both to a contract calling for $350 a week to each boy, plus $150 a week to Mrs. Mauch. In case you've forgotten, $850 a week was a pretty fair piece of change back in 1937.

Well, Billy and Bobby Mauch went on to star in two more "Penrod" films for Warner Brothers in 1938. One was "Penrod's Double Trouble," with Dick Purcell, Gene Lockhart, Kathleen Lockhart and Hugh O'Connell. It was about a reward that was put up for Penrod's return, but a look-alike was returned in his place.

The second film was "Penrod and His Twin Brother," which again co-starred Frank Craven and Spring Byington with Charles Halton and Claudia Coleman. Its plot line had Penrod getting blamed for something he didn't do. His look-alike was really guilty.

Well, Billy and Bobby Mauch had quite a childhood career in radio and the movies, but, later, there was also an adult career for both, but behind the cameras rather in front of them. We'll take a look at that next week.

...and it seems like only yesterday!

Twins worked on both sides of the camera

Last week I covered the careers of two early radio actors and motion picture stars from Peoria, the identical twins, Billy and Bobby Mauch. Being only four years younger than the Mauch Twins, I vividly recall following their careers from local Peoria entertainers to radio to Hollywood. But it was always fascinating to hear about their successes.

After their careers in front of the Hollywood cameras, I lost track of them until the past year when a lady contacted me to say that Billy Mauch and his wife had retired in the Chicago suburb of Palatine, Illinois and that Bobby and his wife still lived in California.

After doing the rough outline for last week's column, I had a few unanswered questions about their careers. Remembering that Billy was supposedly retired in Palatine, I picked up the phone to see if I could find him. To my surprise I did, on the first try.

He not only answered my couple questions, but after I inquired as to their later lives, he began to tell me that story, too, which is also an interesting one. So, I immediately wrote a follow-up column to bring you (and me) up to date. It also proves there can be life in Hollywood after being stars in front of the cameras. So, here's a look at the adult life and continuing careers of the Mauch Twins.

After their last two Penrod pictures for Warner Brothers, Billy continued to do some independent acting and Bobby went back to Warner's as a film editor. When World War II came along they both joined the Air Force and were sent to Roswell, New Mexico, where they took basic training and then were trained as control tower operators.

From here they were sent to Marana, Arizona for control tower duty. One night they were awakened and told they would leave immediately for New York City. The surprise orders came from Washington D.C. from none other than General Hap Arnold. They were to join the all-Air Force production of a show called "Winged Victory," under the direction of Moss Hart. It was a great show, and the twins did a song-and-dance routine in it, while touring about 17 cities throughout the country. Some noteworthy actors Billy remembers in its cast include Edmund O'Brien, Don Taylor and Barry Nelson.

After "Winged Victory," they returned to regular duty and were sent overseas and were stationed in the Philippine Islands where Bobby contracted a tropical illness, and was hospitalized. Billy was transferred to Clark Field in Luzon. At war's end Billy was assigned to return to the Philippines and bring Bobby and a contingent of hospital patients back to the States for their discharge.

Bobby Mauch went back to work for Warner Brothers as a supervising film editor on a Warner's half-hour series called "Behind the Camera." Later he joined Jack Webb's production company as film editor on his famous "Dragnet" series. He worked on 39 of the TV shows.

Billy pursued acting for a while. Then in 1951 he received an offer to go back to Warner Brothers as an apprentice in the film editing and sound department. He learned his trade in sound editing and stayed with that studio until 1976.

One of the movies he recalls doing sound effects on was "Bullitt," starring Steve McQueen. He worked closely with McQueen and recalls it was his first (and only) time to ride in a car going 135 mile an hour. Other productions were "The Wild Bunch," an excellent movie starring William Holden, Ernest Borgnine, Robert Ryan and Edmond O'Brien, and "The Prisoner of Second Avenue," starring Jack Lemmon and Anne Bancroft. When I mentioned I had met Jack Lemmon once in Peoria and again on the set of "The Front Page," in